SHADOWS OF THE NEW SUN

Liverpool Science Fiction Texts and Studies

SHADOWS OF THE NEW SUN

WOLFE ON WRITING/WRITERS ON WOLFE

edited and introduced by Peter Wright

LIVERPOOL UNIVERSITY PRESS

First published 2007 by
Liverpool University Press
4 Cambridge Street
Liverpool L69 7ZU

British Library Cataloguing-in-Publication data
A British Library CIP record is available

ISBN 978–1–84631–057–7 cased
978–1–84631–058–4 limp

Edited and typeset by
Frances Hackeson Freelance Publishing Services, Brinscall, Lancs
Printed and bound in the European Union by
Bell and Bain Ltd, Glasgow

To Marjorie McGivern, Nan,
who couldn't stay to see this one finished – *PW*

Contents

Notes on Contributors

Michael Andre-Driussi gained his BA in English Literature from the University of California, Berkeley. He is best known for *Lexicon Urthus* (1994), a guide to Gene Wolfe's New Sun series. Following that, he published a number of chapbooks on Wolfe's work, concluding with an original Wolfe story, 'Talk of Mandrakes' (2003). With Alice K. Turner he co-edited *Snake's-hands: The Fiction of John Crowley* (2003). He is currently working on a second edition of the Lexicon which will correct many of the errors as well as adding new ones. He resides near Berkeley.

Malcolm Edwards edited the magazines *Vector* and *Foundation* in the 1970s, and was Contributing Editor to the first edition of *The Encyclopedia of Science Fiction*. He started working at Gollancz in 1976, and took over running their sf list in 1982. He is now Publisher and Deputy CEO of the Orion Publishing Group (which includes Gollancz); in recent years his main contribution to the sf field has been the SF Masterworks series, whose first group of titles included Gene Wolfe's *The Fifth Head of Cerberus* – the book which led to the interview with Wolfe reprinted here.

Robert Frazier is the author of eight collections of poetry, and a three-time winner of the Rhysling Award for poetry from the Science Fiction Poetry Association. His most recent book is *The Daily Chernobyl*, winner of the 1999 Anamnesis Press Chapbook Award, published in August 2000 from Anamnesis Press. His work has appeared recently in *The Magazine of Fantasy and Science Fiction*, *Asimov's Science Fiction Magazine*, *Magazine of Speculative Poetry*, *Dreams & Nightmares*, and the anthology *The Alchemy of Stars*. An oil painter, Frazier was president of the Artists' Association of Nantucket, a 600-member non-profit organisation from 1999–2004. In 2005 he curated a museum-level, catalogued exhibit of historical art, *The Art Colony on Nantucket*. He lives on Nantucket Island.

Nick Gevers wrote his Masters dissertation on Gene Wolfe (University of Cape Town, 1991) and subsequently obtained a Ph.D. for his thesis discussing future and alternate histories in SF and fantasy (UCT, 1997). He has since worked very widely in the SF field as a critic – publishing numerous reviews and articles in the *Washington Post Book World*, *Foundation*, *Locus*, *Interzone*, *Nova Express* and elsewhere – and as an interviewer and editor. In the last capacity, he has edited many titles for PS Publishing, including books by Brian Aldiss, Michael Swanwick, Lucius Shepard and Elizabeth Hand. He lives in Cape Town, South Africa.

Joan Gordon is a professor at Nassau Community College on Long Island in New York. She has written readers' guides to Joe Haldeman and Gene Wolfe, co-edited *Blood Read: The Vampire as Metaphor in Contemporary Culture* and *Edging Into the Future: Science Fiction and Contemporary Cultural Transformation*, and is an editor at *Science Fiction Studies*. Her present work explores the intersection of utopia, genocide, and the alien other.

Colin Greenland is the author of *Take Back Plenty*, which in 1990 won the Arthur C. Clarke Award, the BSFA Award and the Eastercon Award, and several other novels, which didn't. He was for several years the Reviews Editor of *Foundation*, where 'Riding a Bicycle Backwards; An Interview with Gene Wolfe' was first published. His interviews and reviews appear frequently in the *Guardian*, occasionally in the *Independent*, and once in a blue moon in the *Times Literary Supplement*. He lives in Cambridge with his partner, the novelist Susanna Clarke.

Melissa Mia Hall is a frequent contributor to *Publisher's Weekly*, a variety of American national newspaper book review sections and online magazines like *Scifi Weekly*. She has taught creative writing for University of Texas at Arlington's Continuing Education centre and she has also begun a freelance art career after teaching at-risk teens. Her short fiction career began with 'Wishing Will Make it So' (in *Twilight Zone* (1981), edited by T. E. D. Klein). She has contributed to Charles L. Grant's *Shadows* anthologies (1983–87); *Women of Darkness* (1988); *Post-Mortem* (1989); *Skin of the Soul* (1990); *Whisper of Blood* (1991); *Marilyn: Shades of Blonde* (1997) and magazines including *Realms of Fantasy*. Her website can be found at http://home.earthlink.net/~blackleatherrequired/hallofmia/.

James B. Jordan is Director of Old Testament Studies at the Biblical Theological Seminary in St. Petersburg, Russia. He is also Director of Biblical Horizons ministries, an educational foundation. He took a degree in Comparative Literature at the University of Georgia (1971), served in the United States Air Force as an historian for four years, and then completed master's studies in theology. He is the author of numerous books, including most prominently *Through New Eyes: Developing a Biblical View of the World*. He presently lives in Niceville, Florida, and receives email at jbjordan4 @cox.net.

Nancy Kress is the author of twenty-three books, mostly SF. Her short fiction has won three Nebulas, a Hugo, and a Sturgeon, and her novel *Probability Space* earned the John W. Campbell Memorial Award. She writes often about the social consequences of genetic engineering. Kress, who is also a columnist for *Writers Digest* and often teaches fiction writing, lives in upstate New York with her very spoiled toy poodle.

Larry McCaffery's books include *Across the Wounded Galaxies: Interview with Contemporary Science Fiction Authors* (University of Illinois Press), *Storming the Reality Studio: A Casebook of Cyberpunk and Postmodern Science Fiction* (Duke University Press) and *Expelled from Eden: A William T. Vollmann Reader* (Thunder's Mouth Press). Currently Professor of English at San Diego State University, he currently lives with his wife, Sinda Gregory, in the magnificent desolation of the Anza Borrego Desert.

Lawrence Person is a science fiction writer living in Austin, Texas. His short fiction has appeared in *Asimov's, Analog, Fear,* and several anthologies. He also edits the Hugo-nominated SF critical magazine *Nova Express,* and is a member of the long-running Turkey City Writer's Workshop. His non-fiction has appeared in *National Review, Reason, Whole Earth Review, The Freeman, The World & I, Science Fiction Eye, The New York Review of Science Fiction,* and Slashdot.org. He owns a very large library. He also makes a mean batch of salsa. He has his own website at http://home.austin.rr.com/lperson/.

Calvin Rich enjoyed a career teaching challenging material, especially British and Renaissance writers and transformational grammar, at high school and college level. When given the opportunity to create a course in Fantasy and Romance, he was delighted to discover a certain writer who chose reader-challenging protagonists. Therefore, when Gene Wolfe provided a torturer-as-protagonist in *The Book of the New Sun,* he happily included his fine work in the course, then was greatly disappointed to learn during the interview that Wolfe preferred that academics leave his books alone. He is now retired and lives in Pacific Grove, California.

Peter Wright is a Reader in Speculative Fictions at Edge Hill University in Lancashire. He is author of *Attending Daedalus: Gene Wolfe, Artifice and the Reader* (Liverpool University Press, 2003), which was based on his Ph.D. thesis, and co-editor of *British Science Fiction Television* (I. B. Tauris, 2005). He has also contributed essays to *Foundation,* the *Blackwell Companion to Science Fiction* (Blackwell, 2005) and *British Science Fiction Cinema* (Routledge, 1999). He still hopes that more people will write and publish on Gene Wolfe.

Acknowledgements

Once again I am deeply indebted to Gene Wolfe, who agreed to this project many years ago and who has remained supportive throughout its compilation and publication. I am particularly grateful to him for the volume's wonderfully resonant title. Gratitude is also due to each of the interviewers, who generously agreed to make their work available to me for reprinting, replied to my enquiries promptly, and demonstrated an unfaltering enthusiasm for the project itself. They all made editing this collection a genuine pleasure. Special thanks is due to Ralph Black at the Writers Forum at SUNY Brockport, who put me in touch with Calvin Rich and who kindly gave his permission to reprint 'Gene Wolfe in Conversation'. Although every effort was made to contact Brendan Baber and Elliott Swanson, all communications have remained unanswered. Hence, their interviews are reprinted respectfully and in the hope that they will contact Liverpool University Press to ensure any amendments can be made in future editions.

Each of the interviews is published as originally written, with the exception of corrected typographical errors and the removal of some introductory material. As a consequence, there is a degree of overlap between some of the interviews in terms of the matters raised and the issues discussed. Nevertheless, there are often subtle differences or developments in the responses Wolfe offers and it seemed appropriate that these should remain to reflect the subjective and contextual nature of Wolfe's replies.

In addition, I should like to express my thanks to Professor Alistair McCulloch at Edge Hill University, who continues to assist in the support of my research; Andy Sawyer, Administrator of the Science Fiction Foundation Collection at the University of Liverpool for his considerable retrieval skills; Jenni Woodward, who assisted me in proofreading the manuscript; and my parents, as always, for their unflinching encouragement.

Part I The Trackless Meadows of Old Time

'Gene Wolfe: An Interview' copyright © Malcolm Edwards, first appeared in *Vector*, May–June 1973, pp. 7–15.

'An Interview with Gene Wolfe' copyright © Joan Gordon, first appeared in *Science Fiction Review*, Summer 1981.

'An Interview with Gene Wolfe' copyright © Melissa Mia Hall, first appeared in *Amazing Science Fiction Stories*, September 1981.

'Interview: Gene Wolfe – "The Legerdemain of the Wolfe"' copyright © Robert Frazier, first appeared in *Thrust: Science Fiction in Review*, Winter–Spring 1983.

'Riding a Bicycle Backwards: An Interview with Gene Wolfe' copyright © Colin Greenland, first appeared in *Foundation: The International Review of Science Fiction*, 31, 1984.

'A Conversation with Gene Wolfe' copyright © Nancy Kress and Calvin Rich, first appeared in *Australian Science Fiction Review*, November 1985. Reprinted by kind permission of the Writers Forum at SUNY Brockport.

'Gene Wolfe' copyright © Elliott Swanson, first appeared in *Interzone*, Autumn 1986.

'On Encompassing the Entire Universe: An Interview with Gene Wolfe' copyright © Larry McCaffery, first appeared in *Science Fiction Studies*, 15, 1988; reprinted in Larry McCaffery, *Across the Wounded Galaxies: Interviews with Contemporary American Science Fiction Writers*, Urbana: University of Illinois Press, 1990.

'Gene Wolfe: An Interview' copyright © James B. Jordan, revised version 2007.

'Gene Wolfe Interview' copyright © Brendan Baber, located at http://mysite.verizon.net/~vze2tmhh/wolfeint.html, 1994.

'Peter and the Wolfe: Gene Wolfe in Conversation' copyright © Peter Wright, 2007.

'Suns New, Long, and Short: An Interview with Gene Wolfe' copyright © Lawrence Person, first appeared in *Nova Express*, Fall/Winter 1998.

'A Magus of Many Suns: An Interview with Gene Wolfe' copyright © Nick Gevers, located at www.sfsite.com/03b/gw124.htm, 2002.

'Some Moments with the Magus: An Interview with Gene Wolfe' copyright © Nick Gevers, Michael Andre-Driussi and James B. Jordan, located at www.infinityplus.co.uk/nonfiction/intgw.htm, 2003.

Part II The Wild Joy of Strumming

Introduction

Peter Wright

Gene Wolfe is one of the most important American writers to emerge in the latter half of the twentieth century. The fact that he publishes in the field of fantastic literature (which includes horror, science and speculative fiction) has meant that his significance has been largely unacknowledged beyond and, at times, even within the genre. Nevertheless, he remains the author of some of the most stylistically distinct, structurally complex and intellectually invigorating imaginative fiction of recent years. Born in 1931, an engineer by training, a Roman Catholic by choice and a writer by inclination, Wolfe is a subtle literary craftsman whose work has yet to receive the wider audience and academic attention it deserves. It is undeniable that Wolfe's fiction is deceptive in its themes and plotting, misleading in its allusiveness and intertextuality and labyrinthine in its structuring, yet it is varied, vigorous, challenging and entertaining. The variety found in his work is not solely the product of diverse subject matter, which ranges from the experiences of a priest aboard a generation starship in *The Book of the Long Sun* (1993–96) to the events unfolding around an amnesiac soldier in ancient Greece in *Soldier of the Mist* (1986) and *Soldier of Arete* (1989). Nor is it found exclusively in his mastery of forms extending from the short story to the multi-volume novel. It arises equally from his notable narrative versatility (Wolfe is as convincing narrating as an all-American high school girl in *Pandora by Holly Hollander* (1990) as he is a phantom haunting his own memories in *Peace* (1975)); his stylistic ingenuity – demonstrated, for example, in the contrast between the spare prose of *The Wizard Knight* (2004) and the baroque richness of *The Book of the New Sun* (1980–83) – and his intricate interweaving of discourses on theology, faith, evolution, philosophy and psychology. This is not to say that Wolfe is given over to static, ruminant works: the truth is quite the contrary. His short stories and novels are brisk, incident-driven, dramatic. They can be as emotionally affecting as they are mentally engaging. There is a vibrant energy infusing Wolfe's fictions; they crackle with a sophisticated and restless vitality.

It seems probable that the complexity of Wolfe's fiction discourages critics and scholars from discussing the subject at length. Indeed, to read Gene Wolfe – and especially to write about him – is not without risk. It is an autobiographical activity, a confession, an admission of puzzlement or wonder or even vainglorious revelation. Yet the sophistication of his work, its varied subject matter, its stylistic range and its collective effect upon the reader all invite greater understanding. It is intended that, in a modest way, this collection of non-fiction and interviews may inspire later scholars to commit themselves to debating new interpretations of Wolfe's fiction rather than accepting dogmatic accounts informed more by received wisdom than by genuine critical or oppositional thought.

Having written *The Book of the New Sun*, *The Book of the Long Sun* and *The Book of the Short Sun* (1999–2001), Wolfe provides in this collection a book of shadows. Typically, things are not as they seem for these shadows are not the insubstantial shades that stretch and shorten, darken or fade with the vicissitudes of light. The shadows in this collection are as indelible as imagination and as powerful as dreams. They are, paradoxically, substantial.

In *The Sword of the Lictor* (1981), volume three of *The Book of the New Sun*, Baldanders' homunculus, Dr Talos, considers the scene before him and asks the protagonist Severian: 'Look about you – don't you recognise this … The castle? The monster? The man of learning? I only just thought of it. Surely you know that just as the momentous events of the past cast their shadows down the ages, so now, when the sun is drawing toward the dark, our own shadows race into the past to trouble mankind's dreams.'[1] Dr Talos's observation – a clear allusion to both Mary Shelley's *Frankenstein* (1818; rev. 1831) and James Whale's cinematic treatment of the story (1931) – posits the notion of history as a shadow cast by light. Condensing Urth's existence into a single day, Dr Talos conjectures that sunrise – the antediluvian dawn of Urth – casts the long shadows of prehistory into the future, where they shape cultures, landscapes, destinies. As Wolfe points out in 'Books in *The Book of the New Sun*', it is at the end of this diuturnal day – as Urth declines under a dying star – that the reddened, westering sun throws posthistoric shadows into the past, where they become dream-visions that trouble the sleep with phantoms. These chimeras will, in turn, shape the future from which they themselves were shaped.

Like Dr Talos's notional view of history as a projection of the sun, Gene Wolfe's literary career can be characterised as a projection of *The Book of the New Sun*. Before its publication between 1980 and 1983, the reader can find foreshadows of Wolfe's tetralogy and its sequel – *The Urth of the New Sun* (1987) – in the themes, techniques and conceits of antecedent short stories, novellas and novels. Following its publication, the central concerns of (to borrow Michael Andre-Driussi's eloquent phrase) the Urth Cycle cast their long shadows over the works that follow. They are found in the inversions and parallels of the *Soldier* novels, in the associated books of the *Long Sun* and *Short Sun* and in the spiritual and moral conflicts of Wolfe's two-volume *The Wizard Knight*.

The shadows of *The Book of the New Sun* are not found solely in Wolfe's fiction, however. They fall naturally over the interviews Wolfe has given throughout his career and in his published and unpublished writing on the creative process (most conspicuously on *The Castle of the Otter* (1982), a book about the writing of *The Book of the New Sun*, which has been reprinted subsequently in *Castle of Days* (1992)). Ironically, these are the shadows that illuminate Wolfe's fiction and provide invaluable and absorbing insights into the author's tangible wisdom.

In this collection, Wolfe shares his understanding of and attitudes towards readers, writers and writing. Part I, The Trackless Meadows of Old Time, includes fourteen of the interviews that Wolfe has given throughout his career. In the earliest, an interview with Malcolm Edwards for the British Science Fiction Association's magazine, *Vector*, in 1973, Wolfe provides a succinct biography, recounting his early life and the circumstances that led to his decision to write sf, his debt to Damon Knight and the circumstances around the publication of his first novel, *Operation Ares* (1970). Here, and in other interviews, Wolfe cites his literary influences, yet to compare him to Dickens, Koestler, Kafka, Chesterton, Kipling, Nabokov, Borges or Proust is to do him a disservice. While one can trace the inspirational role of these authors, Wolfe is a distinct writer, a true purveyor of originality. He transforms whatever themes or styles he adopts into something distinctly 'Wolfean'. These are the shadows within the shadows, the implications that attend Wolfe's modest, ingenuous reflections. When he discusses *The Fifth Head of Cerberus* (1972), its origins at the 1970 Milford Writers Conference and its development into three linked novellas at the behest of Norbert Slepyan, Scribner's sf editor at the time, he does not imply – or even allude to – his real achievement in the text. With *The Fifth Head of Cerberus*'s mesmerising complexity and ambiguities of identity, he transformed science fiction's traditional colonisation story from an account of positive human expansion into a complex postcolonial dialogue between coloniser and colonised. As such, it remains one of the most effective and subtle indictments of colonialism found in recent literature.

Perceiving the implications of Wolfe's reflections and commentaries is essential to a better understanding of his work and the reprinting of his interviews with Edwards and others offers a welcome opportunity for Wolfe's readers and scholars to reassess his writing. In his interview with Joan Gordon in 1981, for example, Wolfe not only enriches the reader's understanding of his youth but also emphasises the danger of accepting his Catholicism as a ready mode of interpreting his work. 'I am,' he says, 'a Catholic in the real communion-taking sense, which tells you a lot less than you think about my religious beliefs.' This is, indeed, the case. As he explains, 'Like every thinking person, I am still working out my beliefs.'

This comment, made in 1981, has remained pertinent throughout Wolfe's career, particularly in the spiritual movement detectable in his multi-volume novels *The Book of the New Sun*, *The Book of the Long Sun*, *The Book of the Short Sun* and *The Wizard Knight*. The *Sun* series are characterised by journeys which are physical, evolutionary, trans-temporal and spiritual. Collectively, they suggest a greater journey, a spiritual passage taken by Wolfe himself, away from the uncertainties and delusions of *The Book of the New Sun* through the moments of revelation regarding the Outsider (in all likelihood the Christian God) in *The Book of the Long Sun*, to the concluding mystical communion of *The Book of the Short Sun*. As such, they constitute one of the longest and most complex narrative movements from psychic delusion to spiritual enlightenment found in speculative fiction. They are, in effect, the working out of the intricate metaphysical beliefs of a complex 'thinking person'.

Given the success of *The Book of the New Sun*, which brought Wolfe and his writing to the attention of a much wider audience than *The Fifth Head of Cerberus*, his memorious ghost's story *Peace* (1975) or *The Devil in a Forest* (1976), his medieval tale of moral choice and sly deception, it is unsurprising that he was interviewed frequently during its publication. In his conversations with Melissa Mia Hall, Robert Frazier, Colin Greenland, Nancy Kress and Calvin Rich, Wolfe discusses the conception and execution of the tetralogy, remarking on its origins, intergenericism, its protagonist's complex characterisation and his exploitation of time travel. The occasional inconsistencies between these accounts only serve to make the mystery of *The Book of the New Sun*, with its deceived and deceptive narrator, all the more intriguing.

Larry McCaffery's interview with Wolfe for *Science Fiction Studies* is certainly the most wide-ranging of those collected here. First published in 1988, it extends beyond the usual questions of autobiography, inspiration and literary practice to include discussions of the nature of language and consciousness, Wolfe's fascination with memory, and a much more profound reflection on the development of *The Book of the New Sun* and its interconnectedness with the novels and stories that preceded it. Rarely has Wolfe's intellectual energy been as eloquently expressed at it is here.

Wolfe's interview with Elliott Swanson is rather different. Its peripatetic structure draws discussions of Wolfe's generic experimentation, his experiences of and fondness for libraries, his attitude to film, the possibility of his stories being adapted for the screen and – most telling – what he likes least about his work: misinterpretation despite his best efforts toward clarity. The fitful nature of Swanson's interview also typifies James B. Jordan's conversation also. Such an approach is not unusual, given Wolfe's increasing *oeuvre* and the questions it raises, which are as diverse as the novels and short stories under discussion. Accordingly, Jordan's interview ranges across Wolfe's religious and political beliefs, science, the practice of being a novelist, the Urth cycle and Wolfe's use of the symbol and notion of the wolf. It is at its most revealing when Jordan discusses the religious dimensions of Wolfe's work – particularly with regard to *The Book of the New Sun* and *There Are Doors* – Wolfe's perspective on feminine and masculine subjectivity, and his treatment of the pagan world in *Soldier of the Mist* and *Soldier of Arete*.

Wolfe's discussion with Brendan Baber is much more relaxed though no less intellectually inclined. Indeed, its informal dialogue only serves to sharpen Wolfe's radical perspective on fantastic literature as 'the truth of the human experience' and his penetrating criticism of realism and materialist philosophy in favour of living 'on the animal level'. Wolfe's preference for seeing things as they are, for understanding clearly the nature of objects and relationships, is valid advice for anyone wishing to analyse Wolfe's *oeuvre* and the elaborate relationships that exist within it.

In 'Peter and the Wolfe', Wolfe takes time to reflect on his then thirty-year career. He talks at length about the sources for several of his short stories and for *There Are Doors*, which segues into a detailed discussion of self-deception and the deception of others as a recurring theme in his fiction. This is a personal reflection in many ways, with Wolfe tracing his preoccupation with memory, the subjectivity of perception, and the manipulation of the individual to aspects of his personal life. It is also notable for Wolfe's perspectives on 'cultivated' readers, readers' reactions to his work and his consideration of what makes a good writer and a good (and a bad) academic. There are distinct lessons to be learned from his astute observations.

Lawrence Person's interview focuses on *The Book of the Long Sun*, its religious dimension, and the contrast in narrative styles between this later work and *The Fifth Head of Cerberus*. Some readers may be surprised by Wolfe's confirmation that Severian 'is not a Christ figure' but a Christian figure, although this, too, is subject to debate. Equally important, perhaps, is that Wolfe finally sets the record straight on his involvement with the development of the Pringles potato chips manufacturing machine. Sadly, more people experience the products of Wolfe's labour this way rather than through his significantly more rewarding (and more nourishing) literary works.

In the final interviews in Part I, Wolfe talks to Nick Gevers regarding the writing of *The Book of the Short Sun* and discussing at length his versatility in selecting styles appropriate to the story being told and dialogue precisely reflective of the characters speaking. For those readers attempting to unravel or decode the connections between the various *Sun* books, Gevers' interview elicits – with some effort – several useful remarks from Wolfe. These comments confirm that *The Book of the New Sun*, *The Book of the Long Sun* and *The Book of the Short Sun* together form perhaps the most complex work of speculative fiction to emerge from the genre.

Nick Gevers' second interview, 'Some Moments with the Magus', undertaken with questions from Michael Andre-Driussi and James B. Jordan, is the most discursive in the collection, yet it reveals a new-found political relevance in several of Wolfe's early stories, notably 'Seven American Nights' and 'Hour of Trust'. Refreshingly, after the candid responses in many previous interviews, 'Some Moments with the Magus' sees the return of Wolfe's sometimes playful, sometimes direct, refusal to answer the questions posed and to sink speculations that appear at least plausible. The interview concludes with a discussion of Wolfe's recent work, the two-volume *The Wizard Knight* and the possibility that *it* may form a 'Rosetta Stone' for the deciphering of 'themes explored with greater disguise in the Briah and *Latro* books'. Such 'metafictional cartography', the mapping of the concealed elements of earlier fiction through parallels with later work, is not a new idea. Its effectiveness as a critical approach remains questionable but, as Wolfe himself concludes, 'I'll be interested to see whether anyone does it.' The challenge has been set; it remains to be seen whether any of Wolfe's exegetically inclined readers will rise to it.

Part I, The Wild Joy of Strumming opens with the seemingly exegetical 'Books in *The Book of the New Sun*', an essay formerly published in NESFA Press's *Plan[e]t Engineering* (1984), in which Wolfe addresses Dr Talos's observation regarding history as the shadow of light. He suggests that the shadows haunting Severian's future Urth are those cast by innumerable books: unread, indecipherable, alien. The conclusion emphasises that recurrence often serves as a formal and thematic device in Wolfe's fiction and reminds the reader of the formidable intellect shaping *The Book of the New Sun* and associated commentaries.

The essays that follow gather together Wolfe's direct and often pithy advice to those readers who wish to write creatively. His guidance is given with the same skill and economy the reader experiences in his fiction. 'Wolfe's Irreproducible Truths About Novels' is a concise example of how candid he can be. For anyone endeavouring to create credible characters – or understand, at least in part, how Wolfe engineers his fully realised fictional figures, 'Balding, Avuncular Gene's Quick and Dirty Guide to Creating Memorable Characters' shows a remarkable appreciation of how easy characterisation can be. 'Nor the Summers as Golden: Writing Multivolume Works' opens as a self-deprecating discussion of the process of authoring 'something that is more like life itself than the other forms are', yet is soon replete with the experiential and intuitive understanding of a writer who excels at the form. Wolfe's wit resounds throughout, most obviously in the gentle humour of 'How to Be a Writer's Family', the informal drollery of 'Libraries on the Superhighway – Rest Stop or Roadkill', and in the satirical edge to 'The Handbook of Permissive English' and 'More Than Half of You Can't Read This'. In contrast, sensible, cautionary advice awaits the reviewer in 'Wolfe's Inalienable* Truths About Reviewing'.

Part II concludes with 'A Fantasist Reads the Bible and Its Critics', a discursive essay that makes cogent observations about authorship, inspiration, the Bible, fantasy and the often overlooked relationships existing between them. The essay is enlivened by Wolfe's wittiness and his relaxed intellectualism. It also raises interesting possibilities for the interpretation of Wolfe's first-person narratives.

There can be no doubt that Gene Wolfe is a luminary both within the genre and in the wider context of contemporary fiction. As such, it is appropriate that much of his work is invested with themes of light and darkness, sunshine and shadow. Indeed, those of his readers who choose to write about his work constitute an additional cadre of shades. The reviewers, commentators, interviewers, academics and editors are all shadows cast by Wolfe himself. There are times when such shadows are appropriate to give sharper form and context; on other occasions, they are unnecessary. When the light is sufficiently brilliant, they simply disappear. In this book of shadows, the light is very bright indeed.

Notes

1. Gene Wolfe, *The Sword of the Lictor* (London: Arrow, 1982), p. 277.

Part I

The Trackless Meadows of Old Time

1

Gene Wolfe: An Interview

Malcolm Edwards

Malcolm Edwards' interview with Wolfe first appeared in *Vector*, May–June 1973, following the publication of *The Fifth Head of Cerberus: Three Novellas* (1972). Although Wolfe had only published his first short story, 'The Dead Man', in 1965, his work had already attracted critical acclaim. 'The Island of Doctor Death and Other Stories' (1970) and 'Against the Lafayette Escadrille' (1972) had both earned Nebula Award nominations (in 1971 and 1973 respectively); and 'The Fifth Head of Cerberus', the opening novella of the collection, had been shortlisted for both the Hugo and Nebula Awards in 1973. Here Wolfe discusses his life and early career.

ME: Could you first of all tell us something about your background, how you came into writing, and why sf?

GW: I was born in Brooklyn, New York. This came home to me, to me who had always called myself a Texan and thought of myself as a Texan, when I read that Thomas Wolfe 'warmed up' for writing by walking the night streets of Brooklyn. He was from the hill country of northwest North Carolina and so was my great, great grandfather – making us, at least presumptively, distant cousins. Hemingway sharpened twenty pencils and Willa Cather read a passage from her Bible, but Thomas Wolfe, bless him, swung his big body down Brooklyn streets and may have been thrashing out some weighty problem in *Of Time and the River* during the early hours of Thursday 7 May, 1931. I hope so. I like to think of him out there on the sidewalk worrying about Gene Gant and flaying NYU.

At any rate I was born in that city at the southwestern tip of Long Island. My parents lived in New Jersey at the time, but they moved and moved. To Peoria, where I played with Rosemary Dietsch who lived next door, and her brothers Robert and Richard. To Massachusetts, where little Ruth McCann caught her hand in our car door. To Logan, Ohio, my father's home, where Boyd Wright and I got stung by bumble bees that had nested in our woodshed. To Des Moines, where a redheaded boy taught me chess while we were both in the second grade. Then to Dallas for a year, and at last to Houston, which became my home town, the place I was 'from'.

I went to Edgar Allan Poe elementary school, where we read 'The

Masque of the Red Death' in fifth grade and learned 'The Raven' in the sixth. We lived in a small house with two very large bedrooms; the front room was my parents', the back one, with mint growing profusely beneath its windows, mine. I had no brothers or sisters, but I had a black and white spaniel named Boots, and I built models (mostly World War I planes, which still fascinate me) there and collected comics and Big-Little books.

The thing I recall most vividly about Houston in the late thirties and early forties is the heat. Houston has almost precisely the climate of Calcutta, and until I was ready for High School there was no air conditioning except in theatres and the Sears Department Store. You went to the movies in the hottest part of the day to miss it; and when you came out the heat and sunlight were appalling. I remember my father wrapping his hand in his handkerchief so he could open the car door.

Our house stood midway between two mad scientists. Miller Porter, who lived in the big house behind us (his father was a brewing company executive), was my own age but much tougher and cleverer, and he built Tessla coils and similar electric marvels. Across the street a chemist for Humble Oil maintained a private laboratory in a room over his garage. If this were not enough there was, only five sweltering blocks away, the Richmond Pharmacy, where a boy willing to crouch immobile behind the candy case could cram *Planet Stories*, or *Thrilling Wonder Stories*, or (my own favourite) *Famous Fantastic Mysteries*, while the druggist compounded prescriptions. Almost unnoticed the big, slow moving ceiling fans vanished from the Richmond Pharmacy and the barbershop. World War II was over and there was a room air conditioner in one of my bedroom windows and another in the dining room; Houston began to lose its mixed Spanish American and Southern character and I was in high school, where I showed no aptitude for athletics or most other things. I joined the R.O.T.C. to get out of compulsory softball. (I was one of the very few cadets who was not made an officer for the year before graduation.) And a year later the 'pappy shooters' of the Texas National Guard because you got paid (I think $2.50) for attending drills.

To my surprise the National Guard was fun. We fired on the rifle range and played soldier, with pay, for two weeks during school vacations. When the Korean War broke out we thought our outfit, G Company of the 143rd Infantry, would be gone in a week. It never went, and though I would gladly have waited around the armoury for the order I found myself committed to attending Texas A&M instead.

A&M, which offered the cheapest possible college education to Texas boys, was at the time I attended an all-male land-grant institution specialising (the A&M stands for Agricultural and Mechanical) in animal husbandry and engineering. For some reason I have forgotten – I suspect because someone told my father or me that it was a good thing to take until you made up you mind what to switch to – I majored in Mechanical Engineering. Only Dickens could do justice to Texas A&M as I knew it, and he would not be believed. It was, I suppose, modelled on West Point; but it lacked both the aristocratic tradition and the sense of purpose. I dropped out in the middle of my junior year, thus losing my student deferment and was drafted for (remember that?) the Korean War. So G Company never went but I did. I was lucky and got my combat infantry badge during the closing months without getting nicked.

The G. I. Bill allowed me to finish my education to B.S.M.E. at the University of Houston. Rosemary Dietsch, whose mother had kept in touch with mine, came to Texas for a visit, and we were married five months after I got a job in engineering development. We have Roy II (after my father, whose real name, however, is Emerson Leroy Wolfe; mother is Mary Olivia Airs Wolfe), Madeleine, Therese, and Matthew; and a three bedroom house.

How did I come into writing? Quietly. And late.

The lights were dimmed and most of the seats were filled. He edged down the aisle, dribbling popcorn and tripping over fat ladies. Eased into a seat and found that he was the picture.

Why sf? Okay, I'll level with you: it is the biggest market for short stories. In fact, sf and mysteries are almost the only short story markets in America today, and the sf market is several times the size of the mystery market. I have written a number of mainstream short stories and I have never *sold* (for money) one. I have written a number of mystery shorts and sold two – for 1c a word. Let me add in passing that I don't believe in these rusty little fences: fiction is fiction and there are no fundamental differences between the supposed types. It would be perfectly possible to write a mainstream sf western about a murder with a strong sex element; if it sold it would probably sell as sf – because the sf audience is the last audience that can stand the psychic strain imposed by the short story form.

I have been squatting here trying to remember what books I liked as a child. The Oz books, which you do not, perhaps, read in Britain, and the best of which were written within a few miles of here (i.e. Barrington, Illinois). *Alice.* A series of books about a goat named *Billy Whiskers* who was always on the bum. When I was in school twelve years later, the head of the department, an old Swede who had been an officer in the American army in both World Wars, asked our class who had read the BW books; and then who had read *Miss Minerva and William Green Hill*; and I was the only one who had heard of either. A very early Disney book: *Bucky Bug* – because it was full of wonderful machinery the bugs had made from junk, tanks that were pill boxes on roller skates and the like. The oldest Disney was rich with this kind of mechanism, which made its last stand in *Snow White.*

ME: The dedication of *The Fifth Head of Cerberus* implies a considerable debt to Damon Knight, and in fact you are one of a group of writers closely associated with Knight, Milford and *Orbit*. What effect do you think these associations have had on your development as a writer?

GW: I implied a considerable debt to Damon Knight in the dedication to *Cerberus* because I owe him a considerable debt; in fact, more than I will ever be able to repay. He was the first editor to buy my work regularly, and the first to pay me good rates. He has given me invaluable advice and been my steadfast friend when he owed me nothing.

You ask about Milford. Read *A Pocketful of Stars* if you have not already. I knew no other writers and no readers before I went to Milford for the first time. In England where (so I am told) things are better, you cannot well conceive the climate of anti-intellectualism that exists in this country outside of a few places like New York and San Francisco. And though I was born in the former I left it in infancy and have lived all my life in Texas and the middle west.

ME: But is the kind of criticism and advice you get at a place like Milford any better than what you get elsewhere?

GW: Yes, but sometimes it can be very bad. In 1969 almost everyone said (for example) that Richard Hill's 'To Sport With Amaryllis' was bad – they were like people biting into cotton candy when they expected roast beef. But you can't get roast beef on the Ferris wheel.

ME: Your first novel, *Operation Ares*, was published in 1970, although differences from most of your other work suggest that it is one of your earliest stories. It's a very leisurely book for the first 150 pages or so, but thereafter becomes increasingly rushed and telegraphic. Was it cut for publication?

GW: *Ares* was written in 1967, and the original manuscript ran over 100,000 words. It was cut to about 80,000, the earlier chapters by me and the later ones by Don Benson, then editor at Berkley. At the time I began it I supposed it to be possible to tell the story of a war in a single novel of not unreasonable length. I still believe this, but it would take some handling.

ME: Are you satisfied with the published version?

GW: No, but I will never revise it, and that for two reasons – first, because with an equal amount of work I could write a new book, and second, because I regard that sort of thing as a species of crime.

ME: Crime against whom, or what?

GW: Against Truth, for one thing; you will say (or if you don't someone else will – I shall use you because you're handy) that a given book or story will carry all sorts of disclaimers to the effect that the author wrote at twenty-five and revised at forty but in point of fact it won't. The publishers won't bother with them – not for long on a book and not at all on a short story. Secondly against Art. Assuming that the writer had progressed (and if he hasn't, of what use is the revision) he will be using the techniques he has developed by years of practice on his own youthful ideas, much as though a parent were to forge the child's homework.

ME: I was fascinated by *The Fifth Head of Cerberus*, but trying to put myself in the author's place, I was unable to see quite how you could come to write the book in this way. How did it come about?

GW: How the book came about is uncomplicated. I wrote 'The Fifth Head of Cerberus' (the first novella) for the 1970 Milford Writers Conference, the last to be held at Milford. As is customary I mailed in the manuscript several weeks before I left for the conference myself – this gives Damon and Kate and any early arrivals (and people sometimes come as much as a week in advance) a chance to read some manuscripts before the pressure gets too high, and gives Damon the information he needs to work out a schedule for the first few days. Damon wrote back in a day or so that he would like to buy the story for *Orbit*, and I accepted; so it was actually sold before I got to Milford.

Norbert Slepyan, who was then Scribner's sf editor, attended the conference, and Virginia Kidd (who has since become my agent) and Damon sicked him onto the manuscript. He said he thought Scribner's would publish it in book form if I would write additional material.

It was artistically impossible to continue the story of Number Five, but when you have imagined an unreal world it is possible to lay any number of stories in it. It considered Aunt Jeannine and David as possible protagonists – I still regret slightly that could not go with Dr. Marsch and Jeannine both – and the rest you know.

ME: Was the idea of the Annese incorporated in the first novella with no intention that it should be developed, then?

GW: At the time I put them in 'Cerberus' I had no plan to develop the Annese further, but I was conscious that they *could* be developed, as I've tried to say. Almost everything can be developed further. The fact that the development occurs in a later story, or in the same story, or does not occur, makes no fundamental difference. Stevenson could have written the childhood of Long John Silver – it was there. I could begin the later adventures of Marydoll tonight.

ME: *Cerberus* is published as 'three novellas'. Yet the three stories are strongly, if unobtrusively, linked; they illuminate one another and finally add up to a unified book. It seems to me at least as much a novel as – to take a recent example – *The Gods Themselves*. Why didn't you call it one?

GW: You seem to be asking why I published my three novellas *as* three novellas when I probably could have called them a novel and not been sued or sent to prison. Why should I? Would they have been better received under that label?

All this suggests the problem of the theme anthology – you know, 'Great Science Fiction About Bees'. It is perfectly true (at least in most cases) that all the stories have something to do with bees; it is equally true that they have nothing to do with each other – they are linked by an external. Now I think the stories in my book are in the opposite situation: the internal linkage is there, but the external links are entirely omitted: the first story is told in the first person, the second in the third person; the third is a mixture of both: a minor character in the first story is the author of the second and a major character in the third; and so on. Now if the public is willing (as it clearly is) to accept 'Great Science Fiction About Bees' as a true expression of its theme, what would it think of my book if it claimed the unity of a novel?

I should add that I rather enjoy these themed anthologies because they force their editors to uncover good but seldom reprinted material.

ME: Would it have been better received as a novel? Hard to say; but I think it might have been better enjoyed. As you say, the internal linkages are there, but by labelling it as it is, surely you encourage readers to over-look them? Put it this way; if someone were to read the third part first, then the first, then the second, would they get as much out of it as some-one who read it consecutively?

GW: I think I see what the trouble is in this novel–novella argument: you feel that if shorter pieces are in any way connected they should be called a novel. I don't agree, but granting your definition then *Cerberus* is, as you say, a novel. I did, of course, intend the stories to be read in the order in which they were published; and it would, of course, be possible for some thick or eccentric reader to decide that 'V.R.T.' was the most attractive title (I might almost agree with him there) and read that first.

ME: Are there any writers who have particularly influenced you? Which writers do you especially admire?

GW: Damon Knight once asked me what books had influenced me most, and I told him *The Lord of the Rings* (which I found out later he loathes), *The Napoleon of Notting Hill* (which he loves), and *Marks' Mechanical Engineer's Handbook*. I still feel this is a pretty good answer, but would add *The Man Who Was Thursday*, *Darkness at Noon*, *The Trial*, *The Castle*, *The Remembrance of Things Past*, the *Gormenghast* trilogy (magnificent no matter how flawed, and it is terribly flawed), and *Look Homeward Angel*, which I feel *is* that 'great American novel' people still talk about; very few people in this gen-eration trouble themselves to read it.

I have read Bradbury, Ellison, Disch, Lafferty, Russ and a few others with great respect, but I don't feel I have been influenced by them – their things are good things but not my thing.

I have read most of Maupassant and feel *Mme. Teller's Excursion* to be his story. I have read a good deal of Dunsany, Oliver Onions and Machen.

And Lovecraft and Günter Grass. If you haven't read them yet I recommend *A Voyage to Arcturus* (though I despise its philosophy), *The Teachings of Don Juan* and its sequels, *The Universal Baseball Association, Inc. J. Henry Waugh, Prop.*

ME: I'd be interested to hear you enlarge on the flaws in the *Gormenghast* trilogy.

GW: I don't want to do that. There is always something sneaking about trying to pick holes in a masterpiece, and this is doubly so when the writer is among the dead of our time.

So I'm going to try instead to talk about the three books a little, the good and the bad, but always with the reservation – which I think you already are willing to concede me – that they are great literature in precisely the sense that *Hamlet* (for example) is great literature. We may complain justly about the gravediggers' jokes or the absurd welter of blood at the end of the last act, but we are throwing stones at the moon and we know it.

A disclaimer first – it's been three years since I read the books. I'm sure it will be possible for you to catch me out on some of the things I say. I can claim, though, that I have performed the fundamental duty of a critic and read my author: I remember very well how eagerly I looked forward to my daily hour with Peake.

You asked if I read the Langdon Jones reconstruction of *Titus Alone*, saying that you understood it to be more faithful to the author's intentions.

No, and I confess to being very wary of 'reconstructions'. In any event, I think the second volume – *Gormenghast* – and not *Titus Alone* is the weakest of the three, and that by a considerable margin. The school (granted that it is great fun at times) is the worst thing in any of the books. After we have enjoyed the scene in which the Professors come to Irma Prunesquallor's ball – in fact while we are in the very midst of it – we realise with terrible disappointment that we have left the castle and have been stranded instead in the middle of just such a nineteenth century English village as Pickwick might have visited. It is very jolly, and never jollier than when one of the teachers mistakes Irma's face, as she peeps around a corner, for an apparition of Death; but it is not the world of Steerpike (that magnificent creation) and Fuschia and Barquentine. It is not even the world in which Craggmire the Acrobat crosses his apartment on his hands tossing a pig in a green nightdress to-and-fro with his feet. It is not Gormenghast at all.

A few other points from the first two books: at one time we are told that there are rattlesnakes outside the castle. If you cannot understand why there cannot be, I cannot explain it. Those are adders. Flay (his fight with Swelter is the best thing in the first book save perhaps for Swelter's corpse floating in the trapped water on the roof with the sword a cross sticking out of it and eventually cascading over the eaves like the body of a dinosaur going over a waterfall) has knees that click when he walks, which is good. When he comes to kill Swelter (I believe it is) he binds strips of blanket about them to muffle the noise, which is very good indeed. But later, when it is no longer convenient for the author that Flay's knees click, we are told that they have stopped, which is just ghastly – I wanted to take Peake by the throat and shake him when I read it. The wild girl comes to nothing, when she promised so much.

The death of the twins is wonderful, unique. As is the very end of *Titus Alone*, when Titus hears the signal gun and turns away. Muzzlehatch, in the last book, is a fine character; as is Crabcalf, who is surely a self-parody of the author. But nothing can console us for the death of Steerpike...except the knowledge (like Titus') that Gormenghast is still there. I think that it is more or less the custom, when writing about a great book, to quote the opening paragraph, or at least a few sentences of it, at the end. I am not going to do that – they are quite undistinguished. Instead I would like to quote the sentence from *Titus Alone* that I copied out on the flyleaf when I first read the book: 'Behind him, wherever he stood, or slept, were the legions of Gormenghast – tier upon tier, with the owls calling through the rain, and the ringing of the rust-red bells.'

I came on it a few minutes ago while I was paging through the books in preparation for writing this letter, and the demon who stands behind my chair is still screaming (as he did when I first saw it) *why not you? Why not you?!*

ME: Most of your stories appear in the various original anthologies – *Orbit*, *Universe*, and so on – which now seem to be proliferating beyond all reason: for example I read recently that one editor had signed contracts with nineteen different publishers for forty-two anthologies! Do you think this will lead, fairly soon, to a collapse in the market? If so, what effect do you think it will have?

GW: I too read that one editor (Roger Elwood) has signed contracts for forty-two anthologies, and it is hard to believe. But Roger has been buying an awful lot of material (I hear); and certainly he has been buying quite a bit from me, viz: 'An Article About Hunting', 'Beautyland'; and 'Going to the Beach', all of them paid for and none yet published. May he prosper.

This question of collapse you raise is an interesting one; it is tied, I think, to the replacement of sf magazines by sf paperbacks, and this in turn is tied to the general lack of understanding of the sf field by the upper management of publishing. To oversimplify, I would say that the proliferation of original anthologies will lead to a collapse when and if the publishers decide that the public is so eager for this type of book that the books can be edited by their junior tradebook editors. When that happens (and I hope it never does) we will see entire books filled with really bad material – and the great mass of the sf reading public (which is much larger, as I feel certain you realise, than fandom) simply does not know enough to understand that a volume edited by Harry Harrison is likely to contain quite a bit of good material while one edited by Norman Nudje is probably a bad investment, particularly if his contents page is populated exclusively by unrecognizables. There are a lot of reasons for this, and they all pull together: it is unlikely that Norman knows or cares much for science fiction, and he will not be given much of a budget for his book. On the other hand, it is highly probable that he will feel confident that he knows what the public wants: he has (after all) seen two episodes of *Star Trek*, he has watched the sci-fi flicks on late TV, he has seen the covers of Ace doubles. Very little that is good will be sent to him, and most of that will be rejected.

In time his book (*Tales from the Void*) will appear. How many bad books will his non-fan reader buy (at $1.25 each, I should say) before he stops buying anything? I suspect two or three.

I also suspect I am not answering the question you want to ask, which is, I think, *As things are now, is collapse imminent?* No.

To answer a question you have not asked, I am much more optimistic about the future of print as a medium than I was five or ten years ago. Motion pictures, the great enemy of print in my boyhood, the popcorn monster that seemed so completely invulnerable when there was no television, and only the theatres were air-conditioned, and an adult paid 35c or 40c and a child 10c or 15c, today is more than half dead. Television itself is noticeably weaker every year, and every year more inclined to occupy itself with completely non-literary material (i.e. sports). The loss of cigarette advertising has been a terrible blow to television, and it seems certain to be followed by others – soon, I think, there will be no more broadcast ads for tobacco in any form (natural-wrapper cigarettes, which are legally cigars, are being advertised here now), no ads for wine or beer, either. Recently, I attended a symposium sponsored by the American Business Press in which the effect of TV cassettes was discussed. The publishers who hadn't tried them were (for the most part) enthused. Those who had were grim.

ME: How much contact have you had with sf fans, fandom, fanzines? Have you been to any conventions? D. G. Compton said once that he was grateful to discover the existence of sf fans because it proved that there were people who *read* his books but had reservations because such activity tended to encourage the continuance of sf as a genre, while we should be tearing down compartments rather than building them. Would you agree?

GW: I went to St Louiscon, two Marcons, Pecon last year and Midwestcon
this year; in a few days I hope to be at Chambanacon. I have a feeling I'm
leaving out something, but that's all I can think of now. I hope to go to
Torcon; and while I was in Cincinnati I was a member of the local fan club
called, I believe, the Cincinnati Fantasy Group. I get *Locus*, *Yandro*, *SOTWJ*,
Geg, *SF Commentary*, *Richard E. Geis*, *Mota*, *BC*, *Starling*, and a lot of other
excellent magazines whose titles escape me now.

I certainly cannot agree with the Compton quote you give. It's one
thing to take sf out of the ghetto; it would be another to deprive it of its
individuality. Space travel and alien intelligences tend to encourage the
continuance of sf as a genre too; but the way to break down these compartments is to have a great many very good books.

ME: Would you describe your method of writing?

GW: You want to know (I should say, seem to want to know) about my
schedule; I suspect you're going to find this so dull you're going to have to
cut out the whole thing. On a work day I get up sometime between six
thirty and seven, shave if I can beat the children to the bathroom, go
down into the basement and write until Rosemary calls me up for breakfast, go back down, if there's time left, until eight. Besides writing I will
have reviewed the carbons of any letters I wrote the night before, and
decided whether to send them or revise them.

At eight I go upstairs, dress, drive to the post office, mail my letters and
pick up the mail. At eighty-thirty I am at my desk at work. At five I am
back home (all of this assumes I am not travelling, of course) go down-
stairs and try to deal with the mail between then and supper, which will
be between five thirty and six. After supper I will shop if I have shopping
to do, or write more letters, or fix something around the house. From
seven to eight I watch TV about three times a week; after eight (if it is a TV
day, after seven if it is not) I try to write until nine. From nine to ten I
read. At ten (unless what I am reading is very good indeed) I watch the
news and TV and the first half hour or hour of the Tonight show, then to
bed. I usually get in about four hours of writing on Saturday and Sunday.

It takes me about an hour/page of finished copy – a half-hour for first
draft, another half for two or three revisions. As I said, I write in the basement, but I try not to yell at my children when they come down and want
to talk to me. At least not the first time. I find that when I start a story I
had better know the ending. Sometimes I change it when I get there, but
if I start without that I'm usually in trouble. I must have the characters
and the end.

No, I don't voice my own opinions through my characters, because one
of them is that each character should be true to himself or herself at all
times; and if one of them isn't it hurts like a boil until I fix it. Obviously I
may agree, from time to time, with something a character says, but that is

purely coincidental and I seldom think about it.

It is very hard to say how much of my output I sell, because I continue marketing things for a long time – I once sold a story (I won't tell you the title, so don't ask) on the 38th submission. I have written three novels I am no longer marketing, so that is a considerable body of work which will remain unpublished. One is very bad, one fair, one, I think, good but badly dated as to content. Of my present output I would say that I sell 80%. Yes, I would like to write full time, and will do it when I feel I can support myself and my family that way.

You think I'm fussy and Damon Knight and Virginia Kidd tell me I'm sloppy, and that gets me off onto a tangent that might be interesting to any *Vector* readers who have followed this thing this long. In 1969 I took part in a sensitivity group programme in which each participant was required to write a capsule description of all the others as the last exercise. I saved the ones I received (I have a stack of binders I call my journal – letters, jottings, etc. dating to March 1960; it now fills two shelves of a sizable bookcase), have not looked at them since I received them, and think it might be interesting to copy them out for you – to my knowledge no one has published this kind of parlour analysis of a writer, but I should add that none of the participants knew I wrote. The descriptions are not signed (unfortunately) but I will indicate when the hand changes. You have to trust my honesty obviously, but I promise to spare nothing:

> Gene's humour is a key to his psychology. It is clever, cutting, deep. Full of double meaning and can be readily sharpened to a keen edge.
> (1) He is ego-centric to the point of excluding other peoples' ideas and closing his mind to opposing discussion.
> When given leadership position he asserts himself in a 'let's get lined up and don't dare challenge my position.' (This has been crossed out, but is still legible – the kind of thing we do with slashes.)
> He is a firm leader and tends to carry his authoritarian attitude as a leader into the discussion. He cuts off conflict as sharply as he can.
> (3) Gene works just as hard as necessary to get the job done. Step on toes, loner – (can't read) – good guy façade.

> *Ray*: Impatient, withdrawal, instructive, hard-hitting, self-possessed doesn't search …
> In the face of conflict, he presents his position once, and then withdraws; typically 'Here's the way it is boys, if you can't see this position now no further contribution by me will help understanding.' If understanding is not reached, he is willing to compromise. His major contributions to the team are invaluable and instructive insights such as analogies (sic), case histories, and psychoanalysis. He does not search for alternate opinions and listens to them through unfiltered ears. (I

think he means *or* instead of *and*, but he wrote *and* – or maybe *nor*.)

He exerts informal direction throughout meetings and as a leader exercises excellent control. His humour is generous hard-hitting, and sells his position. When withdrawing from meetings he exhibits disgust and pouting.

DK (not Damon Knight): He tends to be domineering and responds to conflict by defending, resisting, and counterarguments. He does not hesitate to step on toes to get his point across. His humour is hard-hitting and aimed at convincing his opponents. Although he is very task-oriented, he has a strong desire to be liked and this basic personality conflict tends to cause him to withdraw when he believes that the job is not getting accomplished. He is a good leader because his intelligence commands respect. Only in the light of very strong factual evidence against his position does he change his position without withdrawing from the team effort. He desires to obtain team results by traditional approaches such as timed agendas etc. and hence forces compromises to which he is not committed.

W (?): His skill in coping with conflict situations stems from in-depth probing and critique.

His humour is candid and hard-hitting style that fits the situation. High performance is coupled with deep commitment, deep enough to cause a close-minded attitude in evaluating divergent points of view. He drives himself and others in an effort to produce quality results and meet stated deadlines.

O: The 'sage'. He is highly competitive, anxious for conflict, as he feels that he can sway the opinions of others. His humour is barbed and directed to winning his point. He is a forceful leader, an orator, and yet he hides behind a 'good guy' façade. His contributions to team achievement, though many, are influenced by how they agree with his convictions to self.

Wayne: Conflict is openly faced but generally managed by talking a position of superiority. He has a high level of commitment to goals he considers worthwhile but will withdraw completely when situations deteriorate. (Next sentence crossed out but legible.) He is a very opinionated person which results in taking and expressing strong stands on issues with little room for compromise. Situations are examined in depth yielding deep insights such as that the 'Big Picture' approach is used in problem solving. Leadership abilities are excellent but *he is more a loner than a team man*. Humour is hard-hitting used to make a point and shows deep insights of human behaviour.

ME: Finally, could you tell us something about work you have forth-coming or in progress.

GW: I won't mention the stories sold to Roger Elwood, since I just did. Tom Disch has a 10, 000 novelette, 'Hour of Trust'. Unfortunately his book – *Bad Moon Rising* – seems to have been delayed [I believe it has now appeared – *MJE*], and I haven't heard from him for a time.

Terry Carr has 'The Death of Doctor Island', which I understand has made the lead story in *Universe 3*. This is 'The Island of Doctor Death and Other Stories' inverted – perhaps I should say reversed. Your image in a mirror (as I am sure you realise) does not look in the least like you; in fact it would be completely correct to say that there is probably no one in the world who looks less like you than that image does. It is the reverse of you. Kate Wilhelm says that every story has a certain size and shape (and she might have said colour or colours too); what I tried to do here was to create the mirrored story with a new entity. About 19,000 words.

Orbit 12 will carry 'Continuing Westward', the story of two aviators blown into the future while fighting the Turks in WWI.

'How I Lost the Second World War and Helped Turn Back the German Invasion' tells of Adolf Hitler's ill-fated attempt to market Volkswagens in Britain. Six thousand words, to be in *Analog* one of these days.

'Feather Tigers' recounts the difficulties of aliens whose speculations about the interdependence of that extinct animal Man with the other creatures of the planet embroils one of them in a little adventure. A very light treatment of a subject that interests me deeply – totemism. To be in *Edge Supplement*, a little magazine.

I've hopes of having what is called a young adult novel – a term I dislike – published this year. *The Devil in a Forest*.

There are two novels half or less complete which have been in that state for years – *Frieda from the Fire* and *In Grayhame Prison*. Someday.

And I've 150 pages of *Peace*, the big thing I'm trying to do. I still don't know what it's about.

Just before beginning this I finished the second draft of 'Forlesen', a largely autobiographical novella; and as soon as I've finished I'll begin 'The Dark of the June', the first story of a four-part cycle Roger Elwood has asked me that I do for *Continuum*. And that's it.

2

An Interview with Gene Wolfe

Joan Gordon

In the eight years between his interview with Edwards and the publication of his correspondence with Joan Gordon in *Science Fiction Review* for Summer 1981, Wolfe had become a respected writer of speculative fiction. His shorter works had been nominated consistently for both Hugo and Nebula Awards throughout the 1970s and he won the Best Novella Nebula for 'The Death of Doctor Island' in 1973. Gordon's interview follows the publication of Wolfe's first collection, *The Island of Doctor Death and Other Stories and Other Stories* (1981), and *The Shadow of the Torturer* (1980), his fourth novel after *Operation Ares* (1968), *Peace* (1975) (which received the Chicago Foundation for Literature Award in 1977) and *The Devil in a Forest* (1976). Importantly, *The Shadow of the Torturer* was the first novel to earn Wolfe a wider audience. Marketed largely as a fantasy in both the US and the UK, the first volume of *The Book of the New Sun* shared in the rising commercial success of popular fantasy fiction by writers including Stephen Donaldson and Terry Brooks. It is, however, a much more ambitious and literate work than any of its contemporaries, a fact recognised within the genre and evidenced by its receipt of the Howard Memorial Award and the World Fantasy Award in 1981, and the British Science Fiction Award in 1982. In the interview that follows, Joan Gordon attempts to draw out the impulses and qualities that make Wolfe's fiction unique.

One of Gene Wolfe's novellas, 'Seven American Nights', which appears in *The Island of Doctor Death and Other Stories and Other Stories*, illustrates the special nature of Gene's writing. It is a mix of Oriental arabesque and sordid realism, of dreams and reality, speculation and character development, ambiguity and clarity. No one else could have done it. If I tell you the plot concerns a traveller to the future America after it has fallen, you may think of all the after-the-holocaust SF novels you have read – it is nothing like them. America here is not a charred wilderness peopled by solitary rugged individualists learning the lay of the new land. Instead it is a decaying city filled with subjected souls and haunted by the ghosts of its former strength. The metaphorical and literal worlds of 'Seven American Nights' are equally alive, to us and to the protagonist.

I wanted to be told the secret – how does Gene Wolfe write these stories that shine on long after being read? Though he never answered that question, he has answered others in our extended epistolary interview. Between 1979 and 1981 Gene and I conducted an interview by mail. The topics have been Gene Wolfe, his writing, writing in general and life in general. And that is the organisation of what follows here.

JG: Tell me about your childhood.

GW: My childhood was fairly normal for my place and time. I was raised in Houston while it was still a Southern city. Mother – whom God bless – was a Southern Belle, very energetic, very soft on the outside and very hard on the inside. Do you know the type? Some artistic talent (she used to do Japanese-style brush paintings and I wish I had some of them), a champion-calibre bridge player. I've never really known what she wanted me to be, but I'm fairly sure it was none of the things I've been. A lot of my childhood was by Tennessee Williams, if you know what I mean.

JG: Did you serve in the army?

GW: I was in combat for four months or so during the Korean War; I got the Combat Infantry Badge. It was trench fighting almost like that in World War I. I was shelled a lot but never bombed or strafed. I suppose the main effect the army had on me was to make me see once and for all that regimented systems both do and do not work in the way their designers intended. It's something like doublethink, something like hypnosis. Regimentation succeeds brilliantly when everyone involved wants it to – which is to say it succeeds best where it is needed least: the paratroops, the Special Forces. Combat showed me that the people who act bravely when there is no special danger are not the people who act bravely when there is. I didn't know that.

JG: What are your beliefs, religious and political?

GW: I am a Catholic in the real communion-taking sense, which tells you a lot less than you think about my religious beliefs … I believe in God, in the divinity of Christ, and in the survival of the person. I don't mean by that that I think I will not die, or that (for example) my parents are not dead; the protagonist in *The Book of the New Sun* carries a sword inscribed with the words *terminus est* ('This is the dividing line'). Like every thinking person, I am still working out my beliefs.

  Politically, I am a maverick. I agree with the far left on many issues, with the far right on others, with the centre on still others. I distrust concentrations of power, whether political or economic. I am a strong environmentalist. I believe we are higher creatures than we think we are, and that animals are closer to us than we believe. (I should have said the higher animals.)

JG: Were you an only child?

GW: Yes, I was an only child. It's a wonderful and terrible thing – terrible because one ends up being the last of the tribe, the only one who remembers the customs and teachings of the now-sunken land of home. I remember how we used to sit in the living room, my mother, my father and I and my dog, Boots. The couch and the chairs and the big library table and the radio and the floor lamps are all gone; the house is sold; I am the only one left, the only thing left; if I had to, I could not prove it was not all a dream.

JG: What you said about being an only child seemed very true to me. When the ritual of Home lies in the hands of only three people, it is subject to frequent change and I resist it, substitute my own rituals, fabricate old ones to insert in my memory.

GW: Sooner or later you're going to ask how I started writing, so I'll tell you right now that I started because my bride and I were living in a two-room furnished apartment and I had hopes of raising enough money to make a down-payment on some furniture so we could move out. Twenty-some years later I still need money.

JG: Do you have a routine for writing?

GW: No. I have no routine for writing – I can't afford one. I write when I can, when I have the energy and the time and the opportunity. I write the piece all the way through, then start again at the beginning, then start *again* at the beginning … Everything gets at least three drafts. Most get four-plus. I continue to revise until I begin to wonder if the changes I'm making are really improvements … then I stop and send out the piece. Whenever possible, I allow at least a week between revisions and I usually use that week to work on something else.

I do each draft on the typewriter – including the first – then mark it up with whatever pencil or pen I have handy. I've tried working to taped music (classical, the only kind I like) and it just doesn't make any difference – if I'm working well I don't heard it. Coffee helps. So does iced tea, hot tea and skimmed milk. I drink more coffee than I should and take more aspirin. When I'm through for the night, I take a three-mile walk if the weather lets me. That's usually sometime between nine and eleven.

JG: Gene, what parts of being a writer are a real drag?

GW: I wasn't going to bring that up, but since you insist … People who ask what name I write under as if they had heard of every author in the world except me. A little questing usually establishes that they have never heard of Saul Bellow, Erica Jong or Norman Mailer.

People who assume that every writer has thousands and thousands of copies of everything he has ever done, all provided free by the publisher. (I once asked Doubleday for *two* copies of an anthology, because I had two stories in the book. No dice and they thought the request was quite humorous.) People who quite seriously ask how much I pay the publisher to 'print' my books and stories. People who assume that since I write science fiction I love every trashy sci-fi monster flick ever made. Plus *Space 1999*, *Lost in Space, Star Trek* (which actually wasn't always terrible) and the Saturday morning kiddie cartoon. (I do admit to a soft spot for *Rocky and Bullwinkle*.) There are more, but that's enough for now.

JG: What authors do you admire? Whom have you learned from? With whom do you think you have something in common?

GW: The list of authors I admire, whom I've learned from, and with whom I feel I have something in common is almost endless. Damon Knight, Kate Wilhelm, Joanna Russ, Ursula LeGuin, R.A. Lafferty, Saul Bellow and John Updike, with many more among the living. Poe, Proust, Dickens, Chesterton, Flaubert, Orwell, Thurber, Twain, Melville, Irving, Van Gulik, Kafka, Borges, Dostoevski, Bulgakov …

JG: In what ways do you think your writing breaks new ground?

GW: I find it's almost impossible to say, 'I'm trying to break such-and-such new ground …' without sounding like an ass. I'm trying to express a view of the universe while working it out, of course, but then all serious writers do – that's what makes them serious writers. I am trying to bring good writing (my definition) and whole people to a type of writing that has not been overburdened with them, but that's hardly new ground.

JG: You marked a bibliography of your stories for me with checks to indicate which ones were 'pivotal'. What did you mean by 'pivotal'?

GW: A pivotal story for me is one in which I feel I have succeeded in doing well something I have never really done well before – fairy material in 'Thag', a certain religious viewpoint in 'Westwind', the use of second and third person in 'The Island of Doctor Death and Other Stories', the progression from realism to fantasy in 'The Eyeflash Miracles', even the primitive inventions no one ever actually invented (and which no one now notices) in 'Tracking Song'. Just as 'Tracking Song' is about uninvented inventions of the stone age, 'Straw' is about (partly of course) uninvented inventions of the middle ages.

'Tracking Song' is a wolf totem story, by the way. The protagonist gets his original orientation from a wolf tribe, then lives in a world in which the roles of moose, lion, deer, mink and so on are taken by semi-human beings. Wolves are winter symbols, of course, and birds symbols of spring.

JG: Do you use your own life in your stories?

GW: Weer (the narrator of *Peace*) is a man very much like me – I don't mean that the same things have happened to me, but we have similar souls. Tackie (in 'The Island of Doctor Death and Other Stories') is pretty much the kind of child I was, lonely, naïve, isolated. Nicholas (the boy in 'The Death of Doctor Island') is the boy I might have been and in some ways would like to have been.

JG: I thought the idea, in 'The Woman Who Loved the Centaur Pholus', of technology bringing back (and destroying) mythology, was an especially nice one.

GW: The idea of technology 'bringing back' the fauna of myth is more than just nice. It is going to happen. The ability to create centaurs and so on will be widely available *within our lifetimes*. When I tell people that, they say, 'Oh, no. Maybe a few high-powered scientists could, but ...' How'd you like to take an *undergraduate* course in gene-splicing? (No pun.) Columbia will offer one next year.

JG: But will people bring back mythological fauna or will they instead create kitsch and corn? Have you ever gone into a craft shop and seen the feather and pipe cleaner art that is spawned there?

GW: Some people will create their own designs (in monsters) of course. But the challenge will be to do good work within a set 'classical' design. Obviously, we will see dinosaurs as well as dragons. Anyway, it's surprising how hard it is to come up with anything really original. I just made a quick stab at it and came up with a centiger and a woman with the head of a cat. But my woman would be Bast of ancient Egypt, and my centiger very close to a sphinx.

JG: I'd like to ask the next question the way my students do when they ask me about, say, Borges. Why do you make your stories so hard to figure out? Why all those ambiguities, those surprise endings and un-endings ('The Adopted Father' as sort of an un-ending – the story ends with implied ...), those places where you can't tell what happened.

GW: Why do I make my stories so hard to figure out? I don't think I do. Certainly, I try to make my stories as pellucid as I can, without actually changing the story to another story. Are you seriously saying that Borges' stories are difficult to understand? Some are pedestrian ('Rosendo's Tale'), some are brilliant imitations ('Doctor Brodie's Report'), some are original masterpieces ('Tlön, Uqbar, Orbis Tertius'), but all are as clear as glass.

You say, 'why all those ambiguities, those surprise endings and un-endings ...?' and you instance 'The Adopted Father'. Ambiguities are absolutely essential to any story that seeks to counterfeit life, which is filled with them. Today my wife and I went to a music store, and I heard her tell the clerk that she thought she had seen some prominent performer (I know little about music and do not recall his name) in another store playing the piano. The clerk said there was a local performer who closely resembled the man she thought she has seen, and suggested she had seen this local man instead. My wife is near-sighted but seldom wears her glasses and so is as likely to mistake identities as anyone alive – in fact, she had done just that in a book shop a few minutes before. I was not paying much attention to what the clerk was saying, although they were only a few feet away; and in any case, I am slightly deaf. Had she seen the performer she named? Had she seen the local performer the clerk named instead? Had she seen some third party, a good amateur player? Did I perhaps misunderstand their conversation? (Parts of it were inaudible.) Am I creating all this – spinning a fiction to make my point? This much is certain: you will never know.

What is it that bothers you about the ending of 'The Adopted Father' anyway? Mitch has found the father he needs, Parker has discovered a reason to go on living. Their stories are not over, obviously, but the story I was telling, the story of how they found each other, is over, which is why I stopped typing.

JG: What qualities of your writing might make you more a writer's writer than a fan's writer?

GW: I doubt that I am, but in general the practitioners of any art appreciate its difficulties more. To a child a juggler who juggles red, blue, gold and green balls is as good (I suppose) as one who juggles a knife, an axe, a torch and a champagne bottle. The second juggler is a juggler's juggler, though – someone a good juggler watches to learn from.

JG: The ambiguity I associate with your writing seemed especially controlled in *The Shadow of the Torturer*, as if you were relaxed about space, had a long enough journey to really stretch your legs. Of course, you were very mischievous at the end. I appreciate your architectural need to stop at the gate, but you purposely made me very curious about what was beyond (and inside) the wall. Anyway, the characters, the world, the atmosphere got me. Triskele and Baldanders had little to say but they lived as much as Severian.

I don't think the cape of the torturer on the cover was fuligin (I admit that would be tricky) but the balcony he stands on, straight out of Gaudi, is right.

GW: I could pick several nits about the dustjacket, the worst one being that the executioner there seems to be wearing a shirt. But the important thing about a dj is that it reflects the spirit of the text, and I think that one does.

JG: Why did you pick a torturer for a protagonist?

GW: I don't know how to answer when you ask why I made Severian a torturer, except by saying that I chose to write the book I wrote. If he had been a sailor or a policeman, that would have been a different book.

Torture doesn't *seem* violent because there is no element of struggle.

Believe me, I have thought for hours and hours on the subject of torture while writing these books. The tough part is drawing the line between punishment and torture. If I were to spank my 14-year-old son would that be torture? Nonsense. If I were to give the same spanking to a grown man (assuming I could) surely that wouldn't be torture either – he can stand it better, if anything, than the boy. But if I were to hit harder and harder (again, assuming I could) eventually what I was doing could be called torture by any standard. Thus, the two shade into each other.

And, of course, torture can be purely mental, with no striking, crushing or burning at all.

JG: Would you give me a few tantalising hints about the rest of tetralogy, *The Book of the New Sun*?

GW: I could give you better tantalising hints if I knew what sort of thing you want. All four books will be told in the first person by Severian – does that help? *Shadow* took place entirely within Nessus; most of the action of the other three books takes place outside it. Jonas, the man on the merychip Severian encounters near the Piteous Gate, is a fairly important character in *The Claw of the Conciliator*, and so on.

JG: How close is the tetralogy to completion?

GW: I'm doing the final (or perhaps the semi-final) draft of the fourth book (*The Citadel of the Autarch*) now. *Claw* is to be published this coming March. The third book (*The Sword of the Lictor*) hasn't been sold yet, so I can't say when it will appear. Certainly it will be over a year from now. [Note: 'Now' is November 1980 – *JG*]

JG: How do you feel about academic study of your work?

GW: It scares me to death. The colleges have killed English poetry – which flourished as long as they confined themselves to Greek and Latin – deader than last year's bacon pig.

JG: I wonder if some of the power of SF for its readers lies in that fact that it is disapproved of.

GW: It does, of course, and that makes me feel guilty about writing all these letters and cooperating with you generally. I have always derided and discouraged the academic study of SF in theory, and nearly always cooperated with academics who sought my help. The thing is that although I believe Establishment contact with SF is a bad thing, a thing detrimental to the genre, I also believe that the harm done by the academic wing of the Establishment can be mitigated. I admit I am beginning to see that attitude as hypocritical.

There are two main mechanisms at work here. The first is the realisation (practically a definition of intelligence) that Establishment-approved media are uniformly untruthful. If SF really becomes that untruthful, well and good. But if, as now seems more likely, it is merely *perceived* as having such approval, it will lose many readers it deserves to have. In a dim, half-witted way, that was what the 'New Wave' was all about. (I was claimed as both a New Wave and an Old Wave writer by various critics and commentators, as many of us were). In order to fight off that approval we have to be more or less anti-science, anti-business, anti-government and (of course) anti-establishment. It also helps to be violent and mystical, and I think you'll agree that most of us tend to be.

The other mechanism is the radically negative effect of school-assigned reading. Most kids *hate* whatever they are made to read. (For some weird reason perhaps related to left-handedness, I did not; I even liked *The Mayor of Casterbridge*, though as far as I can recall I was the only one in our English class who did; but it has taken me forty years to outgrow the distaste for athletics I developed when I was forced to take part in them.) Many are now being made to read sf. My own story, 'Eyebem', is already in one high school text and I think is going into another. So you see.

JG: Since I started as an sf fan and later made my enthusiasm my scholarship, it's hard for me to see academic study as *necessarily* deadening. I know it *can* be, and I've read plenty of criticism that is (especially criticism about criticism or about literature as if it were just an illustration of critical theory). But I don't think criticism needs to be poisonous. Learning about something is exciting, and sharing and developing knowledge can be exciting too. Isn't that what scholarship should be?

GW: I don't think the profs *have* to be deadly (I hope I didn't say that); it's just that most are.

JG: As a literature of ideas, is sf important educationally?

GW: Yes, though it does not *necessarily* follow that it should be made a part of some particular curriculum. Your question goes to the heart of my preference for the term *speculative fiction*. Of course we both know that no one coined the sacred term 'science fiction' and then went into a study and wrote the stuff. 'Science fiction' was a purification of old Gernsback's 'scientifiction' – scientific fiction – which he made up to describe a type of didactic story he published in magazines derived from a magazine for radio amateurs. That type of story hasn't been around for a long time; it failed because it (I mean in its pure form) engaged only the mind. If one wants to teach a student something about the nature of the atom, one can do it much better in a few paragraphs in a textbook.

The educational virtue of speculative fiction is that it engages the imagination and emotions as well as the mind, and of course, its thrust need not be scientific in any sense except one so broad as to be meaningless. (Academics sometimes talk about the 'science' of history, the 'science' of comparative religion, and so on, but these subjects are not sciences in any meaningful sense of the word.) If T. B. Swann can write well enough to make me (in the famous phrase) suspend my disbelief in Greek mythology he will teach me some very important things about Greek mythology I could not learn by reading half a dozen textbooks. Swann's work has nothing to do with science, but it is SF as defined by *our* culture – we talk about him as an SF writer, shelve his books in the SF section and so on.

Swann was speculating about what it would be like to live in the mental world of people who *believed* the stuff of Greek myth, just as C. S. Lewis, in the Narnia books, speculated about people who believed in the cosmology of the Middle Ages. It is obviously possible for another author (or for that matter the same author) to speculate again and reach different conclusions, but we can learn from both. And the speculation need not be concerned with past beliefs or erroneous ones – no student perhaps, believes in Relativity *in his heart* unless he has read some book that makes him understand something of how it would feel to approach the speed of light.

JG: How is SF so well suited to the discussion of ideas?

GW: Well, to begin, it is only suited to the discussion of certain types of ideas. *Swann's Way* is a psychological novel – one of the best – and SF is not particularly well suited to discussing the types of psychological ideas with which it is concerned.

With that cavil aside, let me say that your question is like the old theological puzzler, why do great rivers choose to run through most of Earth's larger cities? If a study or novel is largely concerned with a discussion of scientific or sociological ideas, it thereby 'becomes' SF whether so labelled or not in the minds of many publishers and many readers. For example, unless my memory is playing me false, Winston Churchill once wrote a piece called, 'What if the North had Won at Gettysberg?' This was, obviously, a parallel universe story: in this case a story about a universe in which the South had won (Hurray!) and a military historical theorist was speculating about the results of what we know actually happened. It was, clearly, speculative fiction – and most of us would so classify it, although we don't think of Churchill as an SF writer.

But, of course, conventional – *Analog*-and-Ace-Books SF does have advantages when a writer wants to speculate on the types of ideas it handles well. It gives him an audience that is accustomed to such speculation – an audience whose mind is already stretched. That's an immense advantage, because he knows he does not have to baby them into it. They know, for example, that a society doesn't have to be based on commerce – we just happen to have lived all our lives in one that is. They know that it is accidental that Florida's climate is warmer than Maine's, and that a shift in the poles could reverse the gradient. And so on.

Second, SF gives the author who is already familiar with the field (but only to him) a ready-made language of conventions – mechanical human beings with emotions (thanks to Lester Del Rey), time travel (thanks to H. G. Wells), starships that can rove the galaxy at will (thanks to E. E. Smith). *None* of these things exist outside SF, and many reputable scientists say all three are utterly impossible. (It is easy to program a computer to *act as if* it possessed emotions, but quibbles aside, that clearly isn't the same things as having them. To me, the interesting question is whether a computer that had developed consciousness would feel the programmed emotions as real.)

Third and most importantly, the conventions of SF permit the writer to set up alternate worlds that are logical rather than fantastic. Before SF,

Shakespeare might write of the kingdom of the fairies, but that kingdom was governed (and could be governed) only by whim – what Titania wanted she did, unless the greater power of her husband stopped her. (It is surely no coincidence that that play is laid in ancient Greece – its 'logic' is exactly that of pagan Greek religion, in which T. was Juno, O. was Zeus and so on. I suspect strongly that the Greek setting is the remnant of an earlier draft using the Greek gods that Shakespeare was too rushed to change completely.

Anyway that framework can be used very effectively in much the same way beast-fable is used: Hermes/fox, Ares/bear and so on, with each god or fairy or animal representing a human passion or concern. But it cannot be used at all to speculate about real *external* human societies. Real rulers act because of political and economic constraints and only rarely by whim. Oddly enough, it was because of the king's whimsical desire to marry his lovers that the man who did most to get us out of that mess – St. Thomas More – was killed.

The voyage to a fantastic country had been used often before, of course, but so far as I know, he was the first to revive the then-long-dead Platonic idea of a fictional country that was not fantastic but interesting and instructive. He was not the founder of modern SF; I would give that title to Wells. But he is almost more important than the founder. We owe him a monument.

JG: What is good writing?

GW: To begin with, good writing is grammatically correct except when it is intentionally incorrect. A good reader quickly senses the difference between that kind of writing and writing in which the writer does not know (or perhaps care) that his subjects and verbs do not agree in number and so on.

Similarly, good writing is only intentionally ambiguous. Good writing is interesting to read, rather than easy. People like Rudolph Flesch would like to see every sentence as short as possible, because that kind of writing is easy to read, but it bores and exhausts the reader by its easiness. Did you ever know of anyone who backpacked on level ground? In good writing, the length and structure of the sentences are varied. Many are short. A few may take eight or ten lines of type.

Good writing is concrete. That's why our businessmen and bureaucrats can never be taught to write well – it is against their best interests. A bureaucrat says *economically disadvantaged*; a good writer says *poor*; an educational bureaucrat says someone has a learning disability; a good writer says the same person is *stupid* or *lazy*; a businessman (or woman) says *competitively priced*; a good writer says cheap. You'll note that good writers are almost never elected to public office. Norman Mailer and Wm. F. Buckley have tried and failed. (In fact, the only good writer who ever won a major election was Winston S. Churchill, and he was overwhelmingly defeated as soon as the war was over.)

Good writing is rich in tropes without being pretentious about them. It says, for example, that English society around 1850 was like an October day (I am, of course, quoting H. G. Wells), and it says it in such a way that your understanding of both is increased. Furthermore, you feel that the comparison was perfectly natural. Do you remember Partridge (I think it was) in *Tom Jones*, who went to see Garrick play Hamlet and said that if he had seen a ghost too he would have started in just the same way. Like that.

And lastly, good writing is multileveled, like a club sandwich. Savants talk of writing being linear – one thing at a time. But a good writer is often saying two things at once, and sometimes three or even four. When Fielding wrote that bit about seeing *Hamlet* he told us something about acting and something about Partridge at the same time.

Please understand that I would never claim that all my writing is good. I do claim, however, that I try to make it good, always.

JG: What is your cure for writer's block?

GW: My cure for writer's block is to cut out all unnecessary communication. Don't read, watch TV, write letters or talk more than is needed to get through the essential business of the day. Instead, take long walks alone or do manual work – paint a room or dig in the garden. The cure usually only takes three or four days.

JG: I've been thinking about photography of late, especially the big argument – is it art or document?

GW: 'Art' and 'document' aren't mutually exclusive. Photos *can* be documents (all this is just my opinion, of course), although not all of them are. I don't really think that they can be art. A lot depends on craft, a lot depends on equipment (if you ever see a book called *Borne on the Wind*, pick it up – it contains the most wonderful photos of insects in flight … and I could not have taken them because I don't have the stuff) and a great deal depends on opportunity. The most beautiful picture I can remember was taken by a 19-year-old sailor who had never owned a camera before he was sent to the South Pole, and who never saw what any of his pictures looked like until he got back to the US and could get his film developed. It showed the sun over Mt. Erebus.

The only thing that keeps photography from being art is that it is a mechanical reproduction of a pre-existing scene. I certainly agree that there are photographers who treat themselves as artists. There are even some who are treated as artists by other people. But those things prove nothing. There have been a million people who have thought they were artists and been wrong, and probably most of them were treated as artists by at least one other person. There have been a million people who actually were artists but didn't think they were and weren't treated as artists by others. The people who made the cave paintings are examples; so are those who carved the façade of Notre Dame.

The use of techniques – and especially in photography, where 'technique' is almost precisely the same as 'trick' – is not art. A salesman uses techniques to close the sale. A master of the martial 'arts' uses techniques to break your neck, but he is no more an artist than a football player is. In five minutes I could teach you five techniques that would let you come up with pictures far removed from snap-shots. (For example, smearing a little petroleum jelly around the edges of your lens to give a softened border.) But they would not make you an artist. Even if you invented a new technique – and people do almost every day – you would be an inventor, not an artist.

JG: What are we born only to suffer and die?

GW: You may choose your favourite answer from the selection below:

1   *We* are not born to suffer and die. Only you. We have kept this from you until now, but it's time you were told.

2   We are not born only to Suffer and Die. Other firms have children too – Goforth, Killburn and Robb, for example.

3   *You* are born to die so I can get a word in edgewise. *I* suffer until I do.

4   We suffer because if we could not, French fries would have no place to go. We die to keep from suffering.

5   We die so we don't have to suffer and suffer because it beats dying.

6   All of the above.

JG: Thank you, Mr Wolfe.

3

An Interview with Gene Wolfe

Melissa Mia Hall

First published in *Amazing Science Fiction Stories* in September 1981, Melissa Mia Hall's interview follows the publication of *Gene Wolfe's Book of Days* (1981), his second short story collection, but predates the publication of *The Claw of the Conciliator*, volume two of *The Book of the New Sun*. Like Joan Gordon, she cannot resist asking for 'hints' to the contents of the rest of the tetralogy. Wolfe obliges – with further hints.

Boston, the second day of the 1980 World Science Fiction Convention and I'm going to meet Gene Wolfe and interview him. First, I have to make contact. I'm wandering past the cavernous huckster's room with a friend. I glimpse a middle-aged man with a receding hairline, and an amiable air about him, almost childlike, eyes glancing around brightly. I know it's Gene Wolfe although I've never seen him before. I nudge my friend. 'Is that Gene Wolfe?' He says he thinks so and I rush forward just as he starts moving away. 'Gene! Gene Wolfe!' I yell, knowing I must look frantic. He pauses politely, extends a hand. I introduce myself clumsily and compliment him so profusely that he must think I'm lying or insane.

We meet several times during the convention, mostly for short conversations, enough to get to the point about where the big interview set for Sunday noon will take place, but not enough for me to know who he is. He is still the Man who wrote the currently enfolding *Book of the New Sun*, *The Island of Doctor Death and Other Stories and Other Stories* and *Gene Wolfe's Book of Days*.

When the hour arrives for the session with Gene, I am therefore a little scared, very much excited and tired. Like most convention goers, I stay up too late and consequently appear a bit bedraggled. Gene, on the other hand, although he was up late, too, appears wide awake and ready for anything. We sit down and soon the interview begins in earnest. I begin to know Gene Wolfe – a comfortable sort of man, deliberately thoughtful and wryly humorous, just as much a paradox as one of his stories.

MMH: You're noted for your elegantly crafted writing and you've been writing for sixteen years. What's the most important thing you've learned about the craft of writing?

GW: I think the most important thing I ever learned was that you must write to be read rather than write what gives you pleasure to write. In other words, you should be attempting to create something for a reader, rather than indulging your whims.

MMH: Religion, spirit, magic, the pursuit of light, the analysis of darkness, all of these pervade your work. Do you consciously set out in search of them? Do you feel like you're a writer with a mission? What comes first, the message or the art?

[*There is a pause as Gene reflects on this loaded question, his brow appropriately furrowed.*]

GW: The art comes first or the message doesn't come at all. The message comes from me. I am a religious person (Roman Catholic). I am, I suppose, in a very, very minor way, something of a mystic and when you read my material, I think it comes through … I don't believe in writing *with* a message unless that is what you're paid to do. I think a proper writer with a message is a propagandist or an advertising copywriter. He's paid to write with a message. A supposedly artistic and literary writer has no business in writing propaganda.

MMH: You use a large amount of cultural jumping, for example. Tommy Kirk, Mickey Mouse, etc. in 'Three Fingers' – the list is endless. There are constant asides throughout your short stories (Huck Finn, Little Nell, etc.). It's as if you've undertaken a holy cause to further engrave them upon the minds of your reader. Do you realize that you've been doing this?

GW: No, it just happens. I think you would say these things are symbols that have emotional power and a person who is doing literary writing must deal in emotion charged symbols – and so you end up writing about things like death and lions and sacramental meals, perhaps because those are emotional things that wake certain feelings in the deep spring of the individual. I'm using it as I have to, to engage and stir the reader's emotions. And if fiction doesn't do that, then it's failed. That's the purpose of fiction.

MMH: I've also noticed the rich reservoir of humour you tap into from time to time in your work. How important is humour to you?

GW: I don't know. On a schedule of 0–10, it's probably about a 6. Humour is a wonderful thing. It's very under-appreciated. One of the reasons that it is, is that it's no good when it's out of place and it's very frequently out of place.

MMH: Do you feel that there are major themes latent in your work or is that hogwash? What's more important – the plot, the characters –

GW: Oh, certainly – again, if you want to do deep emotional things, you have to deal with major themes. Some traditionals answer that all writing is about Love and Death, which is a title of a Woody Allen movie. But there's a certain layer of truth in it. There are things that are major for people. Living or dying is very fundamental. Getting love, losing love, those are very fundamental things. Exploring new territory is fundamental. Being imprisoned or breaking out of prison, all those are major themes. Major themes are the proper province of literature.

[*We both take a breath and relax a little. The outside light pouring in from the large picture window make his features hard to read. I plunge onwards with an easy question for me but a hard one for Gene.*]

MMH: Do you have any favourites among your stories?

[*He mulls that one for a bit and replies, rubbing his mouth and stretching.*]

GW: Well, I would say my topmost story would be 'The Detective of Dreams' in *Dark Forces*.

MMH: I loved it. (An eerie tale concerning dreams and Christ.)

GW: That's my own favourite of all my short stories. About one story out of twenty seems to come close to what I really wanted it to be when I started it … Obviously, I may be wrong … 'Westwind' is also a favourite. 'The Toy Theatre' is another.

MMH: What have been some of the major influences on your writing?

GW: Obviously, some things are more important than others. Probably the earliest influences I had that were of any significance, were the Oz books and the two *Alice* books which I read as a child. G. K. Chesterton has undoubtedly been a major influence. So has Borges, who was also influenced by Chesterton. So has Dickens … H. G. Wells … Bram Stoker … Mervyn Peake. Modern writers. R. A. Lafferty, Ursula K. LeGuin. Damon Knight has influenced me, not so much as a writer, but as an editor. I think Knight is probably as good as editors ever get.

MMH: What are your primary goals?

[*Gene seems stunned. It's wonderful to watch him truly consider the question before he answers.*]

GW: Wow … WOW. [*Another heavy silence.*] I would like to be a really, really *good* writer, a fine writer. One of the things that took me a quarter of my life to learn was that the only way to really succeed is to do the thing that you do best. I'm one of those unfortunate kids who were bright enough to be a second rate mathematician. It takes more than bright, it takes a real talent for mathematics, a certain genius. And writing is one thing and I've found I seem to do best. And of course, I enjoy it.

MMH: Could you talk a bit about how the Torturer series came into being?

[*Gene sees right through the phrasing of my question and pounces.*]

GW: Oh! My work – everybody always says – what was the idea that led to this story?

MMH: Right, it's a very common question … .

GW: I'm not sure now that I can even recall all of the things that came together to make the Torturer stories. One of them was a certain mystical or pseudo-religious element that I wanted to bring in. I was struck at some point by the realization that Jesus was crucified on a wooden cross and Jesus had been a carpenter. And a carpenter presumably had built that cross and that although the Gospel tells us that Jesus was a carpenter, he's only described as making one thing. The Gospel tells us one thing that Jesus Himself made. Do you know what it was?

[*Gene leans forward, waiting for an answer, wagging a finger at a tongue-tied student who's forgotten to do her homework.*]

MMH: No.

[*Gene's voice rises with excitement; he claps his hands and sits back.*]

GW:It was a whip! If you don't believe me, go back and read the New Testament. He made the whip that He used to drive the moneychangers from the temple. And all that stuff struck me in some half-witted way as *significant*. At the other end of the scale, at that time I was beginning to be worried about the idea that my work was insufficiently visual ... I've been tending to be too verbal, too cerebral ...

[*As I let this sink in, I slump a little in my chair and realize I'm a lot sleepier than I want to be.*]

MMH: Could you give us some hints about *The Claw of the Conciliator*? [*An inadvertent yawn slips out that Gene seizes upon merrily.*]

GW: I warn you, if you nod off during this interview! [*We laugh. I sit up straighter.*] Well, you know the Claw of the Conciliator is the miraculous gem Severian gets stuck with in the first book ... and it really isn't immediately involved in any strange happenings. There are some things that are ambiguously miraculous in the second book, subject to rational explanations, but the rational explanations are a little difficult to buy. The second book begins with Severian in a village which is fairly close to the gate where the first book ended. He spends a good deal of the book in the House Absolute which is the Monarch's palace and then closes with him again on the road to Thrax.

MMH: Why the 'Doctor Island' titles?

GW: Well, the first one, as you probably know, was a Nebula nominee. That was 'The Island of Doctor Death and Other Stories' and it was the only story, as far as I know, that lost to No Award. There were more votes for No Award than there were for that story. It was found afterwards that (this was fairly early in the history of the Nebula) some of the people that voted for No Award were under the impression that that meant they were abstaining in that category, and not voting for No Award to be given ... So, I was talking to Joe Hensley (who's a good friend of mine who I haven't seen now in years) and he said you ought to write one called 'The Death of Doctor Island' because everyone would say – hey, here's a second shot at it, right? I didn't believe him, but it sounded like such a cute idea that I started thinking about how I could turn the original story around and reverse a lot of the roles and have a different story that was sort of a mirror image of the first one. And I did it and it turned out Joe was right, it did win a Nebula. And then ... my wife said three's a good number, you know, so you ought to do a third story ... So, I wrote 'The Doctor of Death Island' and at that point I decided that the business of trying to turn the plot and themes of the original story inside and out again – well – I had come to the end of it.

MMH: Are you in favour of continuing the Nebula Awards?

GW: Yes. Awards reflect their presenters. If SFWA'ans are corrupt, the Nebulas will be corrupt. If fans are, the Hugos will be, too. The value of any award is the value of the giver, which is why decorations bring little respect in the U.S. Armed Forces today.

MMH: What do you have to say about the state of the art, current literature?

GW: The most apparent thing to me in literature, in general – it seems to me that there are no living novelists of towering stature ... the other really strange thing that has happened quite recently is the near death of poetry. Poetry is mankind's oldest literature to retain popularity with a bulldog grip for about 5000 years and the grip has suddenly slipped. I've spent many hours trying to figure out why and there are some things that seem to have some bearing on the problem, but I'm not sure I really know why. It's very easy to blame things like the schools and television but I'm not sure those are valid ... you know, I'll bet you could go through this hotel and not find a person who could name five major living poets.

[*Gene stops gloomily, his face a study in reflection and then resolutely brightens.*]

GW: I think that we are entering now, the real Golden Age of Science Fiction and of modern fantasy. Fantasy is in better shape than it has been since the Middle Ages. Science fiction is in better shape that it has ever been, *ever*. There are more good writers and what's much more important than good writers, there are more good readers.

MMH: You don't feel we've gone past the boom?

GW: We're seeing a downward trend now that is part of a general economic cycle. The reader, who say, a couple of years ago wouldn't have been willing to spend $8.95 for a hardcover science fiction book, today has less money and is being asked to spend $12.95 for the same book ... that is the decline, but the decline is not that the person doesn't want to read it ... I think that the slump the publishing industry is talking about relates much more to publishing in general than it does to the science fiction genre, in the broad sense.

MMH: What was your first published story?

GW: My first published story was 'The Dead Man' which appeared in *Sir* in 1965.

MMH: What was your first novel?

GW: *Operation Ares*. I wrote a short story and sent it to Damon Knight for *Orbit*. Damon, at the time, was acting as an acquisition editor for Berkley Books and he said, 'This isn't really a short story but it would be a pretty good first chapter for a novel and I'll get you a contract for a novel, if you want it.' And I was green enough that I took it. I say green enough because I wasn't really skilful enough to write a good novel at that time. I don't think *Operation Ares* is a very good novel but it was my first book. It came out in 1970. That was a book that was sold about three years before it was produced. Those were three long years …

MMH: Did you have a full-time job at that time?

GW: I've had a full-time job all the time. I have a full-time job now.

MMH: How do you do it?

GW: This is my current schedule … it changes, depending on how things are going. I get up at 5:15 a.m., shave, wash my face and by about a quarter to six, I'm in the basement at the typewriter and I write till about a quarter to eight and then Rosemary has my breakfast ready. I write each morning. But when things get tight, and I'm up against a deadline, I also write in the evening … now I'm a technical editor. I was an engineer for sixteen years. But I am now a senior editor on the staff of *Plant Engineering* magazine. Basically, my writing experience combined with the engineering degree, too, enabled me to get this job which is, frankly, a good job and a lot of fun.

MMH: Okay, I wanted to ask about *Peace*, your first mainstream novel and how it evolved. Did it grow organically? Did you plot it carefully?

GW: No, because it isn't a plotting book … The basic idea is that a man has died and he is haunting his own mind, his own past. This is something very few people seem to understand about *Peace*. If you'll notice the opening line of the book is 'The elm tree planted by Eleanor Bold, the judge's daughter, fell last night.' And, in the closing chapters of the book, Eleanor Bold comes to him and requests permission to plant an elm on his grave when he dies (she's on a reforestation kick or something) and of course, the old legend is – if there's a tree on a grave, when the tree falls, the falling of the tree releases a ghost on the Earth. In *Peace* that ghost prowls through his memories throughout the book.

MMH: Of all your characters, who do you love the most?

GW: Boy, that is tough. That *is* tough. I suppose I would have to say Severian.

[*Gene is totally absorbed in thinking about Severian and absolutely unprepared for the next question I've been waiting to ask. I launch into it slyly, trying not to grin.*]

MMH: When you dream at night, do your characters ever come and talk to you or when your characters dream, do you come and talk to them?

[*Gene jumps forward breaking into a wide smile.*]

GW: Oh, aren't you getting fancy! I really wish I had an answer that is equal to that question. In honesty, I have to say no. But what *does* happen to me, and this is to me very frightening (the first time it happened it scared the pants off of me) is, I actually meet characters in real life!

MMH: Oh, no – !

GW: I wrote a book one time that's never been published. In it, I had a girl who was kind of a liar and a tramp, but she was also sympathetic in a number of respects … and I was driving my car and looked up in the rearview mirror and she was driving the car behind me, exactly as I had visualized her – *exactly* – and that was scary and the same thing happened in a couple of other instances. I will look around and there is that character … talking, breathing. Really, to strip this of any supernatural pretensions, which I don't think it deserves, what I think this really means is that I have the ability to envision characters who are sufficiently realistic that people like that can actually exist.

MMH: You haven't met Severian yet?

GW: No, no, I have not. That would be frightening. Severian – you see him in the book from the inside, but the people in the book see him as a rather grim and frightening figure. Towards the end of the book, Dorcas wakes up with Severian bending over her (in *The Shadow of the Torturer*) and he's been eating pomegranates so his lips and chin are stained with red juice. She gets quite a start out of it. There are other tip-offs in the book as well. He is a large man physically. He is hatchet-faced with piercing eyes. Rather inexpressive and although he is a very decent individual by his own lights, he really isn't very bothered by other people's pain and suffering. And he isn't very bothered by his own … pain has been a part of his life, all of his life.

[*When Gene finishes I find that I've been almost hypnotized. It's difficult to remember what my next question is; I'm still full of thoughts concerning the mysterious Severian.*]

MMH: He's almost a trance-like character, like he's walking in a waking dream. Okay, your contribution to raising the level of sf and fantasy is incalculable. [*A yawn escapes before I can hide it.*] Who do you feel is doing exciting, innovative work in that field?

[*Gene almost jumps out of his chair acting dramatic, points a finger at me.*]

GW: You're dropping off again, Melissa!

He laughs and laughs, repeating, 'Yes, you are!' several times to my hopeless protestations. Finally he concedes to sit back and reply.

GW: Ursula LeGuin, absolutely. R. A. Lafferty has been doing it for years now and has not gotten anything like the recognition he serves … If I had to pick the most underrated writer in sf, I think Ron Goulart would be the one. New Writers? Somtow Sucharitkul.

MMH: Did you know that there is now a field called Gene Wolfe fiction and that no one but Gene Wolfe can write it? How would you describe the fiction of Gene Wolfe?

GW: This is something that I got from Harlan Ellison, who, all kidding aside (and nobody kids Harlan more than I, believe me) who is first of all, a fine person and is secondly, a fine writer – I heard Harlan say one time, and as soon as he said it, realized it was absolutely true, that every writer who's worth a damn has a unique product ... I don't think there's anybody else who writes Gene Wolfe stories or Ursula K. LeGuin stories ... people always tend to say that old so-and-so is another – and then they name some famous writer. H. G. Wells, in the latter half of his career, was called the second Dickens. There never will be a second of any writer that's really worth a damn.

MMH: That's right. Your next books are ... .

GW: The third volume of *The Book of the New Sun* is *The Sword of the Lictor*. The fourth volume is *The Citadel of the Autarch*. You see, before I marketed *The Shadow of the Torturer*, I had all four volumes in second draft because I didn't want to get in a situation where the first volume was set and then I couldn't make changes to make the series end the way that I thought it should end and so I went through two drafts on all the books. This kind of thing is the great advantage of writing on the side as opposed to writing for a living.

MMH: And you'd describe yourself as a part-time writer. [*I want to get this down; to memorise it for posterity.*]

GW: I *am* a part-time writer.

MMH: Astounding.

GW: I'm holding a full-time job. I work forty hours a week. Sometimes more.

MMH: Well, that makes me feel a lot better.

4

Interview: Gene Wolfe
'The Legerdemain of the Wolfe'

Robert Frazier

After the success of *The Shadow of the Torturer*, the remaining volumes in *The Book of the New Sun* received additional approbation. *The Claw of the Conciliator* earned Wolfe his second Nebula in 1981, while *Locus* honoured the novel with its Best Fantasy Novel Award in 1982; *The Sword of the Lictor* received the British Fantasy Award for Best Novel in 1983; and *The Citadel of the Autarch* took the John W. Campbell Memorial Award in 1984. Robert Frazier's interview from *Thrust: Science Fiction in Review* (Winter–Spring 1983) follows the publication of *The Citadel of the Autarch* and sees the playfulness Wolfe expressed in his interview with Hall becoming more adroit.

I first met Gene Wolfe in a hallway in Waterloo, Iowa in 1978. He promptly steered me away from the rather stuffy SFRA party where I knew no human, and engaged me in a conversation that left poetry in the dust. My initial impression of Gene stands essentially unaltered today. He is an amiable and caring man blessed with a wry sense of humour that is both subtle and thought-provoking. He is apt to answer a query with a terse and precise reply, rather than talk on and on in vacuous phrases. Luckily, he is also blessed with great patience.

RF: Let's start with a bit of fat on the fire. Do you consider the marketplace of science fiction as your main writing niche?

GW: I think I understand what you mean by 'marketplace' and 'niche' in this. I think you mean, 'Do you, Gene Wolfe, consider yourself primarily a writer of science fiction?'

RF: I feel like magic circle time. You are going to ask questions back before answering mine. My answer is yes. Do you?

GW: More or less, if you mean for 'science fiction' to include fantasy and speculative fiction and all that – sf in the broadest sense, in other words. The real question, which I am still asking myself, is whether I want to stay where I am. If by 'niche' you mean *permanent abode*, I don't know. I'm not content to have all my work labeled sf and sold in the sf marketplace, because I don't think it is all sf.

RF: Let's try something more straightforward. I am going to guesstimate that you were thirtyish when you started writing.

GW: I was sick a lot as a child, and my mother read to me. Later I read a lot to myself. Shortly after I graduated from high school, I got the feeling I could write – I don't know why. In 1956, after Rosemary and I were married, we needed money for furniture. I decided to try to write, in order to make something on the side. I'm still doing it.

RF: I take it that was no answer.

GW: I was thirtyish in 1965, when I was first published professionally. I had been published by my college humour magazine in 1950, when I was nineteen. I started *trying* to write professionally in 1956 (November or December) when I was twenty-five. You would have to have lived through it to know what a long nine years that was.

RF: With every writer, some time must come when they are staring at their latest cheque or list of sales and realize that writing could become a full-time occupation. At what point did that happen to Gene Wolfe?

GW: It was probably when I sold *Peace*.

RF: Any thoughts of freelancing on a full time basis?

GW: From time to time. No doubt I'll do it sooner or later, but right now I have a son in college and another in high school. Of course, if I were fired tomorrow, I'd start writing tomorrow afternoon.

RF: Do you have a preference between your short story collections?

GW: This must sound dumb; but no, I don't. Both have some of my best stories, and some of my best stories are in neither – 'The Detective of Dreams', for example, and 'Westwind'. I would advise a reader, however, to buy *Gene Wolfe's Book of Days* whenever he or she can find it. Is seems to be awfully hard to get hold of.

RF: Do you have a preference among recent short stories?

GW: Yes. 'The Detective of Dreams', which I just named. And for 'A Criminal Proceeding', which no one seems to like but me, and 'The God and His Man'.

RF: Some of your early pieces sold to *Sir* and *Mike Shane's Mystery Magazine*. Did you consciously begin, after these, to specialize in science fiction?

GW: No. When I thought of what I believed a good story, I wrote it and sent it to every place I thought might possibly take it. I wasted a lot of time and postage sending sf, fantasy and mysteries to places like *Harper's*.

RF: Do you find that the skills you developed then are applicable to longer prose forms?

GW: Yes, short story skills are applicable to novels. As Jack Woodford once wrote, 'A short story is a story that is short. A novel is a story that is long.' What is needed to write at various lengths – short story, novelette, novella, novel, and so forth – is a sense of space of each form. That sense can only be developed – so far as I know – by writing or attempting to write at the various lengths. However, a short-story writer can fake out a novel by plotting it in advance by episodes, writing the episodes, then linking them up. The novel will then be episodic, but some episodic novels are very good – I doubt that you'll have much trouble thinking of examples.

RF: Cheever's *Bullet Park* may be a good one. Let's focus on your short stories. 1969–71 seem to have been good years for you. What changes were you experiencing in your writing then?

GW: I suspect that when you mention '69, '70 and '71 you are thinking of work published in those years rather than what was written in those years. So to set the record straight, let me list some of those stories; that way we'll know more or less what we're talking about. Let's see: 'Paul's Treehouse', 'Remembrance to Come', 'Loco Parentis', 'Morning-Glory', 'How the Whip Came Back', 'The HORARS of War', 'Eyebem', 'The Island of Doctor Death and Other Stories', 'Car Sinister'. Also: 'Against the Lafayette Escadrille', 'Robot's Story', 'The Packerhaus Method', 'Sonja, Crane Wesselman and Kittee', 'Of Relays and Roses'. And 'Thou Spark of Blood', 'The Toy Theatre', and 'King Under the Mountain', 'A Method Bit in B'. Obviously this is a very mixed bag. Some of my best stories, such as 'The Island of Doctor Death and Other Stories', appeared in this three year stretch. So did a lot of my worst ('King Under the Mountain', 'Thou Spark of Blood'). Obviously (again) I was learning – but had not yet learned – the difference between a good story and a neat idea that could be expounded in fiction and perhaps sold. The thing that strikes me more than anything about these is how short everything is. I would venture to say that there isn't a story in there that is more than 10,000 words. The best of them, 'The Island of Doctor Death and Other Stories', is 7,000. The second best, 'The Toy Theatre', is 2,200. I was in the process of discovering the limitations of the short story. In photographic terms, short stories are stills; novellas and novels are movies.

RF: What were some of the background readings and stimuli that went into the creation of 'The Island of Doctor Death and Other Stories'?

GW: The only reading I can recall for 'The Island of Doctor Death and Other Stories' was Wells and a mountain of pulps – all read years before.

RF: What various character ideas, plot ideas, etc. came together to generate 'The Death of Doctor Island'?

GW: Joe Hensley suggested, as a joke, that I do a story with that title after 'The Island of Dr Death and Other Stories' lost the Nebula to *No Award*. I had been swapping theories about thematic treatments, that means what I want it to mean right now, with Kate Wilhelm, and I decided to take Joe up – which I figured would blow his mind – and do a thematic inversion of the earlier story. I had had a very nice sort of little boy; I would have a very nasty sort; thus Tackie/Nicholas. I had had a doctor who *looked* like a villain; I would have one who was one but looked real good; thus Dr. Death/ Dr. Island. I had a real, somewhat gritty island on the Atlantic coast; I would have an artificial island on an artificial world; thus Settler's

Island/Doctor Island. And so on and so forth. I had just read an article about brain-splitting in *Scientific American*. It is incredible stuffy, though as I understand it, further research tends to show that only right-handers are really that flakey in their mental construction. Us southpaws remain much more normal when our brains are cut in two.

RF: Is the story 'The Doctor of Death Island' a twist on the material generated in the previous two 'Death' stories?

GW: Sure, that's what made it so hard to write. Every so often, people suggest further variations on the Island of Doctor Death title. 'Island of the Death Doctor', 'Doctor of Island Death', and so forth. But I did the first by switching around the plot elements of the second, and then 'The Doctor of Death Island' by switching the first two. So in order to do a fourth story that would satisfy me, I would have to switch all three. I'm not sure I could do it, and I'm certain the end result wouldn't be worth the effort.

RF: Who were the first editors to show conviction to these earlier stories?

GW: First, and a long, long time before anyone else, Damon Knight, who you know from Clarion. Later, Victoria Schochet and David G. Hartwell. I always liked Damon a great deal, and I still do. At the same time he frightened and irritated me. He frightened me because he is a genuinely brilliant man who does not suffer fools gladly – who in fact would march them over the edge of a precipice, I suspect, if he could. And I am something of a fool at all times. He irritated me because he liked to suggest one word changes without giving a reason, and because he would never answer a question put to him in a letter. Our working relationship was enthusiastic and strained, if I may put it so. But as a writer, I owe more to Damon than anyone else, expect possibly my mother. I will work with him again at the first opportunity, if he will let me.

RF: Damon claims the novella is a dying form, sadly I am sure. With such works as the 'Death' stories, the 'Cerberus' stories, 'Forlesen', 'The Eyeflash Miracles', 'Seven American Nights', do you still consider it worthwhile writing novellas?

GW: Damon thinks it is ceasing to be commercially possible, I think. Certainly it will always be artistically viable. The commercial demise of the novella is just a special case of the death of magazine fiction. Yes, of course I like writing novellas; I think writers nearly always do. Readers seem to prefer very short stories or very long books as a rule. The magazine novella, I suspect, was pretty much a compromise achieved by editors between the writers' demands for the acceptance of longer works and the readers' demands for short stories.

RF: Whose suggestion was it to market two thematically related original novellas with 'The Fifth Head of Cerberus'?

GW: Norbert Slepyan's. He was an editor then at Scribner's.

RF: Do you think it was a conceptual success?

GW: Yes.

RF: What about *The Devil in a Forest*? It is so non-traditional as a juvenile that it must have been a devil to label by Follett.

GW: Here comes the magic circle bit again ... If by 'label' you mean *as a juvenile*, as I think you do, hell no. Any book in which the protagonist is too young to vote is categorized as a juvenile almost automatically. Believe me, they knew what it was the moment they saw it. Have you read *Huckleberry Finn*? Nine times out of ten it is called a juvenile. I don't know if I'll do another, not soon; I presently have a mystery going the rounds in which the protagonist is a teenage girl, but that is laid in contemporary America.

RF: Will you try any more humour, like the award-nominated 'How I Lost the Second World War ...' story?

GW: I've never allowed my humorous side to fully appear in my work, since experience has convinced me that my humorous side will generally be greeted with fear and loathing. I suppose there are other directions I'm reluctant to pursue. The literary short story is one. There is almost no market at all until a writer gets to the point at which he can maneuver his publisher into putting out a collection.

RF: Another important work was 'The Hero as Werwolf'. What prompted you to write a piece sympathetic to a violent, cannibalistic murderer?

GW: When Tom Disch reviewed that story, he pointed out the missing E of werewolf on the end of my own name. I wasn't conscious of that when I wrote the story, but I suspect he's right. *Werwolf* is a valid old spelling. I used it to point up the fact that *werewolf* means 'man-wolf'. *Werguild* is the price of a man's life. Note also that the protagonist of *Peace* is Alden Dennis *Weer*. I've always been conscious, you see, that I am neither exemplary nor popular, and every so often I try to tell my side of the story. Severian is a torturer, for that matter.

RF: There is a point in the story where the corpse suddenly speaks, which prompted Terry Carr, in a Best-of Annual introduction, to recount an anecdote of your ability to surprise the reader.

GW: I wanted to show that the victim race was in fact superhuman. It was that fact that made Paul a hero, just as a man-eating tiger should be a hero among tigers. It had to be done early on in the story, and nothing is more superhuman than the power to reverse, if only slightly or temporarily, one's own death. All the best surprises and wonder come about like that, growing from the material of the story itself when you're willing to face the consequences of that material.

RF: I found the material of *Peace* fresh and wondrous; was it autobiographical?

GW: Some, but not a lot. My father came from Logan, Ohio. I went there several times as a boy for more or less extended visits, and lived there once for a year or so. Those memories gave me a great deal of background, but that was about the end of it.

RF: *Peace* seems to be told by a *sidhe*, mentioned in the last pages of the book. As if some immortal creature lives by constantly reliving. What exactly *is* going on with Alden Weer?

GW: Weer is dead. In spirit, he is reliving his life, which he confuses with the house he built during his final years. Note that at the end of the book Miss Bold asks permission to plant a tree on his grave. It is the fall of that tree, at the beginning of the book, that has freed his ghost – an old superstition.

RF: A free-association question: what stands out in your memory at the mention of *Operation Ares*?

GW: *The Laughter at Night*, which was my own title for that book. Three years passed between the sale and appearance of *Operation Ares*; when it did appear, it was little noticed. I view it as a journeyman work, about on a par with the average paperback original.

RF: Is there still room for the journeyman paperback original novel?

GW: I see a modest but real increase in market size, the decline of the horror novel – though there will always be room for a good anything – and more humour and science fantasy.

RF: Do you see an untapped potential in the area of science fantasy?

GW: Of course. Science fantasy is about where science fiction was fifty years ago. I wouldn't even want to guess at how big it might be.

RF: Do you view *The Book of the New Sun* as a straight fantasy quest, or as a hybrid scientific fantasy? You have flyers and energy pistols in the first scene of *The Shadow of the Torturer*, matter transmission in *The Claw of the Conciliator*, and the full realization in *The Sword of the Lictor* that Agia, through Hethor, employs alien creatures against Severian.

GW: I view *The Book of the New Sun* as science fantasy – by which I mean a science fiction story told with the outlook, the flavour of fantasy. There are no fantasy elements involved – no 'magic' in the fantasy sense. There is time-travel, but that belongs to sf, not fantasy. There are hypnotism, sleight of hand, and a few other things, but those belong to the world of reality, if not the world of science.

RF: Then science fantasy has the burden of having to explain the seemingly fantastic, or impossible. Are there subtle methods of doing this, other than an awkward explanatory lump at the end of the story?

GW: No, there isn't. As long as you stick to explaining, you're going to have that lump – at the end, in the middle, or in the beginning, which is where most writers seem to want to put it. The trick is to leave clues in the story that make an explanation unnecessary. I say 'trick' because it isn't easy, and there will always be some readers who don't understand. Perhaps

I might add that there are times when you *want* the lump. Typically these are in mystery or mystery-like stories in which the story turns on some character's figuring things out and saying, 'You see, Watson ...' In science fiction and science fantasy these are fairly rare, but they do occur. For an example see the second scene in which Severian and Dorcas are in the room in the Duck's Nest in *The Sword of the Lictor*.

RF: Though there is a need to explain, or at least hint at, the origin of seemingly magic devices in science fantasy, must there also be explanations of the creatures? For example, the alzabo.

GW: I'm by no means sure I agree with the first statement. Certainly I do not feel that every creature must be explained. The alzabo, like the averns, have been imported from another planet, just as the rabbit was brought into Australia from another continent. I doubt that an Australian writer would feel the need to deal with the rabbit's evolution. There are a good number of animals and plants that seem to have no place in the scheme of things and yet exist anyhow. The kiwi and the monkey-puzzle for example.

RF: Is there a body or work that gives roots to science fantasy? I can only think of Jack Vance.

GW: Yes, and like you I think of Vance first of all, particularly in *The Dying Earth*. But remember all those 'ghost' stories in which the supernatural element proved in the end to be natural. They are science fantasy too, of a type. And how would you classify *At the Earth's Core*? Or any other lost race novel?

RF: Or some of Verne's shipwreck stories? I see that concept is sometimes as important as its handling in science fantasy. What were some of your initial conceptions in constructing *The Book of the New Sun*?

GW: The idea of a torturer as hero, first of all. I began by casting my mind around for a truly unusual and fertile background, and came up with the notion of a boy raised in a dungeon where he ran errands for the torturers and eventually became one himself. That I recognized as a dramatic figure against a dramatic background, and I further recognized that the moral ambiguities of the position would provide any number of plot twists. With it I wanted to use the idea of the necropolis, and grave and tomb robbing.

RF: And spiced freely with all that archaic terminology. An interesting recipe to work with. Were any of the terms invented?

GW: None. Some of the terms are Latin; others have been made by divesting Latin words of their endings – mostly in the case of extinct animals.

RF: Each volume contains another unique feature: the stories within the story. What function do they perform?

GW: So many I doubt I can remember them all offhand. They provide pacing – something that is very hard to explain but very important. A long story requires interludes between the periods of climactic action, and these interludes must not be dull and must contribute something of value. They prevent the reader from growing bored with a too-familiar cast; or at least, I hope they do. They act as dividers between the parts of the action that should be divided. They shed light on the world in which the action is taking place. They reveal the character of the teller, in some instances. They sometimes reveal character by allowing me to show how someone reacts to them. They sometimes foreshadow. Dr Talos's play is an obvious example.

RF: The *New Sun* works also have an unusual clarity that I don't readily find in your earlier books. It is so *visual*, if that means anything.

GW: I don't really know. I always try to suit the style of the story to the protagonist. Perhaps what you're really seeing is Severian's straightforwardness, as opposed to someone like Number Five or Den.

RF: Though Severian is no one but himself, were you consciously redefining fantasy traditions by fusing the wizard and the swordsman within his character?

GW: No. Severian isn't really a wizard in any meaningful sense. Swordsman and saviour, perhaps, but that is only to say, hero. A bit of a theurgist.

RF: Then Severian represents a sort of divine interloper rather than a magician?

GW: Can't we find a spot midway? Theurgy is the work of a god, but a theurgist is one who 'works' a god. A magician compels spirits; a theurgist persuades them. Suppose that I found the First National Temporal Bank, with the slogan: 'Your money available whenever you need it.' Now if you were to deposit $100 next month, you could draw out $50 when you were seventeen. That's what Severian does, I think. He has an account at FNT; you and I do not.

RF: His talk with the undine in *Claw* … is very revealing of his past and future. Severian seems to have some control over the immense and purposeful forces at work in his life.

GW: No direct control. He can be said to have indirect control – if you like – because the forces are responding to his actions in an earlier time-cycle; thus their actions 'now' are shaped by his earlier ones.

RF: What are some of the scenes that shape and define Severian, much like his observations shape and define the scenes of the books, or his past actions shape the present?

GW: The grave-side encounter with Vodalus first of all. The discussion with Thecla in which she will found a new religion. His encounter with the false Thecla in the House Azure. She is actually a clone of Thecla.

RF: If Severian were standing in front of us, describe him externally and internally.

GW: You didn't say at what point in his life, so I'll choose him at the time he leaves the Citadel. He is 6'1", and weights 175 pounds. He is pale, with dark eyes, dark straight hair, and good teeth. His face is long and rather bony: high, square forehead, moderately high cheekbones; strong chin. He is muscular; his hands are a little larger than average. He wears heavy, black, knee-high leather boots, coarsely but strongly made; soot-black trousers of a fabric like soft wool; and a long, hooded cloak (unlined) of the same material. He wears no shirt. Mentally he is an unconscious intellectual – that is to say, he is fascinated by ideas, including problems of ethics and morality, but he is not aware that he is an intellectual and for the most part he lacks the vocabulary. He is a great deal less like most men than he thinks he is. Even so, he knows himself to be alienated by his eidetic memory. Subconsciously, he has been further marked by his loss of his mother in infancy. He has difficulty in forming relationships because of that, although he *does* sometimes form them, and he tends towards strong erotic attachments to women who subconsciously suggest the mother he lost. On the simplest level, this means toward women who are physically larger than he – Thea, Thecla, the undine – and to Jolenta, who has unusually large breasts. Of course, everyone is attracted to Jolenta, or at least nearly everyone. On a more subtle level, he is attracted to women who act as guides, Agia, or counsellors, Dorcas.

RF: There must be special circumstances involved with giving your viewpoint character eidetic memory.

GW: The great advantage is that he can plausibly recount in detail events that took place years ago, including just what was said, how someone dressed, and other such details. The disadvantage is the obvious one: he cannot plausibly forget, even when it might be convenient for me that he could. For example, when Severian was a boy running errands in the Citadel, I might have wanted him to get lost. But unless some special circumstance was involved, I couldn't lose him, since he would remember every twist and turn he made.

RF: Have you read other long fantastical series like Susan Cooper's *The Dark is Rising*; or C. S. Lewis, or Tolkien, etc? They seem centred on good versus evil, whereas *The Book of the New Sun* seems to centre on reality versus illusion. Severian's identity seems to be finding him, rather than he it.

GW: I haven't read *The Dark is Rising*. I have read the seven Narnia books and the Lewis series that begins with *Out of the Silent Planet*, as well as *Until We Have Faces*, *Pilgrim's Progress*, and perhaps one or two other titles. And of course I have read *The Lord of the Rings*, as I suppose everyone who reads at all has by now. If I sound a little bitter, it is because I first read the trilogy in 1956, when very few people had – in this country, at least. I spent a couple of months going around telling everyone what a great book it was and having them look at me as though I were mad. You didn't mention

Peake's Gormenghast series, but I have read them too, and I suspect *The Book of the New Sun* is more like them than it is like Lewis' work, or Tolkien's. Certainly *New Sun* is about reality and illusion, but even more, it is about good versus evil in the sense of moral choice. Any child can see that Strider is good and that the Black Riders are bad, but there are indeed times when life is like that – but there are not *many* times. In most cases we have to decide whether we will betray our trust and allow Thecla to die or remain faithful to it while she endures the torments of the damned. Do you remember Huck Finn on the raft, struggling with his conscience, which demanded that he return Jim to his owner? And how at last he went over entirely to evil?

RF: So then the good versus evil is caught up in Severian's identity quest. It is internalised, rather than externally evident in physical confrontations and clearly evil characters. At least for the most part. This makes Severian a truly haunting character then. Does he often enter your thoughts during non-writing time? An image … An action … ?

GW: Yes, he did and still does. What I am most conscious of, however, is not an image or an action but his mental presence, his personality. I am aware, in other words, of what he would think of whatever it is I am doing at the time.

RF: Again, I see the stress on mental processes with Severian. Is he shaped from other characters you have read or worked with; or perhaps from people you have met?

GW: Not consciously. I made him up. I made up Thecla and Thea and Agia and Agilus, Master Gurloes, and Abdiesus. Obviously I wouldn't be able to make up people if I hadn't met real people – no writer could.

RF: Is then the setting of the tetralogy also made up, or do geographic and historical analogues exist for Severian's Urth?

GW: The answer can only be yes to both. I made the setting, but I used elements from real places and periods. Maybe we should clarify the nomenclature a little. Urth is the planet. In the first four books, we never get out of Severian's country, which is called the Commonwealth. There is a lot of Byzantium in the Commonwealth, and a lot of South America.

RF: So you have a map of Severian's trail, and world?

GW: When I was writing *The Shadow of the Torturer*, I made a sketch-map of Nessus, and when I was working on the early chapters of *The Sword of the Lictor*, I made a map of Thrax. I haven't referred to either in a long time, and they may well be lost for good. I have a general map of the Commonwealth – mountains, pampas, Nessus, the isles of the south, and so on – in my head, I see no need to put that on paper. A simpler way of saying it would be to say that I know the course of Gyoll; when that is known, at least 90% of the country comes with it. I was an army cartographer in Korea after the cease-fire.

RF: When did you know that you actually had material for more than one book, or for all four?

GW: That's actually two questions; the answers are widely separated in time. I knew I had enough for more than one when I finished up what I had envisioned as the opening section of a novel and discovered that I had 200+ pages of manuscript. I knew I had enough for four when I finished what I had envisioned as the final book of a trilogy and discovered that it was a great deal thicker than the first two. I am working on a fifth book, by the way, *The Urth of the New Sun*. This at the urgent request of David Hartwell, who wanted me to wind up some matters not covered in the fourth.

RF: Will the fifth book be different from the other four in style, technique, or other significant ways?

GW: Not in style or technique. As for the last, what's significant? The real difference is that the first four were completed before *Urth* was begun. It's a coda, outside the main framework. It will concern Severian's trial by the 'gods' of his universe, his trial as representative of the people of Urth. Also the coming of the new sun.

RF: When you revealed Dorcas was revived from the dead, I somehow knew this was right. You had planted the truth within the book and concealed it. Is the fifth book meant to reveal such truths that are assumed in the fabric of the first four books?

GW: Not specifically or principally, but some of that will take place. I couldn't prevent it if I wanted to, and I don't.

RF: So then it becomes myth-making.

GW: It is a solar myth, perhaps the most common kind of all. I don't mean that Severian is Ra or Apollo, but then Ra isn't Apollo, either, and neither of them are Arthur. For the origins of this sort of thing, we have to look for the origins of mankind itself. As some tribe – probably not wholly human – wandered across the land, there came a time when winter was frighteningly severe. It seemed the sun had vanished for good, and with it, life as well as light. No doubt every sort of magic we can imagine, and many we can't imagine, was tried in the hope of bringing it back, particularly the lighting of small fires. Some authorities say that the *bon* in bonfire is the French word meaning 'good'; others that it is the same as bone. Certainly bones were burned in English bonfires well into historic times, and there is no reason, as Chesterton has pointed out, that it cannot be both. The bones of the sacrifice, the man Graves calls the Sun King, are burned in the good fire to rekindle the sun. To circle about to your mention of reality and illusion, may I point out that the Aztec sun-god's name was, literally, *Smoking Mirror*? Solar myth is tied to reality–unreality from the beginning. Where there is sunlight, there is my shadow. Is my shadow real? Is it my soul? Dunsany's *The Charwoman's Shadow*. Where there is sunlight there is reflection in water. Is that a second soul? If we make a golden image of the sun, we see our own faces therein. Are they still ours?

RF: Ancient ontology?

GW: Today we do not think we regard these questions as serious or difficult, but they are bred in the bone. If there is such a thing as a collective unconscious, you can be sure they will be found there.

RF: And certainly within Severian's unconscious. Perhaps we could end this by telling something about Severian which doesn't end up in the books.

GW: There was a time when Severian encountered assassins in the Secret House who had come to kill Ymar, an autarch a chiliad dead. I may write about that sometime. And the year he spent as a slave of the Ascians. But I doubt that either will make it into print.

RF: Any other works of science fantasy from Gene Wolfe?

GW: I'm sure, but I don't know yet what they will be. I have nothing specific planned.

5

Riding a Bicycle Backwards:
An Interview with Gene Wolfe

Colin Greenland

Colin Greenland's interview with Wolfe, published in *Foundation: The International Review of Science Fiction* in 1984, is the first to interrogate a specific aspect of *The Book of the New Sun*. In his discussion of the posthistoric nature of Urth, Wolfe provides a valuable insight into the conception and execution of one of the most vital fictional realms in speculative fiction.

One of the happier incidents of the Book Marketing Council's October 1983 promotion 'Venture Into Science Fiction' was the first visit to Britain by Gene Wolfe, author of the highly acclaimed *The Fifth Head of Cerberus* (1972) and *The Book of the New Sun* tetralogy (1980–83). In the well-preserved gloom of Durrant's Hotel, I talked to him about posthistory, publishing, and political magic ...

GW: I don't think of myself as setting out to write science fiction; I set out to write certain stories that I like. A great many of them are categorized as sf. I suppose the thing is simply that this market tends to accept me more than the others, and, let's face it, there's an unconscious influence there that you can't escape.

CG: Why do you think it is that the sf and fantasy audience responds so much better to your work? Do you think it's a certain kind of mind that goes with that readership?

GW: I think so. I think I try to see things from a little strange perspective, perhaps, and that's about the only readership that's willing to take that sort of thing. The others really aren't that much of readerships nowadays. What we call mundane or mainstream fiction seems to be either turning in the direction of sf and fantasy or dying off, as far as I can see: people like John Gardner, for example. What else is doing? Professors who are published by a university press ...

CG: The campus novel.

GW: Yeah, and the very sexy, trashy–oh, Irving Wallace type of book ... a few historicals. The historical is really a fantasy form, except that people who read it kid themselves.

CG: It seems to me that what you've done in creating the world of *The Book of the New Sun*, the posthistoric world, is to openly acknowledge the fantastic appeal of history. What you have in that book is a lot of pre-existing, antique things coming back into being in the very far future: social structures repeating themselves, people, functions, jobs, articles, weapons, everything. You coined the word, 'posthistory', but you're not alone in seeing this sort of medievalism in the far future. What's the impulse behind that?

GW: First of all, there's a recognition that if you are on a certain economic level you have to have some sort of set-up that will work on that level. I don't really think my world is all that medieval, but a medieval set-up is a way of dealing with that sort of thing. When you have a relatively impoverished country, as the Commonwealth is, you can't educate everyone, you can't teach everyone to read, you can't publish newspapers, and this means that if you're going to have a democracy you have to do it some other way. This is what they have done, essentially. They have something that is more like Britain than it's like America: fundamentally a democratic top with an aristocratic underclass. If you have the commonality of people poor and uneducated you have to have some way of putting people over those people who can exact obedience and keep the thing organized, otherwise you fall into chaos and somebody comes along who *does* have a way of doing it, and he does it. Not the only possible way but one fairly easy way is with a hereditary aristocracy, who have their own armed retainers, who have their own small strong-points, and who are kept knocked into line enough to make them collect taxes and furnish soldiers when soldiers are needed. This is the social structure of the Commonwealth outside of the major cities. In Thrax, of course, you have a governor who's been appointed by the Autarch because that's a major place; Nessus presumably has something similar, to control the city. But in the countryside what you have are hereditary families who are the governors and actually govern, and of course if they can't then you have to do away with them.

CG: In a way, it's a cyclical thing, isn't it? You say it's governed in the first place by economic considerations. The power and the technology have dwindled and become unavailable …

GW: The technology still exists, but you can't implement it except on a very, very small scale. Those people would know how to *build* an aircraft carrier but it takes much more than knowing how to build it: it takes huge machines, resources and raw materials – and they don't *have* that. All they have is the technology that was behind the aircraft carrier originally. Mining in the Commonwealth is essentially archaeological pillaging because the real mines have been exhausted for so long that nobody really remembers that they exist.

CG: The point about posthistory is that their history is our present.

GW: The old picture-cleaner is cleaning a picture of a spaceman on the Moon.

CG: Talking of social forms repeating themselves according to circumstances, the other example in your work is the colonialism in *The Fifth Head of Cerberus*: French colonial forms imposed upon a planet, with subjugation of aborigines – in the future, the same problems being enacted.

GW: What happens there has happened on Earth repeatedly. People come, and they have very high-minded impulses, they're going to Christianise the savages, expose them to advances, and take them into the social stream. That works until there's some kind of a disagreement and the savages tomahawk two or three people, and then they say, 'Let's clean those bastards out!' That's a repeated thing. You find the people have been exterminated, or nearly exterminated, or they become an underclass, as they are in much of the American southwest, for example.

CG: In your fiction the social context is mediated through very strongly realised individuals. Some of your major themes are enquiries into individual identity, exchanges of identity, communion of identity … One British fan critic, Chris Bailey, described your usual protagonist as a solipsist: he narrates the world in terms of himself, seeing things in a very calm way – things which to us may be surprising, horrific, completely alien, but to him are normality. Do you think that's a fair description?

GW: Oh yes, because I think that's the way it is. If you're born into that society then you're not very likely to be anguished. People who came to the American South before the Civil War were horrified by slavery, but people who grew up in the South – some of them were my ancestors – didn't have those feelings. That was the way things were, that was the way they always had been.

CG: So the boy in *The Fifth Head of Cerberus* goes through the slave-market every day, and he's bored by it.

GW: Oh yes. They're always there. You've seen one slave-market, you've seen them all.

CG: And it's not until the moment when he has to kill the slave with four arms that he realizes. Is your protagonist changed by his experiences?

GW: I certainly hope so, because people are. Severian has grown up in a pseudomonastic community, accepting its values as a boy would. He's a toddler when he's taken in, he's taught by these people, he sees their world, he sees their life. He feels terribly guilty when he allows Thecla to die; he feels bad and thinks he should feel worse when he's exiled. Of course, in *The Claw* he acquires Thecla's personality, but as he goes on he sees a larger world, he develops. One of my least favourite reviews was from Norman Spinrad who said, In the first place the book is horribly padded and in the second place there's nothing that will prepare Severian to become Autarch: where's his background? Well, what he's done is to take everything that I put in there to prepare him to become Autarch and say, That's padding, throw it out: now there's nothing to prepare him. But

Severian has held a minor administrative position in Thrax, he's travelled, he's seen some of the country, he's had some exposure to the war, to military life, he's seen something of the life of a small peasant, and so on and so forth: this *is* the background. For a young man – and Severian still is a young man, all this takes place in less than a year – for a young man to come into power, if he's going to get any preparation at all, he's got to get it quickly. If you're going to really educate him then he spends forty years of his life being really educated and all that he's learned to do is get this education that will supposedly fit him. I satirise this with Master Ultan, the old librarian, who as a young man would have been ideally suited to head the library and who waited for forty or fifty years to head it, and after forty or fifty years of experience and training was completely unsuited to do it, because all he knew was the waiting. Severian is the opposite of that, he's the young man who goes up very quickly.

CG: All his various levels of apprenticeship are terminated early. He moves on to the next one very fast each time. And you make the point in the last book that he is not just equipped to oversee everything but equipped to undersee it as well.

GW: That's what you have to have. If you can't do the routine things you can't tell somebody how to do them and you can't tell whether they're doing them well or not.

CG: We could contrast this – perhaps a bit maliciously! – with Robert Silverberg's *Lord Valentine's Castle*, which Ian Watson identified works on the principle of the Divine Right of Kings. Valentine is an outcast, but restored to kingship because it's somehow innate in him. He doesn't have to learn it.

GW: This is the fairy-story thing that almost all kids get at some time: these aren't my real parents, I'm adopted, I'm the son of the son of the Czar, or something.

CG: – And somebody's going to come and discover me. Why the mystery of Severian's parentage?

GW: Because that's the way the Guild does it. It reproduces itself by taking the very young children, who have to be able to pass underneath that bar they have; and if they can't, they're too old. The last thing the Guild wants is the grown-up journeyman Torturers or the older apprentices wondering who their real parents were and trying to find them; so they're going to wipe all that out, as well as they can, and they're not going to tell.

CG: The logic is right, as you say; but I was thinking of how that mystery keeps working through the book: who are Severian's mother and father? And there's also the false parentage of the boy in *The Fifth Head of Cerberus*. This is something that seems to attract you, this idea of a kid not knowing his origins.

GW: I think that's something we all feel: am I really the granddaughter of the Czar? Even if we don't take it seriously, we have that feeling, and a lot of fiction is taking feelings like that and putting them into the reality of the story. Severian's father is a waiter at the Inn of Lost Loves, as he realizes, and his mother is in there too, but if you haven't spotted her, I'm not going to tell you who she is! You have to go into another book for that.

CG: What's the state of the fifth book now?

GW: It's in first draft. A coda to the tetralogy is the way I like to think of it, and now that things at Timescape Books are so uncertain, I don't quite know what I'm going to do with it.

CG: The thing that's wrong with American publishing is that it's a minor interest of large corporations who are making their money on more lucrative things and don't actually care very much about it. Is that over-simplified?

GW: I don't really agree with that. I think the fundamental matter with American publishing is that it's being run by people who know only the business side and are unable to appreciate either the problems or the opportunities. They've gone through business school, have business backgrounds, and they're trying to sell books as if they were boxes of soap. You can't sell books as if they were boxes of soap, they're a different kind of product. I think this is the problem we have, not just in publishing, but in a great many other industries.

CG: This is just like what you were saying about Severian. You start off at the bottom, you work your way through the experience, and then you're qualified to stand at the top. Maybe more of Pocket Books staff should sit down and read *The Book of the New Sun*!

GW: Maybe they should. One thing, when you deal with publishers in the US, that you find out immediately, is that they have not read the books they're selling, and this is why the pressure is so terrible on artists and on art directors. The artist comes in here and he's got this picture: here's the girl in the brass brassiere, and here's the dragon or whatever it is, and the publisher can look at that and it only takes thirty seconds to decide – but here's this great thick book! And he doesn't read books anyway; it would probably take him the rest of his life, but he'd never read that book. He's working from two paragraphs if he does it at all.

CG: Do you feel that about the way you've been packaged in the States?

GW: I think that's the way that everything is done in the States. This is the reason that people like David Hartwell get fired by people who are not looking at the product because they don't know anything about the product. They can't look at the future of the enterprise because they don't know anything about the product. All that they can look at is, Well, we've had so many returns, and we've had so many sales, and this sort of thing. It's like trying to ride a bicycle backwards. You're looking at the things that you've passed and trying to guess what's ahead, and you run into the fireplug.

CG: How far do you regard at least one of the points of sf as being to point out to people what fireplugs may be lurking there for them to run into?

GW: It's very legitimate, I think. Any good fiction should be, among other things, a way of telling you about life, about what you're going to encounter, whether it's sf or *Huckleberry Finn*. That doesn't mean that it's predictive. But it should say these things are a possibility. What's going to happen to the human race if we never, never find new sources of raw materials? We don't go out into space and mine the asteroids; we don't go under the sea; we just do what we're doing now and we keep doing that until all of it runs out. That's the world of *The Book of the New Sun*. You end up sifting the garbage of past ages to try and find useable things. Much of the area of the land is going to go down into the sea. Mineral resources are just there and if you're still mining by essentially pick and shovel methods, there's only so much metal close enough to the crust that you can reach, and when it's gone, it's gone. It's exhausted.

CG: How do you feel about the Larry Niven lobby that says, Our resources aren't just under our feet, what we *should* be doing is getting out into space?

GW: I think they're absolutely right. I'm very disappointed that the United States doesn't have a permanent space station now. If you look back to the period of the Moon landings, by now we should have that wheel station that you see in *2001: A Space Odyssey*, that should be up there and built and in use. I think that it's right. We've got to go someplace and I can only see two places to go. One is into space, the other is into the seas. There's certainly a great deal of stuff in the seas and it's certainly very available; in space it's less available, but it's virtually unlimited. The Sun puts out enough energy in a day to run the human race for its entire history. What do we take, one ninety-millionth of the energy of the sun? Take two ninety-millionths, that gives us twice as much energy as we've got.

CG: So presumably you'd be in favour of projects like solar energy and tidal power?

GW: Obviously. One of the things that we ought to be aiming toward is not destroying so-called fossil fuels, which are much, much more than fuels, simply by burning them. When the first explorers came to the New World they chopped down billions of dollars worth of timber and they burned it, simply to clear land on which to grow crops. Now we'd love to have that back. And this is what *we're* doing. We're burning coal; we're burning petroleum that really ought to be feed-stocks for other products. It's as if somebody was heating his house by throwing furniture on the fire. Yes, it will burn, and yes, it will heat the house, and it will do everything that you say, but it's a hell of a wasteful way to heat a house. If you have to go out and carry the stuff back from a warehouse, when the warehouse is empty, the house is going to be cold. It might be better to find something that isn't going to be empty like the warehouse, and there *are* things that aren't going to be empty like the warehouse.

This goes back to what we were saying about the aircraft carrier. If you destroy your resources to a certain point, you can't go back because the things that you climbed on originally are now gone. It isn't there. The oilfields of Texas produce something like 10% of what they originally produced – I'm from Texas. I tend to think about that. You can't go back and start a second industrial age on the American continent with the oil from the Texas fields, because the Texas fields are now nearly exhausted. In military theory they speak of a decisive battle, and there are decisive moments in the development of a high-technology civilization. That's what I'm afraid we're doing in space. If we pass the moment, then we'll never be able to do it again, we'll never be able to start with the shuttle or something like that, we won't have the resources. I don't think we're past it yet, I don't think we're going to be past it in my lifetime, but it's going to be possible to pass it, and then everybody will look back and say, Gee, five hundred years ago they had space travel, we can't do that any more.

CG: A thing that particularly appealed to me in *The Book of the New Sun* was the fact that Severian doesn't distinguish between ships and spaceships. It's gone that far.

GW: When you reach the point where you see the Moon as an island, then there isn't that much to distinguish. A ship is something that could take you to someplace far away but you'll probably never go there in your life. Severian never thinks that he's going to go to the extern lands, which are the lands outside the Commonwealth, and he doesn't think he's going to go to the Moon either, and the things that aren't going to take him there are ships, which go to those places.

CG: You've made a speciality of young protagonists, boys not necessarily understanding what's going on around them but coming to knowledge. Since you're not writing children's fiction, it's quite a daring thing to do, don't you think?

GW: Yes, and the great hazard with it is that whatever you do may be taken as being children's fiction. A child isn't so accustomed to the world, and can report the things that are new to the reader as being new to him. He's not calloused about everything, he hasn't pushed it in the back of his mind.

CG: So it's a fresh viewpoint and one which can teach as well as learn.

GW: To learn something you've got to look at the something in a new way, if it's been around you all the time. This is why artists bend over and they look at the landscape between their legs, because this sort of thing makes you look at things in a new way. [*GW makes a frame of index fingers and thumbs.*] If you look at the rising Moon this way it's much smaller. Magically, suddenly, it's smaller.

CG: Tell me about magic.

GW: Magic works on Earth. There's any amount of evidence to show that it does work. We have taken as part of our super-religion, our philosophical orientation, that it doesn't work, so we all go around agreeing with each other that it doesn't work, and we ignore all the evidence that says that it does. In the last election we had a man named John Anderson run as an independent, and he got something like 9% of the total vote. He was probably the best candidate running, if you listened to the speeches, and if you looked at the experience of the three candidates, their experience in government. But the United States is under a spell, and this spell says, No one can win unless he is a candidate of one of our two major parties. Okay, now that spell works, as long as everyone believes it. That's magic. It wasn't there at the beginning. George Washington, our first president, said, Don't have political parties, political parties are evil. They're going to ruin this country that we've started here if you allow them. No parties; pick out individuals that you think are able individuals, that are leaders in their communities, and elect them to national leadership. And we don't do it. We're under a spell and we can't do it.

CG: So we've got a paradox here, that magic is both the thing that works because we all agree that it does, and also the thing that we all agree doesn't work.

GW: That's precisely true, and that is very typical of the way that things happen. The germ theory of disease was proposed sometime in the thirteenth century, by some priest, who said that tiny little animals invade the body, animals too small to be seen. We don't even know where he got his ideas, all we know is that he said this, and the only reason we know it is because of the people who ridiculed him for saying it. It's the only thing that survived. If we say, Okay, I agree that there's no such thing as disease, you agree that there's no such thing as disease, then disease is going to work *beautifully*. It's going to kill a hell of a lot of people. It's when you recognize it and you say, Yes, it's there, it's real, it does work, then you can start dealing with it and if not preventing it totally, preventing a large part of it. It's the things which you don't admit exist that you can't defend yourself against and which have tremendous power over you. Lafferty says somewhere, we think that the great idealistic concepts are somewhere inside us, but actually we're somewhere inside them. That's why we have such a hard time dealing with them. We think we're bigger than courage, or guilt, or something like that, and that's absurd; those are enormous things, they've been around for thousands and thousands of years. We're in them. The socio-biologists say that we are creatures who are created by genes which we call 'our' genes, for the creation of more genes of their design. If that's true then it's equally valid for machines, for example, to look on us as things that are made in order to make machines.

CG: That sounds like a John Sladek idea. The human is the machine's reproductive system. You mention Lafferty; who else do you particularly admire writing sf at the moment?

GW: I just read a very good book by John M. Ford, who I hadn't read before, so I'm going to have to add him to my list.

CG: *The Dragon Waiting*?

GW: Yes. It's an alternate history, but it's good alternate history. He can get inside a Roman and he knows how the Roman thought. He's not faking it, the Romans really did think that way. Who else? ... Unfortunately, there are very few publishers who are doing sf in the US.

CG: Here too – and yet it's supposed to be a very strong popular form at the moment. We've got the cinema reflecting it, we've got it coming out of video games, influencing the design and vocabulary of children's toys and everything, and where is the fiction? Where is the fiction going?

GW: I don't know how it's going to go. Some new publishers may go into it; some small publishers may get bigger. There are publishers who are doing very well with it, but I don't know what's going to happen. It's been hurt by the recession because our readers tend to be the kind of people who are hurt by recession. They're young people without much seniority and very often if somebody's laid off they're the ones. Now they're living on their unemployment money, they can't really afford to spend on books what they were getting when they were making ten dollars an hour.

CG: I hadn't thought about it that way before; but it's been hit in another way, as I see it: there's a recession of form within sf itself. I mean, people are falling back on formulas, on genre, very much more than they were ten years ago.

GW: That's very definitely so. I think that a part of it is the direction of the publishing houses by businessmen. They've seen *Star Wars* and they know what sf should be: it should be rockets, and robots, and rayguns. So there's a lot of pressure on the editors; and some of the editors aren't all that knowledgeable. There aren't many Dave Hartwells around.

CG: There are spaceships and cyborgs and rayguns in *The Book of the New Sun* too, aren't there? You've taken many of the genre clichés and conventions and turned them around. We don't even realize Jonas is a cyborg, but suddenly there he is. What were you doing with all that?

GW: I think that what I was trying to do there was show how the future would be. In the future, rayguns and robots are going to be things that are essentially of the past, because we've got them all now. There's Robotics International, a technical society for engineers that are interested in robots: I'm a member of it. I've taken two courses at Unimation, which is the biggest robot manufacturer in the United States. I went to look at the

Machine Intelligence Corporation in California; they have machine vision systems there. The mobile industrial robot is probably less than five years away. I'm very happy to hear that the United States Army is putting a lot of funding and effort behind mobile robots. Spaceships – we've got this truck that can go into space now. When I was a kid we read in sf about mechanical brains: that's IBM. HAL in 200I: that's 'IBM' shifted over one letter. So those will be things of the past.

6

Gene Wolfe in Conversation

with Nancy Kress and Calvin Rich
originally edited by Earl G. Ingersoll

The commercial success of *The Book of the New Sun* allowed Wolfe to resign from his editorial post at *Plant Engineering* and devote himself to full time writing in 1983. In the following year, he published three small press collections: *The Wolfe Archipelago*, the punningly titled *Plan[e]t Engineering* (which included 'Books in *The Book of the New Sun*') and *Bibliomen: Twenty Characters Waiting for a Book*, a series of fictional biographies. His novel *Free Live Free* also appeared as a limited edition in 1984. They were all overshadowed by the continued success of *The Book of the New Sun*. Resisting the temptation to question Wolfe exclusively on his tetralogy, Nancy Kress and Calvin Rich discuss Wolfe's broader concerns as a writer in an interview that first appeared in *Australian Science Fiction Review* in November 1985.

NK: There are a number of readers, and especially critics, who would say that if life is your concern, fantasy and science fiction are removed from the mainstream. What leads you to write fantasy and science fiction, rather than mainstream literature?

GW: I don't agree with those people. They assume that the ephemera of today are somehow permanent and important, that we will always have yellow buses and fire plugs. What is permanent and important is the creations of the human mind (of which buses and fire plugs are only very minor creations) and the physical world. The first involves fantasy; the second, science fiction, when you put it into a literary context. I don't think that reality can be defined as a knife edge in time. And, of course, if you actually study physics, you discover that the time-knife edge does not, in fact, exist. If you cut time finer and finer, there is no such thing as this present instant. There is only the future and the past.

NK: You stated something similar in an article that you wrote on fantasy; in it you said that the landscape of fantasy is not the landscape of myth, but the landscape of the future. How did you mean that?

GW: Well, I think that it's quite obvious that the human race is increasing in its power to alter the world in the directions that it desires. To take a very obvious instance, we are now just at the beginning of the biological revolution: for example, cloning and the ability to combine biological material from two different organisms. By 'different', I'm not trying to be redundant; I mean different species. As we increase in our ability to shape the world of our dreams in the real sense, we will have the magic flying horse of the *Arabian Nights*. We're going to see the unicorns in this century, certainly in the first half of the next century, because people want unicorns, and unicorns are fairly easy to build once the genetic engineering is there. You start with a horse, and you introduce a few modifications; they you can have the unicorn of myth. You can have the faun or the satyr of myth. I did a couple of stories on this – 'The Woman Who Loved the Centaur Pholus' [and 'The Woman the Unicorn Loved' – *PW*]. If you create a man's head on a horse's body, and if you figure out some way to make the thing live so that it can eat, you are not going to be able to keep it in the kitchen like a cat forever; eventually it's going to break free. The centaur may very well be a better man than you are, and you are going to find that you cannot be his jailer indefinitely, and people will have to deal with the problems that are involved in genetic engineering. Of course, there are much more dangerous things that they will have to deal with – the creation of new diseases, for example.

CR: Do you think that this is one of the reasons some readers, like some of my students, accuse science fiction and fantasy of being so repetitive? They keep saying you use the same materials, the same themes, over and over. I keep telling them to look for the variations.

GW: I think that some of it is repetitive, but there are certain mechanisms that are used in science fiction because they're useful: interplanetary or interstellar travel makes possible a lot of stories that couldn't be written if you didn't have some way of getting your characters to a different planet. So, they're repetitive in that sense; but, I don't think that there are a great many stories around now that are specifically about interstellar travel as a thing in itself.

NK: The same repetitiveness shows up in fantasy. I'm thinking now of your *Book of the New Sun* and the way it uses specific, traditional fantasy motifs, almost as though you were paying tribute to the genre. There is the gift of a valuable and trusted sword that recalls Excalibur, and there is the sense of a jewel of power called [The Claw of the] Conciliator that recalls Tolkien's Ring. Were these deliberate? Is this your way of paying tribute to the genre?

GW: Yes, in some sense of it. The more intentional thing was to try and show in the first place how such a thing might happen and, in the second place, what the effect might really be of getting such a sword, of getting such a jewel or relic. Actually, the Claw of the Conciliator is a relic. About half of the reviewers who have read the book think that Terminus Est is the magic sword. It isn't. It's simply a very old and valuable sword that's very well made.

NK: You mentioned at various times that academic study of your work, the kind of thing that we're skirting around the edges of here in talking about *The Book of the New Sun*, scares you to death. Why is that?

GW: I think that students tend to dislike what they are made to read in class, and I would hate to see science fiction and fantasy lifted out of its position as a sort of criminal genre and given academic respectability, because I think when it has academic respectability, a great many people are going to say, 'It's dull, so I don't want to read that.' I read 'pulp' magazines when kids who read them frequently had to do it with a flashlight under their bedcovers because their parents wouldn't let them read 'pulp' magazines. As a result, they wanted very much to read them.

NK: Your objection, then, to dissection of your work academically is the effect that it has on the readers rather than any effect it might have on you as a writer. Do critics and reviewers bother you when they dislike something that you've written? Do you think there's a circle in which feedback from critics affects what the writer writes?

GW: I think there is with some writers, but I don't particularly think I'm one of them. When a writer is greatly affected by critics, particularly by academic critics, I think that he has to stop reading the criticism. I don't think that that is helpful. When I get a bad review, or a critic tears up my work, I really feel bad, but only for about forty-five minutes. There are people who are wiped out for years by this sort of thing.

NK: Why particularly academic critics? Why are you making that stricture?

GW: Because I think that academic critics are farther from the popular taste than newspaper reviewers. Secondly, they tend to be taken more seriously by the writers who take criticism seriously. They can use stupendous words and refer to the works of James Joyce, and God knows what. It's all very, very impressive, but if it's destructive you ought not to pay attention to it. It's like pounding your head against the wall.

NK: Do you think science fiction readers differ from mainstream readers?

GW: Yes, I think so.

NK: In what way?

GW: I knew you would ask that. I should have said, 'No.'

NK: Sorry.

GW: They do differ. To start with, I think science fiction readers are brighter. When I say, mainstream readers, I'm not talking about the people who read Shakespeare or Dante; I'm talking about the people who read John Jakes' *The Bastard* and so forth. I think that science fiction readers are much less frightened of new ideas, eager to escape the here-and-now, whereas the mainstream reader is frightened to be drawn away from the here-and-now.

NK: So much of popular mainstream literature – the Harlequin Romances, for example – however, is more escapist than science fiction in that it has less connection with any reality that's underneath.

GW: Yes, I agree, but there's a difference. It's a non-frightening escape, whether it's an adventure or not. I think the people who read science fiction or fantasy are looking for a kind of adventure. The people who read Harlequin Romances are looking for a kind of paradise.

NK: And, of course, the adventure can be intellectual, not merely physical.

GW: Oh certainly, certainly. Ideally, it should be both. It should have an intellectual component, or a spiritual component, as well as a physical component.

NK: I sense from what you say, and also from *The Book of the New Sun*, that you don't make a sharp distinction between science fiction and fantasy.

GW: No, I don't. I don't see that a sharp distinction can be made. What we're talking about, really, are publishing categories – which wire rack a book goes on to. Science fiction is always, to some degree, fantasy. If you say I'm going to extrapolate what the science of the next fifty years will be like, that is in itself fantasy: if you pretend that you think that your extrapolation is going to be one hundred per cent accurate, it never is. It may score some astounding hits. Unicorns, I think, are science fiction if you put them in our world rather than in the world of the medieval past. And so you see, we can argue about that indefinitely. If somebody in the 1800s wrote a book about robots or mechanical men – and there were such books written – they were generally clockwork. Then, to someone who never thought such things would exist, that was fantasy. Looking back on the mechanical men, we see that robots, mobile robots, can be made, automata for Disney or what not. Then it's science fiction. But why should the passage of a hundred or two hundred years make the book change its genre? It depends on the preconceptions that we bring to the book.

NK: So that's why *The Book of the New Sun* has so much science and magic – or seeming magic – intertwined, right in the same paragraph sometimes. You're making a statement on science and magic there.

GW: Yes. If you don't think you know how a radio works – most people don't know how it works, they only think they know because it has always been there – then the radio becomes a magical instrument. These voices speak to you from this box. That's a fantasy device. If you're enough of a radio hobbyist that you could buy a kit at Tandy and put the thing together, then it's science fiction.

CR: That's one of the things that struck me first about the book. I admire an author who will take the hard job to do. I think that's another thing you did.

NK: I didn't find Severian unsympathetic, even from the beginning, and asking myself after I finished the first three books why I didn't find the torturer unsympathetic, I think it was partly because you started out with him as a child. I saw how his world had built the attitudes into him that he naturally would have. If you had started out with an execution over which he was presiding, I might have felt differently, but I never found him an unsympathetic character, from the beginning.

GW: Some people simply threw down the first book after the first hundred pages or so, because he is a torturer. And they can't take that. They can't deal with that, or they don't *want* to deal with it.

CR: When you have descriptions of the torturer, it does require a certain kind of fortitude to work.

NK: You didn't release the first manuscript for the four books until you had all of them done. Is that correct?

GW: I had all of them in second draft. I did all four in the first draft, and then I did all four in second draft, and then I did all the final drafts on the first book.

NK: So you knew before the first one was published how it was going to end, and how it was going to come out.

GW: You betcha.

NK: And you stated before that you can't write a story unless you can see the ending at the beginning.

GW: I think it's foolish to try. I think you're trying to do your mental work on paper. A story should point towards its ending. When the ending happens, the reader should say two things: I didn't see that coming, but it was inevitable; I don't see how the writer can write the story that way, unless he knows what's coming.

NK: What is your working procedure when you have a story? Is there a long germination period when you're not doing your mental work on paper?

GW: Yes. I think there is. Fundamentally, the germination period consists of a coming together of a number of ideas. I've always got a number of ideas shaking around in my head and, thinking what if such-and-such a character were to exist, what if these places were to exist, and sooner or later everything clicks – or I should say a number of those ideas click – and I say, 'Gee, that character there is with this place here and this event here and then naturally so and so … ' And when I do that, then I see the story, I understand the fundamental outlines of the story: how it should begin, where it will go, what kind of ending it should have. But sometimes I make false starts, certainly.

CR: You start out then with a 'what if?'

GW: That's one way of phrasing it.

CR: How do you get the 'what ifs', though? Is there any genesis for the kinds of 'what ifs' you start putting together?

NK: Is that the old 'Where-do-you-get-your-ideas?' question?

GW: Yes ...

CR: Is there a kind of exercise you can go through? In my course in 'Fantasy and Romance', I have students practice their own 'what ifs', and some of them find it impossible to get started with them. I just wondered if you had a little exercise.

GW: I've done that kind of exercise any number of times – brainstorming stories by encapsulating each story in a single sentence. I can sit down with a tablet of paper and I can brainstorm more work in a half hour than I can in two years. You can say, what would happen if one of the freaks in a carnival freak show was really what he or she was presented as being? You can have a mermaid, right, with her legs deformed in a certain way, and so forth. What if one freak, the mermaid, was really that thing? Would she know it? Would the others know it? How would they come to know it? What would be the result of it, and so forth?

NK: What story did that idea lead to?

GW: Oh, none. I haven't written that story yet. I was just doing it for you so that you can see how it's done.

CR: After you have brainstormed, then you go back and pick up the most pregnant ideas.

GW: Yes, sometimes.

NK: You mentioned exercises. We've had writers before who have had (and stated) a very low opinion of workshopping stories and of any kind of creative-writing course. They say the only way that you can learn to write is to write. What is your opinion of creative-writing courses?

GW: Well, the only way that you *can* learn to write is to write. That is perfectly true. The only way you can learn to swim is to swim, and the only way you can learn to play the violin is to play the violin. But one of the things that students in a creative-writing course do is write, and because they have some immediate feedback, hopefully from fairly informed, concerned people, they can progress much more quickly than they would if they wrote their amateur story and sent it to a magazine and six weeks later got it back with a printed rejection slip. That was the way I learned to write, and it took me about seven years to do it. I don't think people should have to take seven years to learn.

NK: So the function of the creative-writing class is to sharpen the critical faculty, not necessarily the creative one.

GW: No, quite the contrary. The function is to sharpen the creative one, and not the critical one. But if you listen to responses, your creative faculty is sharpened. I think that's the main thing that we have to be working toward. People are saying things like, 'This is fake, it should be specific.' The next time if the student tries to make it specific, then he becomes more creative, because he has to create something. He can't just say, 'The three men walking in the door.' What were these men? Why were they doing this? People say, 'This is dull. I want it to be more interesting. I want you to put more energy into it.' This turns up creativity. If a student just studies criticism, long courses of dissecting the old masters, then what he learns is criticism and as a creative writer his brakes are locked, because he can see that his stuff is very, very bad, but he can't see any way to make it better.

NK: So given all that, what would be your advice to young hopefuls who want to become science fiction and fantasy writers?

GW: First of all, read widely. I don't think that most students read anywhere near as much as they should.

NK: Not only science fiction.

GW: No, widely, widely, but with particular emphasis on the type of material that they're trying to write. But, secondly, to do what you said – to write. The trouble with many talented 'writers' that I have worked with is that they produce practically nothing. They have quite a bit of talent. Their work, when they do it, is good, but they produce two stories a year. That doesn't go anywhere. It doesn't do anything.

7

An Interview with Gene Wolfe

Elliott Swanson

Wolfe's interview with Elliott Swanson, first published in *Interzone* (Autumn 1986), follows the mass-market publication of *Free Live Free* in 1985. Here, in part, Wolfe indicates the differences between the Ziesing small press edition and the American and British editions of his complex, transtemporally plotted novel.

When future scholars look back in some academic quest to determine the point where science fiction made the jump to literature, one of the writers they'll have to contend with is Gene Wolfe. Born in 1931, he has recently abandoned the editing of a technical magazine for full-time fiction writing. His first stories were published in the 1960s, but it was not until the appearance of the first volume of *The Book of the New Sun* (*The Shadow of the Torturer*) in 1980 that twenty years of writing turned into an 'overnight success'.

ES: Many writers with scientific backgrounds stick mainly to 'hard' sf. As an ex-engineer, how did you dodge the stereotype?

GW: Actually, I have written a certain amount of hard science fiction. I think that someone like myself who has done a good deal of practical engineering has an appreciation of the difficulties of the thing. I don't find myself very comfortable with characters who build time machines in their basements or whip out super-powered lasers from broken frying pans. I don't *believe* it can be done. I did manage to learn that things that should work in theory don't always work in practice, and that most of an engineer's really difficult problems are with people and politics.

ES: The numbing effect of technology seems to be a recurring theme in your writing. How do you see technology affecting our short-term future?

GW: Fundamentally, as we let it. Technology is a tool, not a god or a devil. Radio and television could have been the greatest things since the printing press; but we want elevator music, propaganda, and sales pitches, so that's what we're getting, for the most part. Creating and using technology requires a great deal of training and education, but the public is being sold on the idea that technology does away with the need for education – why learn to spell when you can get a spelling-checker for your word processor? Why learn to read when the educational channel lets you tune in to *Hamlet*? It's a message we want very much to hear, and we're listening as hard as we can. All this was predicted years and years ago, by the way, in a story called 'The Marching Morons' [by C. M. Kornbluth – *ES*]

ES: In *The Book of the New Sun* series, divisions between magic and technology blur – at least in the eyes of most of the inhabitants of that world – creating a new and bizarre mythology. Are the roots of that future mythology identifiable today?

GW: If you mean the various stories from the brown book [one of the fictional works described within *New Sun* – *ES*], they are tales from our own period or much earlier, mixed and blurred in the fashion that stories are by the passage of time. I had a fan write, saying that I probably thought nobody would realize that I was stealing from Kipling in 'The Tale of the Boy Called Frog', but that he had caught it. I tried to be polite and replied I was certainly glad he had. He said just don't try that again. Of course Romulus and Remus are in that story too, as is the pilgrims' landing at Plymouth Rock.

ES: In one of your stories, 'The Blue Mouse', there is a psychological division among soldiers – those who can kill (Marksmen) and those who cannot (Techs). Yet it's the Techs who are truly brutal. Did your own experience as a soldier have anything to do with shaping that story?

GW: Yes, a great deal. In general, combat soldiers are gentle men who have no desire to fight, although they may very well kill you if *you* do. In general, clerks, truck drivers, and cooks feel the need to prove that they're as tough as commandos. There are exceptions both ways, of course. Our company clerk in Korea was probably the most intelligent man in the company, and one of the best liked.

ES: After talking about your views on high-tech, this may sound like a loaded question … Do you write with a word processor?

GW: I write on what is called a 'smart typewriter'. It's actually a hard-wired word processor. I'd like to have a home computer too, but I haven't been able to justify spending that much money yet.

ES: Libraries often slap little yellow-and-red 'SF' stickers on the spines of your books. How do you feel about being genre labeled?

GW: I think that's part of the librarians' job. I was in a library once when a nice little old lady came in asking for ghost stories. The library didn't have a ghost story section, and the librarians couldn't think of any ghost story writers. Any aversion I may have had to labels vanished as I listened to their conversation. At the World Fantasy Convention, my publisher told me that one of the big book chains was unhappy with the jacket of the hardcover *Free Live Free*, because it did not 'say' science fiction. He and his chief editor explained that they had been trying to think of something that would say it without giving away the ending. I reminded them that early in the book a beautiful naked witch uses her portable computer to summon a demon, so maybe the paperback will have a new cover …

ES: Libraries and librarians often crop up in your works – why?

GW: Probably because I used to ride my bicycle to the magical and mysterious Houston Public Library, then one of the largest public buildings in town. It's one of the smallest buildings downtown now, and has become a 'civic centre', or some such. The library is a new, brilliantly lit, and very noisy building that does everything possible to remind you that books are just a sideline. In the town where I live, the library pretty obviously considers itself a branch-office of the high-school library; and Chicago, the nearest big city, has improved its library by getting rid of every last book. Yet libraries were magical places once, and could be so again. It seems to me that just as we ought to let the Postal System spend *all* its time on junk mail and establish an independent organization to handle letters, magazines, and packages, we ought to let our present libraries handle nothing but sound recordings, software, children's clubs, and video tapes, and establish a new, human-sized institution that would cherish books, occasionally loan them out, and say 'Shhh!'

ES: A reviewer said the recent release of your novel *Free Live Free* [Gollancz, UK, Tor US – originally a Ziesing limited edition] 'can be considered a new book'. What kind of changes were made?

GW: The book was cut by about 4000 words, as I remember. About half that came from dropping a chapter, the rest from tightening up the writing. The order of the chapters was changed slightly, and a chronology was added as end matter. The British edition is the same as the Tor edition, by the way, except that it lacks the chronology.

ES: Who, if anyone, have you used as a model in developing a writing style?

GW: Nobody, really … I just try to suit my style to the material.

ES: Which writers do you read?

GW: The brief answer is all of them. Once I told Somtow Sucharitkul that I read everything except westerns, and he said, 'Oh yes, easterns are much better!' Last night I read a short story by Doris Pitkin Buck. Try to find five other people who remember Doris Pitkin Buck. I'm currently reading *Benchmarks*, by Algis Budrys, and I recommend it.

ES: How did someone regarded as a master of the short story come to write a 400,000 word novel (*The Book of the New Sun* tetralogy)?

GW: It was a novelette that got out of hand. I planned a two-part story: Severian as a young man in the Citadel, and Severian returning to the Citadel to force the guild to make him a master. I hoped to sell it to Damon Knight's *Orbit* series. Severian grabbed the story and ran away with it, then pulled Dorcas out of that damned swamp – she was a total surprise to me, and I had a hell of a time figuring out who she was – and I was really

in the soup. Okay, it would be a novel. Then a trilogy. Thanks for calling
me a master of the short story. It isn't true, but I'm working on it.

ES: *The Book of the New Sun* contains enough archaic and arcane words to
keep a reader buried in dictionaries …

GW: When John Carter goes to Mars, he throws Martian words like 'thark'
at us. It seemed to me that a similar story laid on Urth should use terrestrial words as authentic as 'thark'. James Blish said you shouldn't call a
rabbit a smeep. I decided to call it a lapin. Or maybe a hare.

ES: In the *New Sun* lexicon featured in *The Castle of the Otter*, you apologise
for misspelling 'onagers' saying 'I should look these things up.' The implication is that you keep all this weird language in your heard. You're kidding, of course.

GW: Yes, but kidding myself most of all. I really thought I knew how to
spell onagers, and I was wrong. Some of those words I know, some I had a
vague memory of, and some took hours of searching. Obviously enough,
I'm not quite as smart that way as I thought I was. When Ring Larder
wrote those letters from his fictional ballplayer, he misspelled easy words
and spelled the difficult words correctly. He had a hard time getting that
past his editors, but he was right. That sort of letter writer uses a dictionary for the difficult words, but believes he can spell the easy ones. I know
because I belong to the same group.

ES: The world of *The Book of the New Sun* is a recognisable place, with
Byzantine and medieval overtones. Do you see history as repeating cycles,
with bits and pieces constantly going in and out of fashion?

GW: Yes, but not *causeless* cycles. The Greeks developed democracy because the geography of their country broke then into small communities.
The English revived it because the invention of the horsecollar destroyed
the Roman roads, breaking England into little communities. We revived it
again, because of the pattern of colonization along our eastern seaboard.
Not all the Greek cities were democracies, and not all their democracies
were good, because small, scattered communities can produce other things
as well. But whenever you have small, scattered communities, democracy is one likely result. We no longer have it by the way – we have a
republic, a system by which we elect our rulers rather than ruling ourselves.

ES: If you stripped away the narrative material and redoubts in *New Sun*
you'd have a philosophy book. Gene Wolfe's philosophy or Severian the
Torturer's?

GW: Severian's, of course. He's writing the book.

ES: In *The Citadel of the Autarch*, Severian muses that perhaps all women
betray us … Has there been any reaction by militant feminists to women's
roles in the series?

GW: I think Severian means that men want to be loved more than any other thing is loved, and that though they may occasionally attract such love, they never have the power to hold it. I doubt that militant feminists read me or any author that closely. I've had a lot of flak from them because 'there are no women in positions of authority', which isn't true, and because Thecla is tortured. Not long ago, my agent passed along a letter from a female editor asking for horror stories free of 'child abuse and graphic violence to women'. Guess what's okay …

ES: Would you like to see any of your books made into films – other than for the obvious economic reasons?

GW: Not particularly. Film is a junk medium; if that weren't true, you'd see scripts published like plays. Besides, there isn't room enough in a movie for a good book. I'd much rather see films made from some of my short stories, say 'The Detective of Dreams', 'The Toy Theatre', or 'Westwind'.

ES: There are speciality bookstore owners with walls full of screenplays who might argue part of that statement, but what's more interesting is how you connect script publishing with film as a 'junk medium'.

GW: It seems to me that in most cases movie scripts have very little to do with the quality of the picture. I think the reason is that movie scripts cannot have much to do with picture quality, but that most movie scripts are sufficiently bad that successful pictures succeed in spite of them. If this weren't true I think that we would see more published movie scripts than we do. I've never seen a store of the type you described – maybe they're all over America and I've never come across them.

ES: Within the genre, what about films like *Solaris* or *A Clockwork Orange* or, arguably, *Blade Runner*?

GW: I happen to love *Blade Runner*. I think it's a superb movie. It did not do well, but the fact that it's a superb movie doesn't give me much impetus to see some of my own work done as film. I suppose I've seen any number of *Star Wars* dolls, for example, and I think some of them are probably very good dolls. That doesn't particularly make me want to see someone do a Severian doll, other than the financial aspect, which we set aside. Sure, if someone wants to do a movie of one of my things and pay a big buck, I'm going to take the money and run for the train like anybody else, but I'm not going to expect a good movie. I'd be delighted to get one.

ES: Have film rights ever been sold for any of your books?

GW: No. Options have been sold to *The Fifth Head of Cerberus* and 'The Death of Doctor Island', but the rights themselves have never been sold. Early last year, I got expressions of interest on *New Sun* from Goldrush Studios and Lord and Lady, but nothing has come of them. You didn't ask about game rights, but there's been a good deal of talk – and no action – there.

ES: The word is that you're working on an opera. If so, what's it like, and when can we expect to see it?

GW: The idea was to do 'The Death of Doctor Island' as an opera. I'm not writing the opera in the sense of composing the music, which strikes me as being about ninety percent of the job. I'm writing the libretto and Somtow Sucharitkul is doing the composing. It hasn't gone terribly far. The last letter I had from him said that he was still working on it, but we have much farther to go than we've gone, and (to date) it's taken us four years. So don't hold your breath!

ES: The big question – when will the fifth *New Sun* book be published?

GW: I have no idea. I should finish it sometime this year. It will have to go to Simon and Shuster/Pocket, which has an option from which it will not release me, although S & S/P may or may not be more or less out of the sf field. S & S/P may or may not buy it, and if it does, may or may not publish it. In other words, nearly all the decisions are out of my hands.

ES: What else is in the works?

GW: *Soldier of the Mist*, a science fantasy laid in ancient Greece; I'm told it will be out in October. And *There Are Doors*, a parallel universe novel still in first draft. Recently I finished a short story called 'The Peace Spy' about ending the threat of nuclear war, but so far nobody is interested. I've also written 'Empires of Foliage and Flower', the story about the green and yellow empires to which Severian refers in *The Claw of the Conciliator*.

ES: Stealing an idea from *The Castle of the Otter*, how about wrapping things up with a brief Gene Wolfe interviews Gene Wolfe session?

GW: Okay. What do you dislike most about your own writing Mr Wolfe? Answer: That so often is doesn't work – that I can say X, flatly and in so many words, and later have editors, reviewers, and readers, say 'But you never told me X.' I point out that I did, at the top of page twenty-two, or whatever, and they say, 'Well, it doesn't come through.' Obviously it doesn't, and I don't know how to make it. Similarly, at least a dozen reviewers have said that Severian has a magic sword. It isn't magic, he doesn't think it's magic. In *Soldier of the Mist* I gave up and gave the hero (he's called Latro) a magic sword – it cuts things.

8

On Encompassing the Entire Universe:
An Interview with Gene Wolfe

Larry McCaffery

Between 1985 and the publication of Larry McCaffery's interview in *Science Fiction Studies* in 1988, Wolfe published *Soldier of the Mist* (1986), an historical fantasy set in ancient Greece, which won a Best Fantasy Novel Award from Locus, *The Urth of the New Sun* (1987), a coda to *The Book of the New Sun*, and *There Are Doors* (1988), an intertextual tale of obsessive love. Here, McCaffery elicits one of the most comprehensive insights into Wolfe's preoccupations as a writer of such varied fiction.

LM: Could you discuss what sorts of things have drawn you towards writing SF? Do you find there are certain formal advantages in writing outside the realm of 'mainstream' fiction, maybe a freedom that allows you more room for exploring the issues you wish to develop?
GW: It's not so much a matter of 'advantages' as sf appealing to my natural cast of mind, to my literary imagination. The only way I know to write is to write the kind of thing I would like to read myself, and when I do that it usually winds up being classified as sf or 'science fantasy', which is what I call most of my work. Incidentally, I'd argue that sf represents literature's real mainstream. What we now normally consider the mainstream – so-called realistic fiction – is a small literary genre, fairly recent in origin, which is likely to be relatively short-lived. When I look back at the foundations of literature, I see literary figures who, if they were alive today, would probably be members of the Science Fiction Writers of America. Homer? He would certain belong to the SFWA. So would Dante, Milton, and Shakespeare. That tradition is literature's mainstream, and it has been what has grown out of that tradition which has been labelled sf or whatever label you want to use.
LM: That's why I began by asking if you weren't attracted to the freedom offered by sf – it's only been since the rise of the novel in the 18th century that writers have more or less tried to limit themselves to describing the ordinary world around them …
GW: It's a matter of whether you're content to focus on everyday events or whether you want to try to encompass the entire universe. If you go back to the literature written in ancient Greece or Rome, or during the Middle Ages and much of the Renaissance, you'll see writers trying to

write not just about everything that exists but about everything that could exist. Now as soon as you open yourself to that possibility, you are going to find yourself talking about things like intelligent robots and monsters with Gorgon heads, because it's becoming increasingly obvious that such things could indeed exist. But what fascinates me is that the ancient Greeks already realized these possibilities some 500 years before Christ, when they didn't have the insights into the biological and physical sciences we have today, when there was no such thing as, say, cybernetics. Yet when you read the story of Jason and the Argonauts, you discover that the island of Crete was guarded by a robot. Somehow the Greeks were alert to these possibilities despite the very primitive technology they had – and they put these ideas into their stories. Today it's the sf writers who are exploring these things in our stories.

LM: Did you read a lot of sf as a kid?

GW: Every chance I could. I had a very nice grandmother named Alma Wolfe who used to save me the Sunday comics so that when I visited her there would always be a huge stack of Sunday funnies. I read those with particular attention to Buck Rogers and Flash Gordon. Once when I was a kid in Houston I fell off my bike and hurt my leg badly enough so that my mother had to drive me to school for a while in the family car. On one of those drives she had a paperback book lying in the front seat, and when I looked down at the picture on the cover I saw a picture like the one I had seen in the Buck Rogers and Flash Gordon comics, with a tremendous chrome tower and a rocket ship being launched. It was a paperback collection of sf stories edited by Don Wollheim, who was about 22 in those days. My mother had brought it to read while she was waiting for me to get out of school (she was a big mystery fan but had bought this as a change of pace). I asked her if I could read this one when she was finished, and she said I could have it right away since she didn't much care for it. The first story I came across was 'The Microcosmic God' by Theodore Sturgeon, which was my first real encounter with sf. It was at that point I realised these were not just stories I enjoyed – like those of Edgar Allan Poe, or the Oz books by L. Frank Baum and the books by Ruth Plumly Thompson – but that they constituted a genre. From the Wollheim anthology, which was the very first American sf paperback anthology, I worked backwards and discovered the SF pulps – *Planet Stories*, *Thrilling Wonder Stories*, *Weird Tales*, *Famous Fantastic Mysteries* (that was my favourite) and *Amazing Stories*, all of which were still on sale for 20 or 25 cents. As a kid in junior high school, I used to walk six blocks or so up to the Richmond pharmacy, pick up one of those magazines, hide behind the candy case, and read until the pharmacist saw me and threw me out. Since I was usually interrupted in the middle of the story, I'd go away for a few days and then sneak back and take up where I'd left off.

LM: What kind of family atmosphere did you grow up in?

GW: One important thing was that I had a mother who read to me, which is a great blessing I suppose just about everyone who writes has had. My father was a small-town boy from southern Ohio who had been fairly adventurous as a young man but who eventually became a regional sales manager in New York City. He was assigned to Belhaven, North Carolina, where my mother had grown up in a family that was right out of a Faulkner novel; during the six months he was there they met, were married, and then he was transferred back to New York. My father was an almost ideal salesman, somebody everybody liked. I've lived here in Barrington, Illinois for 13 years now, but if my father were still alive and came to Barrington, within two weeks he would have more friends than I do. Neither of my parents ever went to college (I suspect my mother never graduated from high school) but they were tremendous readers. And that world of literature was very important to me while I was growing up because I was an introverted kid who spent a lot of time in his imagination. I had to because I was an only child and I was constantly sick. I had infantile paralysis as a small child (I was so small I don't remember having it), and I was allergic to lots of things, like wheat and chocolate, that aren't good things for a kid to be allergic to.

LM: Did all those stolen hours reading behind the candy case make you decide you wanted to be a writer?

GW: No, I'm afraid it was much more a cold, practical decision. I wrote my first stories while I was at Texas A&M studying engineering. The guy I was assigned as a roommate was connected to the college magazine as an illustrator and he thought it would be nice if I would write some stories that he could do the illustrations for. I wrote three or four forgettable pieces for the magazine, but eventually I dropped out of college (my grades were terrible), went into the Army during the Korean War, and then went back to college on the GI Bill. By 1956 I had married Rosemary, and was working as a mechanical engineer in research and development for Procter and Gamble. We were both making fairly good money but we didn't have any reserves, so as a result we were living in a furnished attic which we didn't much like – it consisted of two rooms, both of which were pointed so you could only stand up in the middle of them. It was then I decided maybe I could write something, as I had in college, and sell it so we could get enough money to buy some furniture, move into a house, and live like real human beings. I tried to write a novel but it was terrible – it never sold and it never will. But I was bitten by the bug. I discovered I liked writing; it had become a hobby; so I kept on writing other stuff until finally in 1965 I sold a little ghost story called 'The Dead Man' to *Sir*, which is one of those skin magazines, a poor man's *Playboy*.

LM: During those eight years you were trying to sell your first piece, why weren't you selling? Was your work really that bad or were you already writing far enough outside the accepted genre conventions that it was difficult to find a home for your work?

GW: It was a combination of everything. It wasn't just working outside the SF conventions – I'm still doing that today, of course, but I'm doing it better. Certainly one of my problems was that I didn't know anything about marketing when I was starting out. But mainly I was simply learning the art of writing. You don't go out, buy a violin, and then immediately get a job with a symphony orchestra – first you've got to learn how to play the damn thing. Writing is a lot like that. There are cases like Truman Capote who got his first five acceptances in one day when he was 17, but he was a very unusual and precocious writer. I remember vividly how afraid I was after I got that first acceptance that it was just blind luck and I was never going to sell anything else again.

LM: You dedicated *The Fifth Head of Cerberus* to Damon Knight, 'who one night in 1966 grew me from a bean'. I suspect there's an anecdote behind that dedication …

GW: The circumstances behind that dedication to Knight are a little complicated but probably worth relating. I'll never be able to repay Damon Knight for his help and support, although I've made some stabs at it in the past. I've received a lot of help from other people since I've achieved some recognition, but the only person who helped me with my writing when I really needed help was Damon Knight. After I had sold that story to the skin magazine, I sent a story called 'The Mountains are Mice' to *Galaxy*; as I mentioned, I was very naïve about marketing in those days, didn't know who was editing what; but it turned out that *Galaxy* was being edited by Fred Pohl. At any rate, I got back 'The Mountains are Mice' with a simple rejection note, which was the way I got back everything in those days. I was working from one of those lists of SF markets published by *The Writer*, so when *Galaxy* rejected me the next magazine on the list was *If*. So I addressed another envelope, sent the story off to *If*, and I got an acceptance from Pohl (who was also editing *If*!) with a cheque. His letter said, 'I'm glad you let me see this again. The re-write has really improved it.' My point is, of course, that there had been no re-write. Once that story appeared I received an invitation from Lloyd Biggle to join the SFWA, which had a listing of markets that included *Orbit*, the anthology that Damon Knight was editing. I wrote a story called 'Trip Trap' and sent it to *Orbit*, and I got it back with a letter from Knight saying something like: I like this story a whole lot but I think it needs to change here from viewpoint A to viewpoint B – and this is why – and then switch from B to C – with more explanations – and a long list of very sensible suggestions of that sort. After I read that letter I lay on the bed for a long while, and I suddenly realized: 'By golly, I'm actually a writer now.' I said something like that to Damon in my next letter to him, and he wrote back, 'I didn't know I had grown you from a bean', which is the line I stole for my dedication to *The Fifth Head of Cerberus*. During the next few years Knight was buying my work, making a lot of useful observations about what I was doing, and basically giving me confidence in myself when no one else was.

LM: In looking back today, were there any stories that you would point to as being 'breakthrough' pieces?

GW: The real breakthroughs were taking place before I started selling anything. There was a point at which I wrote a story called 'In the Jungle' that was never published, about a kid who wanders into a hobo jungle. At the time I wrote it, I thought it was a milestone in American literature. You know the way *Romancing the Stone* starts with that woman writer staring at the typewriter and crying, 'My God, I'm so good!'? Well, I felt that way about that story, so I sent it out to about 18 places and then watched the rejection slips pile up. Two or three years later I pulled that story out, looked at it, and realized the story I had in my head had never gotten down on paper. What I learned to do in those apprentice years was make those stories run down my arm.

LM: Some of your works proceed in a relatively straightforward, linear manner, but many of them unfold in a more complicated fashion, with the events being filtered through memory, dream, unreliable narrators, stories-within-stories, different points of view. What draws you to these sorts of 'refracted' methods?

GW: First off, my intent in using these approaches is not to mystify my readers. My agent once said to me, 'I know you thought no one would "get" this in your story but I understood what you were up to.' I wrote back that if I thought no one would get it, I wouldn't have put it in there. There's no purpose for an author deliberately making things obscure. What I am trying to do is show the way things really seem to me – and to find the most appropriate way to tell the particular story I have to tell. I certainly never sit down and say to myself, 'Gee, I think I'll tell a story in the first person or third person.' Some stories simply seem to need a first-person narrator, others are dream stories, another might require a third-person narrator. What I try to do is find the narrative approach that is most appropriate to the subject matter.

LM: And since a lot of your work seems to deal with the nature of human perception itself – the difficulties of understanding what is going on around us – a straightforward approach would be inappropriate.

GW: It's the hackneyed notion: 'The medium is the message.' As I work on a story, the subject matter often seems to become an appropriate means of telling it – the thing bites its tail, in a way – because subject and form aren't reducible to a simple 'this or that'. 'That' and 'this' are interacting throughout the story. That's what I meant when I said I'm trying to show the way things really seem to me – my experience is that subjects and methods are always interacting in our daily lives. That's realism, that's the way things really are. It's the other thing – the matter-of-fact assumption found in most fiction that the author and characters perceive everything around them clearly and objectively – that is unreal. I mean, you sit there and you think you're seeing me and I sit here thinking I'm seeing you; but what we're really reacting to are light patterns that have stimulated certain nerve endings in the retinas of our eyes – light patterns that are reflected from us. It's this peculiar process of interaction between light waves, our retinas, and our brains that I call 'seeing you' and you call 'seeing me.' But change the mechanism in my eyes, change the nature of the light, and 'you' and 'me' become entirely different as far as we're concerned. You think you're hearing me directly at this moment but you're actually hearing everything a little bit after I've said it because it requires a finite but measurable amount of time for my voice to reach you. Fiction that doesn't acknowledge these sorts of interactions simply isn't 'realistic' in any sense I'd use that term.

LM: Maybe because of your awareness of the interrelatedness of form and content, you seem to be among a relatively select group of sf authors (Delany and Le Guin would also come to mind) who appear to pay as much attention to the language and other stylistic features of their work as to the plot development or content (in the gross sense). I assume you do a lot of rewriting, but what sorts of things are you focussing on when you're doing these revisions?

GW: I do a minimum of three 'writes' for everything I do – an original and then at least two rewrites. A lot of stuff goes through four drafts, and some of it goes fifteen or even more drafts; basically I'm willing to keep revising until I get it right. What I'm focussing on in these rewrites varies. It's certainly not all just trying to get the language right, although that's important, especially when I'm trying to capture a specific atmosphere or cultural attitude in a story. I remember that when I started 'The Fifth Head of Cerberus' I completely rewrote those opening pages at least eight or ten times because it seemed essential to capture that certain flavour I wanted the story to have, the feeling of stagnation which affects a lot of what's to follow. I particularly remember struggling with that passage about the vine scrambling up the wall from the court below and nearly covering the window. But since character usually seems to be the single element in my works I'm most interested in, a lot of the rewriting I do involves me trying to fine-tune character. This is especially true when I'm working on a novel, where character has more time to predominate, rather than in stories, where often the idea or plot-twist seems more important. It's always a problem for me when I have a character like Malrubius in *The Book of the New Sun*, who shows up in widely separated places – I want to make sure he's the same person on page 300 as he was on page 10. Of course, sometimes I like the man on page 300 better than I had liked him earlier on, so then I have to go back and re-write page 10 to make him match the way he appears later on.

LM: You exhibit not only a near-encyclopaedic knowledge of words and their origins but you obviously have a great feel for language and for inventing contexts in which different lingoes can be presented. And yet one theme which recurs in many of your works (and throughout *The Book of the New Sun*) is the *limitations* of words, the way language distorts perception and is used to manipulate others. Is this a paradox – or an occupational hazard?

GW: Any writer who tries to press against the limits of prose, who's trying to write something genuinely different from what's come before, is constantly aware of these paradoxes about language's power and its limitations. Because language is your medium, you become aware of the extent to which language controls and directs our thinking, the extent that we're manipulated by words – and yet the extent to which words necessarily limit our attention and hence misrepresent the world around us. Orwell dealt with all this in *Nineteen Eighty-four* much better than I've been able to when he said, in effect: Let me control the language and I will control peoples' thoughts. Back in the 1930s the Japanese used to have actual 'Thought Police', who would come around and say to people, 'What do you think about our expedition to China?' or something like that. And if they didn't like what you replied, they'd put you under arrest. What Orwell was driving at, though, goes beyond that kind of obvious control mechanism; he was implying that if he could control the language, then he could make it so that you couldn't even think about anything he didn't want you to think about. My view is that this isn't wholly true. One of the dumber things you see in the comic books occasionally is where, say, Spider-Man falls off a building, looks down and sees a flag pole, and thinks to himself, 'If I can just grab that flagpole, I'll be okay.' Now nobody in those circumstances would actually be doing that – if you're falling off a building, you don't put that kind of thought into *words*, even though you're somehow consciously aware of needing to grab that flagpole. You are thinking below the threshold of language, which suggests there is a pre-verbal, sub-level of thinking taking place without words. Orwell didn't deal with this sub-level of thinking, but the accuracy of his insights about the way authorities can manipulate people through words is evident in the world around us.

LM: Your work often appears to rely on fantasy forms in order to find a means of dealing with these 'pre-verbal' aspects of consciousness. For instance, several scenes in *The Book of the New Sun* seemed to be dramatising inner psychological struggles that aren't easily depicted in realistic forms. I'm thinking about, say, Severian's encounter with the Wellsian man-apes in *The Claw of the Conciliator* or his later confrontation with the alzabo. These scenes seemed to function very much like dreams or fairy tales in which our inner fears or obsessions – those non-rational aspects of people that seem out of place in the mundane world of most realists – are literalised, turned into psychic dramas.

GW: That's a good way to put it. One of the advantages of fantasy is that I don't have to waste a lot of time creating the kinds of logical or causal justifications required by the conventions of realism. I can have that alzabo simply come in the front door of that cabin without having to justify his arrival (keep in mind that even in a standard sf novel I would have had to do something like have a space ship land and then have the alzabo emerge from the ship). That's one of the limitations of forms restricted to descriptions of everyday reality or of events that are scientifically plausible. Of course I'd argue that while the alzabo and those other creatures Severian meets may appear to be dream-like, they also very much exist within a continuum of human potential – they're not really 'fantastic' at all, but embodiments of things that lie within all of us. And it seems important for people to be able to occasionally confront these things (that's what dreams and fairy tales have always done for people). The alzabo is a monster, sure; but it's something many people fear a great deal when they work for a major corporation: we fear we'll be swallowed up by Proctor and Gamble, become just a cog in its innards or so much a company man that we'll just be a voice coming out of its mouth. Its beastliness is also what people don't like to recognise when they look in the mirror. Now if you're a human being, you probably realise that it's possible for you to degenerate into a beast; people who don't acknowledge this have actually degenerated in a different way, have lost a certain amount of self-insight. And you can regress into being an ape, if that's what you really want to do. When people want to bring out their animality, they usually do so by drinking, which helps them turn off their higher brain centres and become a lot like the creature we imagine the Neanderthal man was like (I hope I'm not slandering the Neanderthal man here!) People drink or use drugs to get rid of the *pain* of being a human being (maybe the pain of consciousness itself), to find ways of going back down the evolutionary ladder. Every once in a while in the *Tarzan* books, Tarzan gets sick of civilization and desperately wants to go back to being an ape. That desire may seem scary to most people, but it's inside all of us.

LM: Who were some of the writers you were reading back in the '50s and '60s who might have influenced the development of your work? I take it they weren't exclusively sf authors – your story 'The Fifth Head of Cerberus' echoes Proust in various ways, for instance.

GW: Reading *anything* exclusively is dumb. I had someone ask me once in a letter how long I could read sf before I would bum out. I replied by saying that I never bum out on sf because I never read it exclusively. I always mix my sf reading with ghost stories and mysteries and straight novels, what-have-you. At any rate, I recall that when Damon Knight asked me back in the '60s whom I was reading I wrote back and said 'J. R. R. Tolkien, G. K. Chesterton and *Mark's Engineer's Handbook.*' Chesterton is not very popular these days, but in my opinion he was a great writer who will come back into vogue. *The Man Who Was Thursday* is a tremendous novel and *The Napoleon of Notting Hill* is a wonderful forgotten fantasy work. I was reading other people in those days as well – Proust, Dickens, Borges, H. G. Wells. Proust, of course, was obsessed with some of the same things I deal with in *The Book of the New Sun* – memory and the way memory affects us – except that he was writing his remarkable works eighty years before I was.

LM: This issue of memory is central to a lot of your work – *Peace, The Fifth Head of Cerberus*, each book of *The Book of the New Sun*, and a lot of your stories. Can you say anything about why you return to it so often?

GW: Memory is all we have. The present is a knife's edge, and the future doesn't really exist (that's why sf writers can set all these strange stories there, because it's *no place*, it hasn't come into being). So memory's ability to reconnect us with the past, or some version of the past, is all we have. I'm including racial memory and instinct here ('instinct' is really just a form of racial memory). The baby bird holds onto the branch because of the racial memory of hundreds of generations of birds who have fallen off. Little kids always seem to know there are terrible things out there in the dark which might eat you, and that's undoubtedly because of hundreds and hundreds of little kids who were living in caves when there were terrible things lurking out there in the dark. This whole business about memory is very complicated because we not only remember events but we can also recall earlier memories. I allude to this in *The Book of the New Sun* when I make the point that Severian not only remembers what's happened but he remembers how he used to remember – so he can see the difference between the way he used to remember things and the way he remembers them now.

LM: Just now you didn't cite as influences any of sf's New Wave writers who were emerging during the 1960s while Michael Moorcock was editing *New Worlds*. Were you aware of those authors?

GW: I was not only aware of what they were doing but I even placed one story in *New Worlds*. What was happening with the New Wave was that a lot of sf authors with literary backgrounds, rather than scientific backgrounds, were applying what they knew in their works in just the same way the people with engineering and scientific backgrounds – Heinlein, for instance, or Asimov – had applied those backgrounds earlier. This approach didn't work fundamentally; at least it never became popular. As art it worked in some cases, while in others it didn't – which is true about everything, I guess.

LM: Why didn't these 'literary' approaches catch on with SF audiences?

GW: Probably because a lot of experimentalism was handled in such a way that it alienated readers, many of whom were raised on the pulps and didn't give a damn about 'literature' in any kind of elevated sense. I was personally sorry to see it not catching on since some of what it was trying to do certainly struck a responsive chord in me. When Harlan Ellison put together his *Again Dangerous Visions*, he included three stories by me, so I was associated with the New Wave. It was a time in which a lot of people were yelling at us for what we were doing, and we were yelling back at them. Actually, at various times I was put into both camps by different people, which was fine with me.

LM: In some ways, the three interlocking novellas of *The Fifth Head of Cerberus* operate like a Faulknerian novel, with each succeeding section revealing aspects of the larger puzzle which only comes into focus when the book is completed. Did you realise when you started out that you were going to develop this kind of structure?

GW: Not at all. I wrote the title story for Damon Knight's *Orbit*, where it originally appeared. That same year I went to the Milford Conference and presented the story there. Norbert Slepyan of Scribner's was there at that meeting and he liked the story quite a lot – so that he said that if I could write two other stories of roughly the same length he'd publish them as a book. We agreed I'd write one of the pieces and, if it was good, he'd be able to offer me a contract at that point. So I wrote "A Story" by John V. Marsch', and he was sufficiently impressed that he issued me a contract. At any rate, the specific interrelations that you see were developed as I went along.

LM: The opening sentence of 'The Fifth Head of Cerberus' echoes Proust, you set the story in a place called Frenchman's Landing, and you draw various other French elements into the story. What prompted you to use all these references to France?

GW: It had struck me for some time that it is ludicrous to assume, the way practically every sf story assumes, that people who go to the stars and set up colonies there are necessarily going to be Americans. I saw I could counter this parochial notion by setting my story in a French colony. Frenchman's Landing is actually modelled essentially on New Orleans, which has always had a strong French influence. Somebody – I think it was John Brunner – did an sf book that opens with the words, 'The Captain bore the good terrestrial name of Chang.' When the first space captains go into outer space, there'll be a lot of Changs out there.

LM: Presenting the sections of *Cerberus* out of their chronological sequence forces the readers to re-evaluate information received earlier. Did you ever give any thought to rearranging them so that they would appear in chronological sequence – that is, with the John Marsch sandwalker story appearing first?

GW: No, because I didn't want to show what John Marsch had been researching – the material that make up his 'story' in the second novella – until I had actually introduced John Marsch the researcher in 'The Fifth Head'. I decided to present the Sandwalker story as a legend or story that Marsch had uncovered, rather than as straight reportage, because I wanted to keep all three stories set in roughly the same time-frame – the 'present' of the opening novella. Since the period in which the Sandwalker scene was – in terms of the 'present' found in the rest of the book – taking place in the distant past of the planet, it made more sense to say, 'Here's a legend that has survived from that period' rather than simply jumping into the past and presenting it directly. In the last piece, 'V.R.T.', I finish up by showing what had become of Sandwalker's world (this is only hinted at in 'The Fifth Head') and by showing what eventually happened to Marsch.

LM: All this 'showing' in 'V.R.T.' is made intriguingly ambiguous by the confusion about who 'Marsch' really is.

GW: In the end, of course, it's important that the reader not be confused about this, although part of the fun is supposed to be figuring out what's happened. I leave a number of clues as to who the narrator actually is. For example, both V.R.T. and the narrator are shown to be very poor shots whereas Marsch is a very good shot, and there's other hints like that. If you hire a shape-changer as a guide, there's a definite possibility that he's going to change into your shape at some point. Which is what happens.

LM: Could you talk about the way your stories or novels tend to get started for you? Is there any consistent pattern?

GW: The only true answer I can supply is that I have a bunch of different kinds of things knocking around in my head until something jars me into realizing that these things can come together in a story. Typically I'll read something or see something or dream something and I'll think to myself: 'Gee, that would be interesting to put into a story.' It's usually later on that I think up a character or person who might fit into the context of that original 'something' in an interesting way. Then at some point I recognize that I could incorporate all this material – I could take *that* and *that* woman and *that* ship and *that* situation, and put them all together in a story. There's a wonderful 'Peanuts' cartoon that pretty much describes what I'm talking about: Snoopy is on the top of his doghouse and he writes something like, 'A frigate appeared on the edge of the horizon. The King's extravagances were bankrupting the people. A shot rang out. The dulcet voice of a guitar sounded at the window.' Then he turns and looks at the reader and says, 'In the last chapter I'm going to pull all this together!'

LM: But I take it that you've usually pulled things together enough in advance so that you know, once you're actually sitting down to begin writing the story, where it's heading.

GW: Absolutely. I wouldn't start a work unless I had at least a vague idea of where I was going to end up with it. Of course, sometimes I have a difficult time getting to where I'm heading. That's what happened, on a grand scale, when I began work on *The Book of the New Sun* – I knew roughly where I was going, but as I was trying to get there, I discovered there was a great deal more between 'here' and 'there' than I had anticipated.

LM: Where was it that you knew you were heading when you began *The Book of the New Sun*?

GW: I knew I wanted Severian to be banished and then to return to the Guild in a position of such authority that the Guild would be forced to make him a Master of the Guild. And I wanted to have Severian be forced to confront the problem of Thecla and the problem of torture and the role of human pain and misery. At that time I had not yet read *The Magus*, so the thought didn't come from there, but I was very conscious of the horror not only of being tortured but of being forced to be a torturer or executioner. I didn't want my readers to be able to dismiss violence and pain with some platitudes about 'Oh, violence – how terrible!' It's very easy to say how terrible it is to beat a man with a whip, or lock him up for thirty years of his life, or to execute him. These are indeed awful things. But when you are actually in authority, you find out that sometimes it's absolutely necessary for you to take certain distasteful actions.

LM: Severian makes the point somewhere that if he didn't execute some of the people he does, they would be out killing people themselves ...

GW: And he's right. What are you going to do with someone like John Wayne Gacy – who used to live about eight miles from where we're sitting right now – if you're not going to be willing to lock him up for the rest of his life? If you let him out, he's almost certain to start killing more innocent people. I wanted Severian to have to face at least the possibility that being an agency of pain and death is not necessarily an evil thing. That's one recognition he must come to grips with when he decides to leave a knife in Thecla's cell to help her commit suicide. He's partially responsible for the blood he sees seeping from under her cell door, just as every member of a society is responsible for the blood shed by people it decides to execute. Of course, when Severian later receives a letter from Thecla telling him the suicide was a trick permitting her to be freed unobtrusively, that creates all sorts of other dilemmas for him – and for me as well. I had started out assuming I was writing a novella of about 40,000 words whose title was to have been 'The Feast of Saint Catherine', but now I began to see this material had greater possibilities. The writer has a problem when ideas, characters, and so forth don't seem to come, or when they aren't good enough when they do come. But when they're too good and too numerous, he has another. By the time I had finished with *The Shadow of the Torturer*, I had completed an entire novel but Severian was hardly started. Instead of winding up the plot, I had begun half a dozen others which needed to be worked out. Eventually I decided I needed to write a trilogy to be able to develop everything sufficiently; and when the third book turned out to be almost twice as long as the first two combined, I finally expanded things into a tetralogy. When I was done, I discovered that I had arrived where I had set out for – but the trip to that place was very different than what I had expected.

LM: What gave you the initial impulse to make Severian a torturer? Was it that abstract notion of wanting your hero to deal with the nature of pain and suffering?

GW: No, the possibility of having a character who was a torturer was one of those initial ideas that wasn't tied to anything for a while. It first came to me during some convention I was attending at which Bob Tucker was the guest of honour. For some reason Bob felt obliged to go to a panel discussion on costume, and since he wanted someone to accompany him, I went along (otherwise I wouldn't ordinarily have gone since I'm not a costumer). So I went and heard Sandra Miesel and several other people talk about how you do costumes – how you might do a cloak, whether or not it's good to use fire as part of your costume, and so forth. As I sat there being instructed I was sulking because no one had ever done one of my characters at a masquerade. It seemed as though I had done a lot of things that people could do at a masquerade; but when I started to think this over more carefully, I realized there were few, if any, characters who would fit in with what Sandra and the others were saying. That led me to start thinking about a character who would fit – someone who would wear simple but dramatic clothes. And the very first thing that came to mind was a torturer: bare chest (everybody has a chest, all you have to do is take your shirt off), black trousers, black boots (you can get those any-where), black cloak, a mask, and a sword! Here was an ideal, easy SF masquerade citizen. All this stuck in my head somehow: I had this dark man, the personification of pain and death, but I didn't yet know what to do with him. Then gradually a lot of things began to come together. For instance, I read a book about body-snatchers that captured my fancy (body-snatchers were the people who used to dig up corpses and sell them to medical schools for the students to dissect). And I also had in mind that it would be interesting to be able to show a young man approaching war. So I began to put things together: I could have my young man witness the body-snatching scene that I was now itching to write; this same young man could be the guy who is pulled into the war; he could be a torturer, and so on.

LM: It was a bold stroke to make your hero into a man who's both a professional torturer (with all that this implies) and yet also a man who possesses the capacity for passion, love and tenderness. That reinforces your point about the multiplicity of selves existing within us all.

GW: And I was particularly interested in the way that multiplicity points out the potential lying within everyone for good and evil. Whether we like it or not, that potential is part of what makes us people. We tend to look at somebody like the death-camp guards in Nazi Germany and think to ourselves, 'Thank God I'm not like that! Those guys weren't people – they were fiends in human form.' But those guards weren't 'fiends'. They were human beings who became pulled into a certain game whose rules said it was okay to be a death-camp guard in Nazi Germany. Later on we came along and changed the rules on them. It was important for me to be able to show the way evil expresses itself in people because I think it's essential that we recognize the existence of this potential within us all. This recognition is the only way we can safeguard ourselves from this sort of thing. As long as we go around saying, 'I'm not capable of doing anything ugly, I'm the guy in the white hat', then we're capable of doing just about any damn ugly thing. If you're watching a man on his way to the scaffold and you can't realise 'this could be me', then you've got no right to hang him. I dealt with a similar idea in 'The Island of Doctor Death', where at the end of the story I had Dr Death tell Tackie that if he starts the book again then (as he puts it), 'We'll all be back.' If you don't have Dr Death, then you can't have Captain Ransom. You can't have a knight unless you have the dragon, positive charge without a negative charge.

LM: Once the scope of *The Book of the New Sun* became obvious you must have sat down at some point and developed some kind of detailed outline.

GW: Actually I never use an outline when I work. Even with something like *The Book of the New Sun*, where there's an elaborate structure, the outline exists only in my head and not on paper. The only exception to that was with a book I did a while back called *Free Live Free*, in which a lot of the action took place in an old brick house on a city street. For that book I had to draw a floor plan of the two storeys of the house because otherwise I found myself getting tangled up in such details as: Could you see the street from this window? Could you see from this room to that room? When Ben Free is in his room, can he hear the steps of someone walking overhead in their room? So I had to figure out where the bedrooms and bathrooms and stairs all were. But of course a floor plan isn't really an outline in the usual sense.

LM: In a sense all four volumes of *The Book of the New Sun* form a single novel in the same way that the individual books that comprise Proust's *Remembrance of Things Past* form a single work. But as you were working on the volumes individually, were you aiming at different formal effects that would be more appropriate to what you were talking about? For instance, when I went from *Shadow* to *The Claw of the Conciliator*, I felt that *The Claw* was presented by means of more peculiar effects – it seemed less direct, to rely more on stories-within-stories (and there's that long play inserted into the text) …

GW: I saw the book falling into four distinct segments: a presentation of Nessus, getting from Nessus to Thrax, Thrax, and the war. And despite some slop-over, you'll find me pretty much focussing from book to book on those areas, each of which required me to develop a way of story-telling that would be appropriate for my focus. For instance, when I finished *Shadow* – and keep in mind that I didn't complete a final draft of the first volume until I had all four already in second draft – I was very conscious that in *Claw* I was going to get outside of Nessus and show the atmosphere and surroundings of that world outside. In order to do that I needed to show cultural elements of this world which would allow the reader to understand it: What kind of clothes did people wear? What kinds of stories do they tell, jokes do they make? That sort of thing. That required a slightly different approach, maybe gives the book a different texture from the others.

LM: I was constantly struck in all four volumes by the richness and variety of textural detail – I'm not just referring to physical details but to your meticulous attention to a wide range of cultural, anthropological, and linguistic elements.

GW: From the very onset one of the things I had in mind was to show a big, complex civilization, an entire society that I would make plausibly complex. I've always been irritated (and usually bored) by the Simple Simon civilizations you find presented in most SF novels, where you have a galactic empire spread over umpteen light years but which turns out to have a culture that's as uniform as, let's say, Milwaukee. Except for instances in which a culture's liveable area is small – essentially one island or an equally isolated area – and those in which there is a small population possessing a high technology, this assumption of a simple, uniform culture covering an entire world is simply incredible.

LM: You mentioned earlier that one of the first ideas you had for *The Book of the New Sun* was presenting a young man approaching a war. Did your own experiences going to war in Korea serve as inspiration for this?

GW: Very much so. When I dropped out of Texas A&M I had gone through that rite of passage in which war at first seems impossibly remote and then you find yourself gradually pulled into the actual fighting. At the time I was drafted I didn't think I would ever end up fighting, maybe partly because the war seemed so distant. Oh, my father was worried and wanted me to join the Air Force or something, but an enlistment was a

six-year commitment, whereas the draft was only two years, which seemed
a lot more attractive. Keep in mind that the Korean War was much more
remote to the American people at the time than the Vietnam War was to
your generation. You didn't have the live TV coverage and all the constant
media barrage. Anyway, I can vividly recall watching myself being slowly
sucked into this vortex. When I got to Korea I rode a train all day and all
night up to the front lines, a slow train which gave me a lot of time to
think about what was happening. When I stepped off the train, I could
hear the guns firing in the distance; and at that moment it came to me:
'My God, I didn't miss! Here it is! Here I am!' You can find a similar kind of
progression in *The Red Badge of Courage*, but I wanted to develop mine
within an sf setting.

LM: Despite the sf setting, I was often reminded of the Civil War or World
War I while reading your battle scenes. Did you do a lot of specific research for these scenes?

GW: I didn't research anything specifically for them, but they probably
came out of a lot of reading I've done about the Napoleonic Wars, the
Civil War, the two World Wars, and so on. In presenting the war itself, I
was trying to guess what war might be like for a decadent society in which
there was still some high technology left but most of it was unavailable.
There was an actual time here on planet Earth around 1960 in which
there was a civil war being fought in what used to be the Belgian Congo.
In that war, there were tribesmen with spears who were being led into
battle by European officers with submachine guns, supported by jet planes.
I wanted to show what that kind of war might be like, not taking the
Belgian Congo situation as a literal model but simply as the kind of thing
I was interested in. So I showed some people riding animals at the same
time that others are using laser canons and all kinds of advanced weap-
onry.

LM: Did your war experiences have the kind of permanent effect on
your sensibility as it apparently had on other writers, like Mailer,
Hemingway, and Vonnegut?

GW: I'm sure they did, but it's difficult to say exactly how. I only caught
about the last four months of the war – I was there for the cease-fire and
for quite some time afterwards. I saw just enough action to realize what it
was like. I got shot at a few times, shot at a few people, was shelled. You
don't go through those experiences without getting a different outlook on
life than you would have had without them. Just before you arrived this
morning, I was talking on the phone with Harlan Ellison about a recent
incident in which he wound up decking Charles Platt, and he mentioned
how many of his friends had censured him for his violent reaction. Well, it
would never occur to me to rebuke Harlan because I accept that if you're
not violent at certain times you're going to wind up being the victim of

violence. The fact that you stand there and let someone hit you in the face doesn't do anything to eliminate violence (it may even contribute to further violence) which is one of the underlying themes in *The Book of the New Sun*.

LM: What kind of research was involved in *The Book of the New Sun*?

GW: The main research was on Byzantium and the Byzantine Empire, which was a stagnant political entity that had outlived its time in much the same way that the Urth of the Commonwealth had. One of the things that bothered me about the reviews I got *on The Book of the New Sun* was how often they compared my world with that of Medieval Europe. Insofar as I was trying to create any kind of parallels with an actual historical period here on Earth – and obviously I wasn't aiming at developing an exact analogy – I was thinking of Byzantium. Incidentally, I also got into trouble with some reviewers over my presentation of the Ascians, who were my equivalent of the Turks. If you read the book carefully, it's clear that the action is taking place in South America and that the invading Ascians are actually North Americans. What I didn't anticipate was that nine-tenths of my readers and reviewers would look at the word 'Ascian' and say, 'Oh, these guys are Asians!' This confusion got me accused of being an anti-Asian racist – which I'm not. Actually, the word 'ascian' literally means 'people without shadows.' It was a word used in the Classical world for people who lived near the equator, where the sun is dead overhead at noon and thus produces no shadow. I felt it would be an interesting touch to show that the ordinary man-in-the-street in the southern hemisphere wasn't even conscious that their attackers are coming down from the northern hemisphere (they aren't even aware that there is another hemisphere).

LM: That kind of suggestive use for archaic or unfamiliar words is evident throughout the tetralogy. I'm sure a lot of readers had the same mistaken impression I did that you were making up these wondrous, bizarre words – especially since the use of neologisms is so common in sf. Could you talk about why you chose to use mainly 'real' words rather than inventing your own?

GW: I should clarify the fact that all the words I use in *The Book of the New Sun* are real (except for a couple of typographical errors). As you know, in most sf about unknown planets, the author is forced to invent wonders and then to name them. But that didn't seem appropriate to what I was doing here. It occurred to me when I was starting out with *The Book of the New Sun* that Urth already has enough wonders – if only because it has inherited the wonders of Earth (and there's the alternate possibility that Earth's wonders have descended to it from Urth). Some sf fans, who seem to be able to tolerate any amount of gibberish so long as it's invented gibberish, have found it peculiar that I would bother relying on perfectly legitimate words. My sense was that when you want to know where you're going, it helps to know where you've been and how fast you've travelled. And a great deal of this knowledge can be intuited if you know something about the words people use. I'm not a philologist, but one thing I'm certain of is that you could write an entire book on almost any word in the English language. At any rate, anyone who bothers to go to a dictionary will find I'm not inventing anything: a 'fulgurator' is a holy man capable of drawing omens from flashes of lightning, an 'eidolon' is an apparition or phantom, 'fuligin' literally means soot-coloured. I also gave the people and other beings in the book real names (the only exception I can think of is the Ascian who appears in *The Citadel* – 'Loyal to the Group of Seventeen'). 'Severian', 'Vodalus', and 'Agilus', for example, are all ordinary, if now uncommon, names for men. And if you'd like to call your baby daughter 'Valeria,' 'Thecla', or 'Dorcas', she'll be receiving a genuine name many women in the past have had (and some in the present). As for the monsters' names, I simply named them for monsters. The original Erebus was the son of Chaos; he was the god of darkness and the husband of Nox, the goddess of night; furthermore, Mount Erebus is in Antarctica, the seat of Erebus's dark and chilly power.

LM: I noticed you gave one of your creatures – Baldanders – a name from Borges …

GW: Yes, I took the name of Baldanders, the giant who is still growing, from *The Book of Imaginary Beings*, which may not be Borges' best work but which I have felt free to steal from disgracefully (even second-rate Borges is still very good indeed). Borges is capable of making up much better books and monsters and authors than anyone can find in libraries.

LM: Did you find working on your non-sf novel *Peace* to be different in any fundamental sense from creating your other works?

GW: Not at all, perhaps because the subjective nature of the book gave me so much freedom. It was the book I wrote after *The Fifth Head of Cerberus*, and there was enough continuity – *Peace* is also a book about memory and about the meaning of stories, story as a thing – that it seemed simply like the obvious next book for me to write. It remains my favourite book of all the novels I've written.

LM: On what basis?

GW: By asking myself how close the book came to being what I wanted it to be when I started it, how close I came to my own goals, which have naturally been different in each case. You never reach those goals 100%, but some books wind up being closer to your initial ideal than others. So far, *Peace* is the book which seemed to wind up closest to that ideal.

LM: Was *Peace*'s main character, Dennis Weer, someone you personally identified with?

GW: I identify with all my main characters, but certainly Weer is very much modelled on me, with his engineering and food industry background, his introversion, his sense of isolation. My mother's middle name was Olivia, which is probably a dead giveaway. The house on the hill is basically modelled on my mother's father's house, which I visited when I was a child. My grandfather was an absolutely incredible man who made a tremendous impression on me – he was one of those types of guys who was a Scottish seaman as a kid, jumped ship in Texas, fought Mexican bandits as a US cavalryman in the 1880s, became a circus performer, and wound up as an old man with a wooden leg, a pitbull, and a lot of corn whiskey which he'd drink out of a jug. The grandfather in *Peace* who lights the candles on the Christmas tree is pretty much based on him, while the town in the novel is largely a fictive representation of Logan, Ohio, where my father was raised. So there's a lot more direct autobiographical material I'm drawing on here than in my other books.

LM: *The Book of the New Sun*, maybe especially *The Citadel of the Autarch*, deals with the nature of death and the afterlife, the role of human beings in the scheme of the cosmos, all sorts of grand issues. Are the basic insights Severian eventually achieves into these issues essentially ones that you personally share?

GW: They're very close indeed, which is why *The Citadel* is my favourite of the four books. (Everyone else seems to like *The Shadow* best.) I tried to prepare the reader for some of these insights by earlier placing Severian within that immense backdrop of war. Severian is a soldier, and like any soldier in any war, the immediate parts of the battlefield he's in seem vitally important, essential, whereas it's really just a very small part of a very large picture. Having established Severian's relationship to the larger picture of what's going on around him, in the latter part of the book I wanted to suggest that, 'Look, this is just a small backwater planet – one of many, many planets – and this isn't even a particularly interesting or pivotal period in its history; and the Solar System to which this planet belongs is part of a galaxy similar to quite a number of similar other spiral galaxies; and all this exists in a universe that is just one of a whole series of recurring universes. What any individual human being sees, no matter how vast the vista, is just a tiny corner of what is happening in creation.'

There's a scene in C.S. Lewis's *The Great Divorce* that made a lasting impression on me. That book is about a one-day bus excursion for people who are in Hell and want to go to Heaven for a visit to see what's there; towards the end of it, everyone is saying, 'Wow, everything here is so beautiful, look at these gorgeous trees and waterfall and animals – but where is the infernal city we just left?' At this point the angel who's leading them around says, 'It's right there in that crack between those two rocks – *that's* the infernal city you've come out of.' I wanted my readers to experience a similar shock of recognition at their own insignificance at the end of *The Citadel*.

LM: The outlook expressed at that conclusion seems fundamentally religious in orientation.

GW: I don't scoff at religion the way many people do when they look at anything that has to do with speculations about things we can't touch. I am a practicing Catholic, although I don't think that designation would give people much of an idea about what my beliefs are. People tend to have a very limited, stereotyped view of what it means to be a Catholic, images taken from movies or anti-Catholic pamphlets; but there is much more to it than that. I know perfectly well, for example, that priests can't walk on water, that they are merely human beings who are trying, often unsuccessfully, to live out a very difficult ideal. But I certainly don't dismiss religious or other mystical forms of speculation out of hand. I read it and try to make my own judgements about it. And in *The Book of the New Sun* I tried to work out some of the implications of my beliefs.

LM: Who are some of the contemporary writers you admire?

GW: Among sf writers I'd include Algis Budrys, Joanna Russ, Ursula LeGuin, Damon Knight, Kate Wilhelm, Michael Bishop, Brian Aldiss, Nancy Kress, Michael Moorcock. And Theodore Sturgeon, Clark Ashton Smith, and Frederick Brown, who are dead now but not forgotten. One other sf writer I greatly admire is R. A. Lafferty, who writes very strange stuff that's hard to describe (the St Brendan's story in *Peace* is my version of an R. A. Lafferty story); he's an old man who's developed a cult following, a much-neglected figure I think. Among the non-sf writers I most enjoy are Nabokov (*Pale Fire* is a truly amazing book) and Borges. Robert Coover's *The Universal Baseball Association* is one of my favourite novels. I love a novel called *The Tar Baby* by Jerome Charyn, a writer I know nothing else about. Of course, there are a great many earlier writers I'm fond of: Proust, Dickens, E.M Forster (whom I'm now just reading); Chesterton, whom I've already mentioned, George MacDonald, Poe, and Lovecraft (Lovecraft is usually regarded as an sf writer but to me he is the real successor to Poe). I've read of lot of Arthur Conan Doyle. And I grew up with Kipling, which is one reason I used his lines from 'The Dawn Wind' as an epigraph to *The Citadel of the Autarch*.

LM: You've grown up in an age which has seen both the development of nuclear weapons and the landing of men on the Moon. The use of science and technology seems to be leading us to two different futures, one unimaginably awful, the other filled with marvels and wonder. Which path is technology taking us?

GW: There are more than two paths we can head down. I feel both optimistic and pessimistic about what we've been doing with technology. As you say, it has already been used to produce both wonderful and terrible things. The greatest ecological disaster to yet hit this planet has come from technology – the invention of plastics. (If I could go back into the past and repeal a single discovery of mankind's it would be the discovery of plastics.) On the other hand, we're getting into space now and doing some amazing things with the life sciences, including cybernetics and robot development. Technology is like a punch or a gun: it's good or bad depending on what you do with it. The world is full of people who assume you can get rid of evil if you can just get rid of the punch in the jaw or the gun.

LM: But if that gun is firing nuclear weapons or that punch in the jaw is going to destroy an entire nation …

GW: I don't believe we're heading for a nuclear holocaust. (If I did, I wouldn't be living this close to Chicago!) Using nuclear weapons is too much of a clear no-win situation for both sides, so I don't think they'll be used in a war, at least not under the present circumstances. War usually starts when one side feels it can achieve a quick, clear-cut victory – Iraq invading Iran recently is a classic example of this because Iraq thought it could simply march in and win an immediate victory. Hitler had sold himself so completely on the idea that the Germans were strong and pure, while the rest of the world was weak and degenerate, that he was able to convince himself and a great many other people that Germany could achieve an easy victory in Europe. It's difficult for me to see how anyone in Russia or the US could convince themselves they could use nuclear weapons to achieve that kind of easy victory. Of course, there's another scenario that's much more dangerous – the one where one side feels pushed up against a wall and decides they've got to fight now or they'll eventually be destroyed. That situation worries me a lot more than the other possibility.

LM: But even assuming there is no nuclear holocaust, it seems essential for people to do some basic rethinking about the management of our resources; otherwise the issue of how technology is going to evolve will simply become moot. Once we exhaust our resources, we'll be left in the kind of world you're describing in *The Book of the New Sun*.

GW: That possibility was very much on my mind when I was creating the Urth of *The Book of the New Sun*. I was trying to come to grips with the end-result of the do-nothing attitude so many people-on-the-street have about the future. These people seem to feel that space exploration is a lot of bullshit ('there's nothing really out there we can use'), that undersea exploration is a lot of bullshit ('there's nothing down there for us'), that we should just go about our business the way we are and be 'sensible'. But what is going to happen if we keep on being 'sensible' in the way they're suggesting? If we keep clinging to our old home (the planet Earth) and sit around waiting for the money and resources to run out? The Urth I invented in *The Book of the New Sun* is the world which has followed that course, a world in which people have been so limited in their vision of the future that they saw no other option except what was immediately in front of them. They've been practical and down-to-earth, they've gone on planting their cabbages. Well, there's nothing wrong with planting those cabbages, God knows; but when you ignore any possibilities except those cabbages, you wind up living in a world something like Urth, with its exhausted mines and exhausted farmlands. You get a land which may have had a long period of relative peace and stability, but it's a period of slow decay. I keep tropical fish, and I remember there used to be a fad among fish owners about trying to keep a perfectly balanced environment in the tanks – they'd seal everything up to see how long it was until the fish died out. Sometimes it would take eighteen months or more, but eventually the last fish always died and you were left there staring at a tank full of scummy green water. That's what the Urth of the Commonwealth has become (and what we're headed for unless we look to the future more adventurously) – a tank full of scummy water.

9
Gene Wolfe Interview

James B. Jordan

At the turn of the decade, Wolfe published three widely differing novels. *Soldier of Arete* (1989) continues the story of Latro, the amnesiac narrator of *Soldier of the Mist*; *Castleview* (1990) is a heavily intertextual recruitment fantasy that plays in intricate ways with Arthurian myth and remains Wolfe's most poorly received novel since *Operation Ares* (1970); and *Pandora by Holly Hollander* (1990) is a charming murder mystery narrated by an all-American high school girl. Two short story collections, *Storeys from the Old Hotel* (1988), a British anthology that brought Wolfe the World Fantasy Award in 1989, and *Endangered Species* (1989) were also issued. *Letters Home*, a collection of correspondence from Wolfe to his mother during his posting in Korea, and *Young Wolfe* (1992) an anthology of short fiction, both appeared from United Mythologies Press and form the starting point of Jordan's interview.

As Jordan explains, 'this interview was conducted during the 1992 World Fantasy Convention, held at Callaway Gardens, Georgia, Oct. 29–Nov. 1. The interview was conducted outside in a garden for two hours on the morning of October 30.'

JJ: A lot of what you publish comes out from small presses and sources. If you are not an insider to the SF fantasy world, you would not know where to get it or even know it had come out. Is there any comprehensive outlet for Gene Wolfe's stuff?

GW: Not that I know of. Mark Ziesing handles some of it, but he's probably as close as they come, and he has far from everything. I just don't think there is a good answer to that. I have done some stuff with Dan Knight's United Mythologies in Canada.

JJ: Is he the one that did *Young Wolfe*?

GW: Yes, he did *Young Wolfe* and *Letters Home*. And we may do another one, I am not sure. And then there is Cheap Street. The problem with Cheap Street is that they are anything but cheap! I would like to subscribe – get the Cheap Street series of books and so forth – and to be honest, I cannot afford it. I can't afford every few months to spend $75–$100 on a collector's piece, or at least I don't feel I can. I have better uses for the money.

JJ: My audience – the people that I write for – as I guess you've gathered is what is usually called evangelical Christians, a conservative, protestant audience. And I am interested first of all in discovering a little bit about your religious beliefs, if you're willing to talk about that. Were you brought up within the Catholic Church?

GW: No, I am a convert. I was raised in a rather lax fashion as a Presbyterian. I don't think my father had any particular religious convictions. My mother had been raised as a Presbyterian and so I was nominally a Presbyterian. It was largely an answer to give when people asked you.

JJ: And how did you become a member of the Roman Catholic Church?

GW: I married a Roman Catholic and had to take instruction in it in order that we could have a Catholic wedding. I think that is still a rule of the church, although those things are so laxly administered that you cannot always be sure. I became interested in it, read and studied, and talked to people about it and so forth, and eventually converted.

JJ: Became persuaded of the truth of it.

GW: Yes.

JJ: At that time what kind of theologians did you read, or did you read theology as such?

GW: I didn't read a lot of theology. I read some modern books of explications of Catholic theology for laymen and that sort of thing. I would like to be able to say I read St Thomas Aquinas in the Latin and so forth, but I didn't. It would be a lie. I read some books of Thomistic theology and biographies of St Thomas Aquinas.

JJ: Chesterton's?

GW: Yes, I read Chesterton's book on St Thomas Aquinas. I discovered Chesterton and ended up reading everything of Chesterton's that I could find. I had gone through very much the same thing earlier with C. S. Lewis.

JJ: Ignatius Press is attempting to reprint all of Chesterton in a whole set. Are you collecting those?

GW: That is right, so they are. In fact they have reprinted a lot of newspaper columns that I had not seen in my initial sweep through Chesterton when I read everything I could find.

JJ: I imagine at that time it was hard to find.

GW: It was fairly difficult to find. I have also since discovered that some of those newspaper columns, as I originally read them, had been heavily edited by someone other than Chesterton for book publication. I detest that sort of thing, particularly when there is no indication given in the book that it has been done, because you think that you are reading what Chesterton wrote for a newspaper in 1905, and in fact the history paragraphs have been changed almost out of recognition.

JJ: That has happened with C. S. Lewis too, according to Catherine

Lindskoog, and she seems to have the facts to back it up.

GW: Oh, yes, *The C. S. Lewis Hoax*. With Lewis it is posthumous stuff that apparently is not Lewis at all. I was one of those people who read *The Dark Tower* and got very suspicious because I was familiar with Lewis and I think I am pretty good at spotting styles. I used to belong to a chain letter that included Gardner Dozois, Jack Dann, Chelsea Quinn Yarborough, Mike Bishop. And we would write long newsletters about our doings and then put them in a packet and they would be sent around. This was before they had computer bulletin boards and all that sort of stuff. And I could almost invariably identify the writer from the first paragraph or two. The writer was only overtly identified with the signature, because it was done in letter form. But the styles of the people who were writing were sufficiently different that I could very easily pick out most of them without difficulty. And I am a good imitator. I could write imitation Shakespeare that you would think was probably legitimate Shakespeare because there is a lot of Shakespeare for me to look at. I have sort of a knack for doing that sort of thing. I think I could write much better imitation C. S. Lewis than a lot of this supposedly posthumous stuff that is coming out. I could do it better than this guy does and I think practically any decent writer could do it better than this guy does, because he's not a writer. The reason that there is not more of that than there is, is that the people who can do it would rather write under their own name and take the credit for themselves. Why should they waste their talent in forging work for a dead man?

JJ: You have used a variety of styles in each of your novels. That is one of the characteristics of your work. I assume you will keep going. Is the series you are working on now [*The Book of the Long Sun*], to be in any of the particular styles you have used before?

GW: I don't think so. It isn't a highly very stylized series at all, largely because it is third person. I basically feel that you should write the story in the style that corresponds to the story that you have to tell, and I have tried to do that; but it comes out as a pretty much straightforward journalistic prose, I think.

JJ: Hemingwayesque?

GW: Well, no. Hemingway, I think, has a very identifiable style, which I've never tried to imitate. I think I could do a fairly decent job of it if I wanted to, but I've never particularly wanted to.

JJ: Was Jack Vance's style an influence on the style of the Severian novels?

GW: Oh, I'm sure. I'm sure. A lot of that was my deciding to rewrite *The Dying Earth* from my own standpoint.

JJ: Wonderful book.

GW: Yes it is wonderful. And of course when you read wonderful books sometimes you think, 'Gee, I would like to do that'; and you go off and do it, trying to make it different enough that you are not really ripping off the author, but rather writing something in the same vein using some of the same ideas. I have never concealed a debt to Jack Vance and a debt to Clark Ashton Smith as far as that goes. I think Vance is very much in debt to Clark Ashton Smith.

JJ: Do you know Vance?

GW: I have met him twice I think. I certainly don't know him in the sense of being on friendly terms with him.

JJ: I gather he is not an active participant in the SF world.

GW: As far as I know he is not. A lot of it, from what I understand, is that he has severe eye problems. He is very nearly blind. I had him sign a book for me one time and I was wearing a name badge and he was asking how I spelled my name. I held out the name badge to him and he asked me again how I spelled my name, and I realized that although it was fairly large type, he couldn't make it out. His vision was that bad. Maybe it is better by now. I certainly hope so.

JJ: So Lewis and Chesterton would have been among the formative influences in your paradigm.

GW: Oh yes, very definitely.

JJ: Could you name others, within the area of theology and Christianity?

GW: The problem with this it is hard to see where to stop. Later you say, 'Gee, I should have included so and so', and you didn't think of that person at that time. J. R. R. Tolkien, just to start with. Charles Williams, not as much as the others, but to some extent. David Lindsay's *A Voyage to Arcturus*, which is really strange, and I think very theologically oriented. Much of the theology I disagree with, but I thought it was marvelous as a work of fiction. It is a marvelous example of someone's expressing his theological beliefs in a novel.

JJ: Now you are reading George MacDonald?

GW: Yes, *Lilith*. I had not read anything previously except *Curdie and the Goblin* and *At the Back of the North Wind* and those types, and they are quite good but they are basically fairy stories. I had read others that were about that good, but I don't think they had any great theological impact, any great feeling from that standpoint.

JJ: Let me turn to political philosophy if I might. Your first novel, *Operation Ares*, really has that as something of a theme, John Castle. I guess that 'J. C.' is deliberate somehow. Does that novel reflect your ideas?

GW: I think it reflected them at the time that I wrote it. I don't think it does now. I think I was much more like you said you were. I was much more a doctrinaire conservative when I was a good deal younger. You said that was true of you and it was true of me. I reacted away from the general political current in this country post-Roosevelt and became pretty much a 'William F. Buckley conservative' for a while, and then kind of split off from that. I am now in the unhappy position of finding no one that I agree with.

I am big on freedom. Freedom is the bedrock political value that we need to hold on to. Patrick Buchanan said that in his speech at the [1992] Republican convention, and he is about the only person that I have heard saying it. Today I think people are so used to being free – to having some degree of freedom – that they don't appreciate it; but people are noticeably less free now than they were, say, thirty years ago.

JJ: Buchanan opposed the war in the Middle East [the first Gulf War], and I tended to agree. It seemed to me that to become involved in a conflict between two Islamic nations was of questionable wisdom.

GW: The war in the Middle East was fought for oil. The idea was to keep oil at market prices available to the United States. Saddam Hussein was also fighting for oil. His idea was that if he could corner a large proportion of the world's oil market he could pretty much set prices himself and get a great deal of money with which to finance his war machine. He was right; he could have done that if he had succeeded. Like so many dictators including Hitler, he tried to be his own strategist. Remember the man that, when asked if he could play the saxophone, said 'I don't know; I've never tried.' If you have never done strategy – if you have never meddled around with it – you can't do it because there is a whole science that has to be acquired to be a decent strategist, and he didn't have it. He very clearly didn't have it. Hitler didn't have it either. And instead of leaving these things to people who are competent, the people with the power try to do it themselves. One of the great things that is wrong with American business is that whose with the power to make decisions are often not those with the ability to make those decisions correctly.

JJ: From things you have written in the past, I wonder if you feel it might be just as well to have the price of oil double or triple so that we would be forced to come up with different sources of energy.

GW: I think we might very well say, fifty years down the road, 'Boy, that was a good thing that happened to us.' I think the private automobile has been a disaster, quite frankly. You saw Gay Haldeman last night who came up to our table. Her mother has just been killed in a automobile accident. The private automobile has squandered enormous resources and enormous energy and I think it has developed a very ugly civilization in which everything has to be built around automobile roads and parking – which isn't necessary; it just happens to be what we've got.

JJ: What could we have as an alternative in our kind of society?

GW: In our kind of society? Well obviously we could have public transportation for the longer range: railroad, some air, although I think we have too much air now. We could have less travel, because I think we have an awful lot of unnecessary travelling going on now. And bicycles for shorter range. All of those are very viable alternatives. I once wrote a little piece on this and I am not sure where it appeared. The thing that most people don't understand about it is that you can't rely wholly on public transportation, because if you rely wholly on public transportation you are at the mercy of the unions who control the mechanism. So you have to have private transportation; but I don't think you have to have one man sitting in 5000-pound machine, which is the system that we have today.

JJ: Are there people who write in the area of politics that you read now, or do you spend your time reading fiction and doing research for your novels, and let that mainly pass by?

GW: I don't read a lot of political essays because I find most of them very predictable. I know by and large what these people are going to say after I have read a little bit of it and I generally disagree with them pretty violently. So no, I don't read much in that area. What I read is much more news than political essay.

JJ: In the *Castle of the Otter* you mentioned Lamarckianism and I had written down here to ask if you've kept up with the scientists who were working with that area today.

GW: I didn't know that anybody was working in the Lamarckian area today, to be honest with you. I think somebody should be because I have never been convinced that Lamarck was wrong. I have never seen any convincing evidence that Lamarck was wrong. What we do is we set up Lysenkoism, which is a straw man, and we call it Lamarckianism and then we disprove it – and it is very easily disproved and is in fact very unpersuasive to begin with – and then we say Lamarck was wrong. Or we say Darwin was right and therefore Lamarck cannot be right, which is not true at all because the two theories are not mutually exclusive. It's like saying that Newton was wrong because Einstein was right. Newtonian physics really is the way that you calculate a whole lot of things. Billiard balls and bullets and railroad trains and so forth are all answerable in terms of Newtonian physics. So to put Einstein against Newton says something that Einstein himself would never have said.

JJ: [In a letter preparing for this interview] I asked you about Rupert Sheldrake's work, with which you are not familiar, but in his second book, *The Presence of the Past*, he critiques the modern atomistic view of causality. He argues, from research and testing, that aside from genetics there is also the form and shape of things, a sort of platonic doctrine of form, but one that is embedded in history. He presents evidence to show that there are ways in which plants, animals, crystals, etc. can undergo changes as a result of changes in the environment. I'd thought you might be familiar with that.

GW: It certainly sounds interesting and probably like something that I would tend to agree with. Because though I think that Darwin was right, I don't think that Darwin had the whole answer and I don't think he has it now. The kind of thing that he postulated does take place but it seems to me clear that there are other mechanisms involved as well.

JJ: I asked in the letter if you were familiar with Frances Yates's book *The Art of Memory*, which is a treatise on the entire business of building a house in the mind and the impact of that in the renaissance, particularly in the pre-literate world.

GW: I am familiar with the memory palace concept, which originally derives from Simonides, a Greek poet of the fifth century B.C. I've heard of Yates's book, but have not read it. I have made use of the memory palace system in the *Soldier* books, of course. I have *The Memory Palace of Matthew Ricci*, and have read parts of it.

JJ: Let me ask you about being a southern Catholic novelist. You wrote me one time that you do like to see yourself as a southern novelist, or perhaps a Catholic novelist. Those can be two different things, though overlapping. How would you define a southern novelist, and how do you see your work as in that school? Or is that a fair question?

GW: It is the kind of question that a critic would answer much better than I can. I think there is a great deal of regional background that southerners tend to have that northerners don't. There is the experience of growing up essentially as part of a conquered population, which is something that northerners deny, quite frankly, but nevertheless is quite true. As for being a Catholic novelist, I think the interesting thing about the Catholic novelist today – or maybe I should say *should* be the interesting thing about the Catholic novel today – is that it is the Christian tradition that is urban rather than rural. And I think that your type of Christians are very largely rural people. I think my type of Christians are very largely urban people.

[*A wasp begins to buzz around us.*]

GW: Ack! I really hate those things. We have a crabapple tree in our yard, and it drops crabapples all over, and I don't get them cleaned up in time. So we have a yard full of bees and wasps for a month. I've been stung more than once, and I really, really don't like it!

JJ: Among Catholic novelists who would you consider in that field? Francois Mauriac? Shusaku Endo? Or are you thinking mainly of Walker Percy, Flannery O'Connor?

GW: The last, I suppose. I haven't read widely – I haven't read the Catholic novels specifically as a genre. Perhaps I should. The problem I have is that there are a thousand directions in which I ought to be going, and I generally can't go terribly far in any of them.

JJ: Urban versus rural: I wonder if you would continue with that.

GW: I think the Catholic tradition in America is derived largely from people who got here after the farms had been claimed. The early settlers – some Irish but mainly Scotch, English, German and so forth – came here, and being intelligent and reasonable people staked out claims to the good land and started growing corn and such. The Catholic strain in the American life comes from Poles and Italians and so on, and the later wave of Irish immigration during the potato famine, who arrived after the good farms were pretty much owned already. You couldn't go out and get those, and so these later people became policemen and hod carriers and building contractors and school teachers and so forth. And that urban environment is where the American Catholic tradition is located, as far as I can see. Father Andrew Greeley, whom I have never met, is probably nevertheless my favorite priest, and he is very much aware of that and tends to write about it. I think he is right.

JJ: Does that conviction show up in any of your writings, or is that just what you believe a 'mainstream' Catholic novelist should devote his attention to?

GW: I think that the mainstream Catholic novelist is not going to be able to avoid that completely even if he tries. If you are a Christian you cannot help writing as a Christian. You can disguise it, but there are still acute people who will see through the disguise and say, 'Aha, back in here is a Christian background.' And I think if you're Catholic the same thing is true: people will say, 'Back in here is a Catholic background.' Somebody was describing a Brian Lumley novel to me today and I said, 'Is he Catholic?' I have not read the novel. (I have read very little Brian Lumley; I wish I had read more. I intend to read more after meeting him here at this convention.) But the outline as it was being presented to me made it sound so much as if he were writing from an English Catholic tradition.

Of course, before I ever went to England I thought that there were no Catholics there, and if they were they would reflect the same kind of thing that we have in Northern Ireland today, which is just horrible incredibly awful stuff: people putting bombs in cars and killing little kids in the name of Jesus Christ on both sides! You can't imagine a more unchristian thing than this neighbor-killing-neighbor thing that Northern Ireland goes through! But when I went to England I found there were plenty of Catholic churches and that nobody was scrawling graffiti over them or throwing rocks at the people who went to Mass, or any of that sort of thing. Rosemary and I went to Mass whenever we were so inclined. So Lumley might very well be Catholic. Chesterton obviously was and so was Tolkien. Both were English Catholics.

JJ: In *The Urth Cycle* (let's call it that), obviously memory is a large theme and you have brought the sacraments, at least the sacrament of baptism, into play repeatedly in the book. There are an awful lot of occasions where people pass through water and experience some type of death and resurrection. There also seem to be images of the eucharist.

GW: There are diabolical eucharists: people who are eating corpses in order to get the memory of the dead person. And of course when a Catholic receives communion he is receiving the flesh of Christ in a mystical sense. He is doing what Christ asked him to do, which is to absorb a little piece of Christ into himself to make himself more Christ-like; and so we go forward in the Mass and we consent to that, saying that I wish to be more like Christ. Whoever is giving out communion, the priest or someone assisting the priest says, 'The body of Christ' and holds up the host, and you say 'Amen', meaning 'Yes, I agree this is the body of Christ', and then you take it and eat it.

JJ: Now the climax of that inversion seems to be when Severian actually eats the brains of the preceding autarch. Did you see that as another form of the diabolical communion? Or something that was necessary? It seems to be necessary to the novel.

GW: What I was doing was to say that in order to be a good ruler you must be familiar with the tradition of *that* rule – of that country and of the people in the past who have administered that country. No, not diabolical in that case. The diabolical thing is more Vodalus and the grave-robbers.

JJ: Who are into it just for thrills.

GW: Well, yes they are doing it for trivial reasons. Evil is always a distortion or an exaggeration of something that is good. People don't understand that now.

JJ: Are the other sacraments of the Catholic church present in the novel? Are Severian's various liaisons along the way false forms of matrimony, or in some sense symbolic of it?

GW: They are more manifestations of the search for love, which I think is a great quest of life. What we go into life really looking for is love. And as you've said in your letters, I don't think of Severian as being a Christ figure; I think of Severian as being a Christian figure. He is a man who has been born into a very perverse background, who is gradually trying to become better. I think that all of us have somewhere in us an instinct to try and become better. Some of us defeat it thoroughly. We kill that part of ourselves, just as we kill the child in ourselves. It is very closely related to the child in us.

JJ: Is Valeria the ideal love for him?

GW: No.

JJ: Where would you say it lies in the novel?

GW: I think that the true ideal of love for any person is God. It isn't another human being. If my wife were here she would be deeply offended by that [*laughter*]. I don't mean that God is the only thing that a person can love. I think the *final* object of love is God.

JJ: Right. But within the horizons of a human life, is Severian still searching in the end?

GW: Very much so.

JJ: 'Man is a wolf to man.' You actually quote that in *Soldier of Arete*. You've traded on the wolf idea a lot, obviously, but that brings up the question of horror fiction. Both of the panels you have participated in at this convention have been about horror. You are not really a horror writer, though, and you don't write just to shock. But there are many times in your novels that you have deliberately brought the reader to the place where he is shocked or horrified in order to, hopefully, invoke a reaction against what you are presenting: This is bad and you should be shocked.

So, on the wolf-theme: In your story 'The Hero as Werwolf', what were you hoping to get the reader to think about?

GW: I was trying to get the reader to think about the real nature of love between man and woman. In the first place, the girl in 'The Hero as Werwolf' is retarded and cannot speak. And, secondly, in the end she has to damage very badly the man she loves in order to set him free. I think I was trying to say, first, that you must not think that the person you love has to be a whole lot like you in order for that love to be real and working. And second, that we all, if we are going to be honest, have to hurt people in order to do them good. We have to tear away parts of them in order to do them good.

JJ: The young man in 'Hero' has a wounded foot, as does Severian. Does that come from the Bible, as a sign of the kind of character who receives the foot-wound rather than head-crushing, as Genesis 3 speaks of it?

GW: I'm not sure. If so it was unconscious. I don't think I did that consciously. I think it may very well reflect Biblical reading.

JJ: That is a theme in the Scripture, and Jacob winds up with a limp in Genesis 32. It is as if, as you have pointed out in especially in the Severian novels, it is necessary for God to bruise and wound us in order to make us grow.

GW: This is the same thing. God is the ultimate Lover above the human lover, and God has to do that. It would be very nice for me, I think, if I didn't have to work, and if I never got into any kind of trouble, and everybody thought that I was wonderful, and so forth and so on. In the long-range view, that isn't how you make a larger and better person. You meet people who have really been through it and really, truly suffered – who have been, let's say, a prisoner in the Hanoi Hilton for years, or something like that. Then you discover, yes, they got something out of it that I don't have.

I don't mean that I don't flee from pain and so forth just as all of us do.

I'm at least as cowardly as the average person, probably worse.

JJ: I don't think we are supposed to embrace pain. On the other hand, we understand the purpose of it when it comes ...

GW: We try to.

JJ: ... whether the dark night of the soul or something else.

GW: You always tend to say, 'Why this? Couldn't it have been something else?' It is the problem of pain, which C. S. Lewis has an essay on. I still run across people who talk about pain as if nobody had ever dealt with it before. The idea of pain is to keep you from doing those things that are destructive. And they say 'Surely there is another way that God could teach us.' Yes, there are other ways, but you would complain about those other ways, too, just as you complain about pain. It would only change the dressing of the situation, not the situation itself.

JJ: And if you believe that God has good intentions, then whatever the pain was, it was indeed actually the best remedy. Now, along these lines, is the torturer of which Severian is the shadow, is that God? Is Severian the shadow of The Torturer?

GW: No, I think the idea there is that of the torturer coming between the victim and God and casting a shadow, serving as the oppressor or as a satanic figure. Severian is engaged in working his way out of his profession, which is torture.

JJ: So although there are analogies between what God has to put us through and what a torturer does, that was not your view. It was rather an inversion at that notion?

GW: Well, I wasn't seeing the torturer as the hand of God, if that is what you mean. No, I don't think so. I think that Satan does what God wishes him to do; it is just that he doesn't want to. And I think the torturer is in the same position. He is frequently doing what God wants him to do but he is not trying to please God by doing it.

JJ: Right. He is the Assyrian that God brings in against the Israelites.

GW: Yes.

JJ: Now, in my letter I asked a question that I figured you would not like. I wrote that there seemed to be a number of women who are less sympathetic than male characters in many of your books. You strongly disagreed, which I expected.

GW: Well, as regards some of the characters.

JJ: Let's begin with Ann Schindler. What struck me about her in *Castleview* was this section where one woman is saying the rosary and Ann Schindler starts to 'pray' by thinking through a recipe. What came to my mind was the Biblical phrase 'whose god is their belly'. It seemed to be a form of idolatry.

GW: But I wasn't showing that Ann was a bad person; I was showing that she was in a barren culture. That the only thing that she could come up with was this, and I intended this to be humorous rather than condemnatory. I thought Ann was basically a good person. I am sensitive about this because a reviewer called her a pitiless satire of the middle aged housewife or something like that, which was by no means what I had intended.

JJ: She is a woman who hasn't taken her husband's name, so I would not think that she is your average middle-class housewife.

GW: No, she certainly is 'liberated' in some degree. But she is also courageous, intelligent, inquisitive, and she quite genuinely loves her husband and her daughter. She is not faking that. She actually loves Will, not as much as Will would like, but she loves him. And she loves her daughter Mercedes enormously, fiercely.

JJ: I want to ask you about Laura in *There Are Doors*. Having only been through it once and scanned it yesterday, I'm still not exactly sure about what Laura is.

[*The wasp returns! GW ducks and tries to avoid it.*]

GW: My wife is pro-wasp and anti-spider, while I am pro-spider and anti-wasp.

JJ: He's over here on my coat now.

GW: I hope he stays there! [*Laughter.*]

Laura is my idea of what a pagan goddess might be who survived into the Christian world. One of the places where I probably split off from conventional Catholic thinking is that I believe that the gods of paganism were real. I don't think that they are entitled to the worship that they received from the pagans. I think what many of the biblical writers are saying is, 'Yes, these are real powers, but it is wrong for you to give to them the honors that are due to God alone.' And I think that that is exactly correct. Now, if Aphrodite were to survive into the contemporary world, what would she be like? Well, Laura was a shot at trying to show what she might be like.

JJ: Is there an attempt to redeem Laura on the part of the church?

GW: On the part of the author, not on the part of the church.

JJ: I ask because the Italian restaurant is one of the doorways between the two worlds.

GW: Yes. You said that Mama wanted Laura to marry Green, and she does want her to marry Green. That is because she thinks that Green is a nice guy, which he is. He is kind of dumb, but he is a nice guy. Laura is a nice girl, which is kind of true. And she would like to see them get together. She has that maternal married woman desire to see more married couples and children and so forth.

In *There Are Doors* I wanted to do something that I think has only rarely been done. It certainly has been done, but it isn't done very often. I wanted to present a protagonist who isn't very intelligent. Green isn't. He has almost no virtues. By that I don't mean that he has many vices, but he is not outstanding in any good way. He is a man of very limited intelligence, not terribly courageous, not terribly energetic or enterprising or any of those other things. He is the sort of man who would be quite content to work all his life in a dead end job and never try to get very far outside of that – except that he meets Laura. That is what changes him. Laura is looking for lovers, but Green is looking for love and he has found it, or he thinks he has found it. And whether she loves him or not, he loves her enormously. He can deal with the idea that she doesn't love him, that she doesn't have any particular feeling for him. It makes no difference to him; he still loves her.

JJ: Now, as I read the novel the first time, it appeared to me that Tina and the dolls like her were given to train the men of that world in an idolatrous worship of Laura as the goddess, and that would be an anti-Christian idea. And that Green's affection for her and his overwhelming pursuit of her would be similarly problematic.

GW: This is the Christian world. That world is not the Christian world. That world is kind of a warmed-over pagan world. And that is what I tried to show it as. People always fault me on it by saying I did not work out what a world would be like in which men died after intercourse, but I feel that I did.

JJ: You raise that question in the book itself.

GW: How different would it be? I don't think it would be as different as a lot of people want to think it would be. You would have a lot of men who would refrain from intercourse either throughout their life or at least un-til the very end of their lives. And you would have a more feminine ori-ented society. A feminine viewpoint would have more influence than it does in our society. Although it does have a great deal in our society, it would have still more there.

JJ: And you believe that there are significant differences between femi-nine and masculine viewpoints.

GW: Absolutely. We're too biologically different not to have differences in viewpoint. Of course, we have to get away from the idea that one side is good and the other bad, which we have been struck on now throughout recorded history. The great majority of men have held that women are somehow innately evil; and the great majority of women saying when they dared, and often thinking when they dared not speak it aloud, that men were all beasts and brutes and so forth. The terrible thing is that so much of the bad stuff we say about each other is true. But we keep yelling for other people to be good without trying to be good ourselves. We are the only people we can make good. I can make me good, or I can at least try, and you can make you good; but neither one of us can do much for the other.

JJ: At the end of the novel Green goes off in pursuit of Laura in Manea near Overwood, and that leaves the novel open. Do you intend to come back to it?

GW: I might. I didn't intend to go back to it at the time I wrote it.

JJ: Does he make any mistake running after her?

GW: Oh no, no. I don't think he's making a mistake. I think he is making the great correct decision of his life, which is to go after such love as he sees.

JJ: Even if what is there at the end is likely to be hollow? Because she doesn't really *love*, does she? She just wants lovers.

GW: But how is that going to be at the end, and how much is that going to matter to him? He has found something to love. I think the trouble with a whole lot of people in this world is that there is nothing at all that they care deeply about. And it is certainly the trouble with Green. But now he has found something to care deeply about and he is making the correct decision. He has not made the mistake of saying, 'It is too much trouble and so I'm not going to do it.' I have a friend named Paul who is only a little bit younger than I am. I am 61. Paul must be about 50. And he is training now to be a missionary and he is going to go most likely into South America and do missionary work. And I think he is absolutely right. I know Paul, and he has finally found what he needed to find all his life and he is making the right decision. It is not going to be comfortable and it might be painful, and it is darn hard for a man his age to throw off everything and start studying all the things he has to study in order to be ordained in his church, the Church of Christ, and become a missionary, but that is what he is going to do. That is the right decision for him.

JJ: North in this book reminded me of Gordon Liddy.

GW: Very much so, very deliberately so. I originally started out with the idea of modeling him on Oliver North. He had a different name at that time. And I later came to realize that [Oliver] North was not the sort of person I thought he was. But Liddy really was and I read Liddy's book *Will*, which is an astonishingly good book, and I sort of caricatured Liddy to some degree.

They aren't very many of them, but there really are people like [my] North. North is unconsciously oriented to a death-wish that he can't control. He is trying to get himself killed. Because he is, he raises every confrontation to the level of a life and death struggle. He is the sort of man who shoots the policeman who stops him to give him a speeding ticket. I have nothing against Liddy, and was not intending to take a shot at him or do him harm. I just felt that what he presented of himself in *Will* was fascinating as a type of person, somewhat self-destructive.

JJ: Another thing that I raised that you didn't like at all was from the novel *Peace*. Let me make a case and then you show me where I am wrong and we can maybe discuss how this comes about. But as I reread *Peace*, I reread a lot of it and I found that you have a story in there, you have four suitors for Olivia. Olivia is Olive Branch Peace. That reminds me of the fairy stories where several brothers pursue something.

GW: Well, we do in those fairy stories in the course of the book.

JJ: Julius Smart is the one who wins her hand. He is a man who takes over a pharmacy. A pharmacy dispenses drugs. Dispenses grace. The man who was there before was giving out drugs that were very damaging and Smart doesn't like that idea. He cleans the place up. She is unfaithful to him but he forgives her. He is said to be a symbolic figure and the central character in the book. He owns the company for which Weer works but when he comes around to inspect Weer and all of the fellows fake up as if they were doing good work and are not willing to be seen for what they really are. And all of those things pointed in the direction that Julius Smart would have symbolic weight attached to him and is something of a revelation of a Christ figure. You, however, objected to that idea. I wonder why …

GW: I certainly wasn't conscious of doing it while writing the book. I guess that is about the best that I can say.

JJ: Is he symbolic and central to the book?

GW: I didn't intend him as a symbolic figure I don't believe. I intended him as an ordinary, middle class American. If he symbolizes anything he symbolizes the mass of ordinary working class, lower-middle class America.

JJ: Okay. I wanted to ask you this about *Peace* too. It came up in the discussion yesterday when one of the panelists said that he tried to write a mainstream novel, but that it was not until he finally added a fantasy element to it that it took off in his mind. So often this novel has been interpreted not as a ghost story or as having any supernatural elements but simply as the ruminations of an old man. Why isn't it that? In other words, why didn't you just write it as an old man thinking over his life. What added dimension is there to it that caused you to want to make it a man who is already dead thinking over his life?

GW: Because I wanted to lend to the memories certain supernatural strengths that an old man thinking over his life wouldn't have. I wanted to do the rooms as re-creations of rooms that he had known as a very young man and I didn't think that anybody would actually do that – that it had to be a supernatural stick or a mental quirk or something of that sort. I wanted some interplay between the remembered figures and the present reality, and so on, that I could not have gotten with just reminiscence.

JJ: Okay. It is a very Proustian novel all the same I suppose.

GW: I think it is Proustian and I am a great Proust fan. I have read *Remembrance of Things Past* I think about two and a half times. I don't read it more because when I start reading it I stop reading everything else. Unfortunately,

I am in a position of having a lot of things that I have to read or owe it to other people to read so that I can give them promotional quotes, or things that I need to read to research something I am writing currently, non-fiction and so on.

JJ: I know you have to make a decision among the novels to be awarded prizes at this conference so you have to read all of them.

GW: Well, I had to at least start all of those. The World Fantasy Award was not only for best novel but for best non-fiction and for best story collection and for best short story as well.

JJ: Oh, my, you had a lot to read.

GW: All that. And the only way that you can possibly do it is to begin each work and stop as soon as you say to yourself 'I am not going to vote a prize for this work', and then go on to the next one. And if you find that you can't stop then you had better rethink the decision 'I am not going to vote a prize for this work', because if it is not that good how come you can't put it down? But I finished very few of the books that I started for that. The best one by the way which is a very Christian, very Catholic novel is *Mojo and the Pickle Jar* which was my top pick for the World Fantasy Award; and I couldn't convince any of the other judges it should even be in the running, I think probably because it is too Christian.

JJ: Who is the author of that?

GW: A man named Douglas Bell who lives down in Texas around Dallas somewhere whom I have never met and know nothing about him except his name and that I saw a jacket picture of him on the book. But it's about a young, not very good man in Texas who is working in his uncle's roadside cafe when a Mexican girl comes in with something in a jar, in a pickle jar. The heart of a saint. And she is being pursued by the minions of a cocaine baron because she has been involved in a drug deal that has gone wrong. And the young man is Mojo, the girl's name I think is Juanita. Right out he tries to help her. They go on the lam from the people who are trying to kill them. But they are carrying with them this miracle-working religious relic. It is a good piece. I would have been very happy to have written it.

JJ: Do you read Timothy Powers or James Blaylock much?

GW: I certainly haven't read Blaylock much. I have read Powers a little bit more than Blaylock.

JJ: In *Peace*, is Weer in Purgatory working toward peace?

GW: Yeah, I think probably he is.

JJ: Is that something you thought about when you wrote it?

GW: That is not the way I conceived it when I wrote it. I conceived it more that he was a ghost trying to make sense of his own life. And I think that is another way of saying that. Goodness knows we don't know much about Heaven and we know even less about Hell and we hardly know anything about Purgatory at all. What is it? And if you believe in ghosts – and I happen to believe in ghosts – what's going on with them? Long, long ago, one of Shakespeare's contemporaries said that hell is not a place; it is a state: Wherever I am, hell is. *Dr Faustus*, by Christopher Marlowe. And I think that he is right. The old attempts to locate Heaven above the clouds, and Hell in the bowels of the volcano and so forth, I think are not only obviously naive, but they are fundamentally wrong in that they are looking for countries in the sense that North America or Ireland or whatever are countries, and I don't think that is what those things are. I think they are states.

JJ: The book of Revelation uses the image of the lake of fire in front of the throne of God, which I think implies that everyone winds up in the same place, except some like it and some don't.

GW: Well, I think that may very well be. It's a question, I think, of the soul's relationship with God after death. If that relationship is fundamentally good then the soul is in Heaven. Jesus kept saying the kingdom of Heaven is here. It is not in the far future, it is here and now. And it is here and now for those whose relationship with God is correct.

JJ: Let me ask you about *Soldier of the Mist* and *Soldier of Arete*. Are those historical novels or fantasy novels?

GW: Well, they are historical fantasy. What I tried to do …

JJ: To put it another way: Do we have fallen angels here, or perhaps some kind of powers that really were operative in the world before the arrival of the kingdom of God?

GW: That is my personal belief. I think that the gods of paganism were real. But what I tried to do was to write about that pagan world as the pagans themselves wrote about it. If we read modern historians we are reading a very rationalistic viewpoint of this, which says that all of these people were absolutely wasting their time by building temples to Ares or Apollo or you name it, and by offering sacrifices in worship and all that, because there was nothing there. Nothing at all there and that whether it is true or not that certainly is not the way the people who were doing it felt. They were convinced that there was something there and they had all sorts of legends and so forth about the appearances of the gods, and in fact there is one place in Acts where Paul and another one of the apostles are mistaken for Zeus and Mercury – rather, Zeus and Hermes! Here we are, mixing the Latin and the Greek, which is what I was trying to get away from! They are mistaken for Zeus and Hermes in human form because people in those days expected that you could see Zeus and Hermes in human form. I am not so sure they were wrong. I am not convinced that they were wrong. We love to think how much smarter we are than people of ancient times or biblical times or so forth, but I am very dubious about that.

JJ: I agree with you. There aren't many people who think that any more. We have the influence of rationalism in our society. I think that what most of us are taught about the ancient world is too often nonsense. One of the primary things being the fact that the church fathers say that the Hebrew scriptures were known around the ancient world and I imagine that they were. They weren't secret documents. People like Aristotle were curious for anything they could get their hands on.

GW: People like Aristotle read any book that they could find because books were rare. When I was a kid reading fantasy and science fiction and that sort of thing, it was hard to find that type of material and anything that you could find you read.

JJ: Yes I agree, even when I was young it was still that way.

Now, you do seem to have some symbolic overtones in *Soldier of Arete*. Certainly with Latro, or Lucius, which I guess was his real name and which means wolf. There is a wolf aspect in his being from Rome, being a descendant of Romulus at least in some way, and then Ares being the primary agricultural and martial god of Rome, Mars. He actually seems to incarnate Ares on occasion. In the mythology, Aphrodite, although married to Hephaestus, is carrying on an affair with Ares. She seems to come to him one night. These things happen …

GW: I thought she was married to Ares.

JJ: She is married to Hephaestus, Vulcan. She cheats with Ares. Vulcan catches them in the net and there is a certain amount of punishment that Ares goes through as well.

GW: Okay, I still think there are other poets in which she is married to Ares.

JJ: There may be other versions.

GW: Anyway.

JJ: Is there a larger picture here? I raise the question when Lucius leaves Greece he leaves Io and Polos in the care of Pindar. Polos means a small horse. Io at least for you means joy. Is he leaving joy and myth in the care of poetry? Is there a symbolic dimension?

GW: Yeah, there is. Every once in a while you say, 'Gee, that's neat; I'll do that.' And you do it. I wasn't writing the whole book that way. The book isn't intended as an allegory. The book really is intended to show the problems faced by a genuinely good man who can't remember. Because it seems to me that is the problem of our society. We have a genuinely good society, by which I mean it is made up of people who by and large are quite decent individuals. But our society has no memory because it has no awareness of history.

JJ: Right.

GW: And so we have this America blundering around on the world stage more or less as Latro does. Latro is strong and able and tries to be a force for good but he can't remember.

JJ: That is an interesting perspective on it, I hadn't thought of at all. One of my wife's professors taught in a Moslem country for a while and said he woke up one day and observed some children tossing kittens up into the air and hitting them with a baseball bat against the wall while their mothers just sat by and watched. He said, 'I am not a Christian, I am an atheist; but I am a Christian in that I could not tolerate that. There has been an influence in our society that has made us different.'

GW: Yes, yes, right. We vastly underestimate the importance of Jesus. We think we don't. We have all these churches and we say, 'How can we be underestimating Jesus?' Well, we don't, until we start trying to figure out what it would be like if He had never lived. When you really start trying to figure out what it would be like if He never lived you realize that He is a much more pivotal figure than we give Him credit for. All of these people, everybody at this [World Fantasy] convention are in that sense Christians, although most of them would tell you that they are not and some of them would tell them quite truthfully that they are Jews who practice Judaism in one of its various forms and so on and so forth. Nevertheless, they have been influenced by Christ much more than they realize. We are very lucky to have had Him. We are very fortunate.

A friend of mine learned to read Turkish. And he got hold of a Turkish joke book and read it. And I said, 'What were the jokes like?' He said it was horrible. They were all about ugly tricks that were being played on blind people and things like that. This is what we have escaped from, and we don't realize that it is there and we came very close to falling into it. We very easily could have, and we still may.

JJ: It is a striking thing that if you read the book of Leviticus [ch. 19:14], it is right there: You will never put a stumbling block in front of a blind person and you will never curse at the deaf. That kind of thing is unique. But as you say it is common in other cultures.

In the preface to *Soldier of the Mist* you tell us that Latro knows a little bit of Hebrew but the only people like that he runs into are Phoenicians. I wondered if the fact that the Phoenicians are the ones who rescue him in the end and take him home had a symbolic overtone to you.

GW: Not tremendously. It was just at the time I was planning a third book and I wanted to get him into the Semitic world and out of the Hellenic world that the first two books were laid in very largely, and to involve him with the Phoenicians and the Jews and the Syrians and that part of the world. When I originally conceived the series I wanted to do a tour of the ancient world so to speak. And I had hoped in fact to get him into the new world where there were the Mayan and the various American Indian civilizations. I really dislike the term Native American. I realize Indians is not a very good term for them, but I don't think Native Americans is a

good term either. Anyway, I wanted to do all those things, but after the
second book David Hartwell, my editor, called me up and told me not to
write the third one. He now denies that, by the way, but he did.

JJ: He thought they were so difficult to read?

GW: David said it was too difficult to sell well, and David is as good at self-
deception as most of us, so I didn't. I went off and did something else. Now
I don't know if I will ever write what I was going to write, *Soldier of Sidon*.
Sidon [long i] or 'siddon' [short i]? I would pronounce it Sidon. [*Soldier of
Sidon* was published by Tor in December 2006 – *PW*]

JJ: Well, Sidon in English, or Seedon [long o] in ancient speech. My
impression is that words that are used commonly you say in their Angli-
cized forms and ones that are uncommon you try to say in the way they
would in the ancient world.

GW: That is certainly a good rule, but the question then is what is common and what isn't.

JJ: That's right. Especially nowadays.

GW: Who is to do the determining? People today, half of them have no
idea who Julius Caesar was. They have heard the name but if you asked
them, 'What did Caesar do? Why is he an important historical figure?'
they wouldn't be able to give you much of an answer.

JJ: Latro's world seems to be a really horrible world and one that you
would want to escape from. Were you just being ruthlessly honest there
or were you seeking to evoke that response in the reader? This is not
where we want to be; we want to be in a world that is more Christian.

GW: I think certainly that is true. I think I was reacting against an ideali-
zation of the ancient world that many people have. One of the ancient
authors has this story – I think it is an ancient author – about the woman
who goes to Plato or one of the great philosophers and describes this ideal
society that she and her friends are going to set up. And they are going to
have ritual dancing and do all these Ursula LeGuin things. And he says,
'But who is going to do all the work? You are going to need food and so
forth.' She says, 'Oh, we'll have slaves.'

JJ: Of course.

GW: That was very much the idealism of the ancients: ideally someone
else will do it.

JJ: Right. But then, a gradual diminution of slavery and the development of liberty is a long-term impact of Christianity.

GW: Well, also machinery, simple technology. I'm an engineer and I intend to take credit for what we can. I think the steam engine probably did
more to free slaves than any human being. More than Abraham Lincoln
did or U. S. Grant.

JJ: And so many of these fundamental technological advances were
made in the so-called Dark Ages when the church was in charge of things.

GW: Well, the church very largely saved ancient civilization. We know much of what we do know about ancient civilization because the Church preserved that for us. That is one of things we owe the Church. I am not one of those people who try and say the Church has never done anything wrong. The Church is an organization made up of human beings and has existed for 2,000 years. It's had enormous opportunities to go wrong and it often has, but the thing that I think separates the Church from most other human institutions is that the Church has always tried to go right. It just hasn't always succeeded. Most of our human institutions are very willing to strike a bargain with the devil if they think they can get good enough terms. That is always a bad thing to do.

Do I have a wasp in my hair?

JJ: No. You do have a ladybug on your shoulder, though.

GW: Oh, that's fine. Ladybugs are okay.

JJ: *Soldier of Arete*, even more than *Soldier of the Mist*, is a bit hard to follow in terms of plot. And I remember when it came out Orson Scott Card really complained about it. In *Analog* or one of those magazines he had a review that said, 'Nobody reads Gene Wolfe with more care and affection than I do, but I can't figure out what this book is about. What is wrong with this author?' Does that kind of complaint bother you?

GW: Oh, yes.

JJ: Or do you feel as if you wish you had left more clues, or do you feel, 'Hey, read the book and look at it again and you will find the answers.'

GW: I try not to leave a clue more than once because it bothers me a lot when it is left more than once in somebody else's book. If you've told me once that the hero is left-handed, I have registered it or at least I hope I have registered it, and if you tell me five times then I feel that you are writing for somebody that is a lot dumber than I am. So I try and leave my clues once and generally try and leave all the clues that I think the reader is going to require, sometimes more than they require, because you don't generally find situations in which you have exactly as much information as you need to solve the thing. If it is solvable at all you probably have more. If you have only a very few items then it probably isn't solvable with the information that you have. What you need to do in a real life situation is to go out and get more clues. If you know anything about actual police work, very little of it consists of reasoning from clues and the great majority of it consists of finding more clues. Because when you have found enough then you have very little difficulty in understanding what they mean.

JJ: In the *Soldier* novels you seem to have in the background a war between the moon and the earth. Is there anything there beyond the fact that those who worship the moon had conquered territory that formerly belonged to Gaea?

GW: I was trying to show the difference between the old matriarchal or more female-oriented society and the more patriarchal society that in fact displaced it. I think that the majority of the things that the women's libbers write is nonsense, but every once in a while they are right like everybody else. Everybody is right once in a while and this is one of the things they are right about. There really was a much more female-oriented mother-goddess worship, and the obvious key point is Delphi. If you read about Delphi in classic time you are very clearly reading about a shrine at which a goddess has been displaced by a god. The priests at Delphi in classical times were not permitted to wear shoes and they had to sleep on the ground. And they were priests of Apollo and this makes no sense for priests of Apollo. It makes a great deal of sense for priests of the earth goddess, which is what they originally were, and they carried these traditions through. And I was trying to show that war, that struggle, in terms of its divinity.

JJ: So the moon goddess is actually allied with her brother.

GW: She was. And she was a part of the new mythology that was displacing the old mythology. Basically the Zeus-centered mythology was displacing the Gaea-centered mythology.

JJ: Okay. I was not sure what was happening at the initiation of Sparta at the end. Do you mind shedding light on that?

GW: That was all real. That all happened. What they did …

JJ: What the Spartans did?

GW: Yes. The Spartans were the most totalitarian people that I have ever come across. They made the Nazis look like boy scouts. They really did it, and they did it for a hundred years, and they were so totalitarian as to be almost unbelievable. One of the strange things about Sparta was they had the two kings as I am sure you realize. I don't know of anybody else that had a double monarchy like that, with two kings, like the Spartans had. One of the strange things is that the kings really represented the good past in Sparta. They were relics from the time when Sparta was a Greek state much like other Greek states. They were slowly being constricted and crowded out by the totalitarian ethic that seized power – it was like they had G. Gordon Liddy as an immortal dictator – that seized and effectually ruined Sparta.

The king who died at Thermopylae, Leonidas, armed the Helots [state-owned serfs/slaves]. It was death for a Helot to touch a weapon. If you saw a Helot with his hand on your bow, you were supposed to kill it. Leonidas, who was one of the Spartan kings and was certainly a very brave leader in war – there is no question that he was a man of immense physical courage – also had the immense moral courage to say, 'We are going to need these men. Let's stop this nonsense. Let's arm them and use them as troops because we need every man that we can get.' And he did.

And so when the Spartans were fighting the Persians, their light infantry and their skirmishers and so forth were bands of armed Helots. At the end of the war they said, 'We are going to reward you Helots by giving those who did most in the war their freedom. And they will be not equals, who will be able to run for office and vote and so on and take part in the government, but they will be free individuals living in Sparta and free as such people were. And so you are to name for us those Helots who were your leaders in the late war, those who should be rewarded like this.'

Then they held a ceremony that I described in detail exactly as it was, and they gave each Helot who was to be awarded his freedom at the climax of the ceremony a young Spartan as his companion to lead him through the ceremony. And at a given signal each companion killed the Helot that he was responsible for. And they were all killed except Latro, whom they did not intend to kill because he was not really a Helot. And he survived and all of the rest of them who had gone into the ceremony were butchered. And they really were. This really took place. This is the reason that I say that these people were totalitarians.

The University of Michigan's football team is called the Spartans. And you could have no clearer indication that the University of Michigan does not really understand what was going on in the ancient world. No way would they allow that if the people who are running the University of Michigan understood what the real Spartans were like. They were certainly not like our football players by any means.

JJ: I thought that was what was going on but I wasn't sure. And I wasn't sure why Latro was there but I can see it now. That depresses him terribly.

GW: Oh yes, yes. Latro is under tremendous psychological pressure because of the fact that he can't remember, and this has added an enormous burden of guilt to him because he survived. Remember now that this ceremony with the ancient gods is very significant to him. He is an ancient man and he belongs in all this and now, when all the others have died and he is the sole survivor, he gets an enormous amount of guilt out of this and goes into clinical depression.

JJ: Does the novel anywhere explain why Latro has been struck in the head?

GW: I don't think it does. My idea as I said originally was that he desecrated the temple during the battle of Plataea. A lot of the battle of Plataea was hand to hand fighting in the temple and it occurred to me that the temple could not have been kept in very good order when a bunch of Persians and Greeks were trying to kill each other in it. Of course the initial idea for the whole series of books was that Xerxes would get a band of Roman exiles and enlist them as mercenaries in his army. If you have read Herodotus you know that there is an enormous catalog. There were ancient tribes that we know of only because there was a group of them serving as mercenaries in Xerxes' army or sent by tributary kings and so forth. Xerxes seems to have gathered together every fighting man he could scrape up. Of course what happened – I guess I am going far off the subject – but what happened was that he lost the battle of Salamis, which meant that he lost control, which means he lost the ability to supply this huge army that he had put into the field and he had to withdraw most of it because he couldn't feed the troops. And you know, a small band of raiders or plunderers can live off the land; but when you are talking about hundreds of thousands of men, they cannot do it; the land hasn't got that much food.

JJ: So that was something that might have come up in the third volume if you had not been discouraged from writing it?

GW: Absolutely. The black man, whom nobody ever talks about but whom I intended as a major figure, was an Ethiopian. And Xerxes actually had Ethiopians who were armed with Stone Age weapons – spears tipped with antelope horn and that sort of thing – and he had these people in his army. So the black man was one of those Ethiopians who were sent by the King of Ethiopia as mercenaries. The King of Ethiopia was paid to send warriors to the army that Xerxes was going to invade Greece with.

JJ: He could have had American Indians in his army from what I can tell about the ancient world.

GW: I think you are saying that there was a lot more interaction within the ancient world than we in the New World give them credit for. Absolutely right.

JJ: They have found Peregrini Irish monk inscriptions in places in America but the establishment view just will not admit that it could be true.

GW: I know one of the leading scholars in this, Cyrus Gordon. I had dinner with him; well I have had dinner with him twice. Once in a restaurant, but the one I was thinking of he had us over for dinner, and we ate with him. We had a friend who is now deceased, Sharon Baker, a talented writer who was really just getting started and she was 55 or so when she died of cancer. But Sharon was his niece so she introduced me to him. He is a pariah because he keeps bringing up this stuff and saying, 'But look, look at the evidence!' And they keep saying, 'Oh, he is an old crackpot. Send him off. That nut.' He is saying, 'But why was the army of Yucatan arranged just like an Assyrian army?' They say, 'That's just a coincidence.' He says, 'But why was the loom used in the Yucatan just like the loom that was used in the Mediterranean about 1000 B.C.?' They say, 'Oh well, that is a coincidence that they developed the same sort of loom.'

And can I tell you, this is a hobby-horse of mine. I shouldn't use up our time with this, but I am an engineer by trade. We know how the wheel was invented. Archeology has established how the wheel was invented. The wheel was invented by people who started out by laying down logs and putting big stones on the logs and pushing them. When you do that you have to pick up the end log and you have to carry it around to the front so that it feeds in under the stone. When you do this, your log takes on a coke bottle shape. There are engineering reasons for why it wears in this pattern.

Say that there is a rock here and here is our log and it is going to go over the rock. Now if the rock is in the middle then the full weight of the load is right here on the rock. If the rock is over on one side only one half of the load is on the rock so the middle wears faster and you get coke bottle shaped logs. And you learn eventually that the coke bottle shaped logs work better than new logs. You start getting guys with hatchets to carve the coke bottle shape into them from the beginning because that is easier than wearing them in. Because if there is a stone in the middle and your log is coke bottle shape you just go over it. You don't have to push the load over it. You just sail over it. That makes the load easier to push.

Then somebody said, 'Well, we've got all these baskets full of gravel and stuff that we also need to build the pyramid. Instead of carrying them on our backs, why don't we put them on top of the rock and push everything?' Well, that works. That's easier than carrying the gravel in a basket on your back. So they do that.

Then they have all the big rocks in place and they say, 'Gee, we really miss those big rocks because it was easier than carrying the basket. Let's make a fake rock out of wood. It won't be very heavy and we can put our baskets on it.' Okay that is easier again, so you do it.

Then somebody says, 'Well, look, suppose we have posts going right down here so that that last log can't get out.' Well, you try that and the log rubs against the post. You learn if you put the post inward where the log is coke bottle shaped it doesn't rub up as much and you can take mutton fat out of the tail of the sheep – everybody knows that makes things slippery – and grease it and then it hardly drags at all. And what you end up with is a very big, very clumsy four-wheeled cart. And this is how the wheel was invented.

If you read the anthropologists about the Indians they will tell you the Indians did not have the wheel. But they did. The thing is that the only wheel that they had was tiny little wheeled toys. A little animal on a little platform and four wheels. Obviously they did not develop the wheel. They got it from somebody who had already developed it. And this somebody could not put a big cart or chariot aboard the ship. It took up too much room. You could put a hundred little wheeled toys aboard the ship and trade them. Right? Well the Indians had never seen anything like it. 'Well, gee, that is neat. You can pull it along and it follows the kid around.' It is a nice trade item and you can carry hundreds of them aboard your Phoenician ship. But the Indians never took it any farther. They were not able to look at the wheeled toy and say, 'Why can't we make a big one like that?' They never took that step.

JJ: I am tempted to say there was a book a few years age by a chemist who argued that the Pyramids in Egypt were not made of stones dragged up but they were bricks cast in place with a chemical regent to fill it. Take a box with shells in it, pour in a reagent, and make the brick right there in place. He is saying they had the technology to do this. That we have cut these stones open and that is what they look like. And that there is no reason to believe people in the ancient world didn't understand this. I don't know enough to critique the thesis, of course.

GW: I don't either. I hadn't known of the book. It is certainly a very interesting idea. There are stones in South America that are so closely fitted that you wonder if somebody hasn't been doing something like that. Now maybe they just very laboriously carved these stones so that they fit right into each other, but you would think they would just carve them flat like Joe blocks so they would do that but they don't. They wave round and so forth but they fit. They key into each other nicely.

JJ: What were you regarding as the theme in *Castleview*? You told me that the castle is a Winnebago, from one perspective.

GW: From Morgan le Fay's perspective it is a travelling home. She can send her house, her castle whatever you want to call it.

JJ: Is this a pure fantasy novel?

GW: Oh yes, I would say it is a purely fantasy novel. I was trying to show really the connection of the modern world to the medieval world more than anything else. That's the theme.

JJ: And it has a lot to do with perception? For some people the band that runs through the town are cowboys and Indians, for others they are Arthur and his knights, for others it seems to be a spaceship.

GW: When you research these anomalous stories and accounts you get this sort of thing. You get two witnesses who have very different stories depending on how they perceived some third thing that we don't know what it was. So I tried to show it like that.

JJ: So basically you have Arthurian characters in the modern world who are some way or other archetypes of the characters in the twentieth century characters that we see?

GW: Yes, they are twentieth century characters who are rather like the people of the middle ages. The people of the middle ages weren't that different. And I was thinking of the old business about everybody being descendant from Charlemagne – you are and so am I. You know that if you look at the number of ancestors each of us must have had, we come up with a number by the time we get back to the time of Charlemagne that is something like eight times the actual population of Europe at that time. Europe only had something like 12 million people in Charlemagne's time and our number of grandparents and great-grandparents doubles with every generation. It works out to an enormous number and so any-body who was living in Europe at that time and who did in fact have descendants, and Charlemagne had something like fourteen children, is almost certainly – the almost is really a weasel word – is statistically cer-tain to be descendant of Charlemagne.

Okay, if there really was an Arthur – and there was because he is men-tioned in ancient chronicles – and he left a number of descendants, which is at least plausible, then we are probably all descended from Arthur. And what Morgan le Fay is looking for is a descendant who is a satisfactory Arthur figure for her. But not only is Wrangler descended from Arthur and Will Shields is descended from Arthur, but Bob Roberts is descended from Arthur and Ann Schindler is descended from Arthur, because we all are.

I was telling my wife I am what is called a free-lance. A real 'free lance' was a medieval knight who had no feudal obligations and could hire him-self out. He hired his lance and you had one more lance in your heavy cavalry charge when you hired this man. You also got whatever retainers he brought along with him. But now somebody like me is called a free-lance. I work mostly for Tor Books. Tor Books is owned by St Martin's Press. St Martin's Press is owned by the British Macmillan Corporation, which is owned by the Macmillan family, which is headed up by the Duke of something or other who is the head of the Macmillan family, so I am really a free-lance in the employ of this Duke. Things have not changed nearly as much as we would like to think that they have and I was trying to show some of that.

JJ: Well, we have really discussed this and you have answered it be-cause a number of reviewers assume that you are writing a modern type of novel wherein everything is a matter of perspective and it is supposed to be confusing, and somehow or other that is a profundity. But actually, the clues are there and you are not writing that type of novel. There might be puzzles, but the reader is supposed to figure them out.

GW: Yes. Everything may be confusing but that is how things are. It is not true that you can't get through the confusion and figure out certain things that are happening. Life seen superficially has very little pattern to it. There is a lot of confusion and so forth. That doesn't mean that you can't learn some things about it and see things in it if you are willing to look at what is going on and think about what is going on. It seems to me this is a puzzle that we are all set.

This is one of the principal things that distinguish us from the beast. I know perfectly well that animals can reason in a very limited degree. I think that animals are self-aware. I have no question that animals are self-aware. I'm talking about higher animals, not snakes and lizards and such. But I don't think animals are reflective. I don't think that animals try and make sense of things in the way that we do. The animal may be under the stars every night for all of its life, but I don't think it ever looks up at the stars and wonders what that is. I don't think that animals see anything analogous to the constellations and so forth that human beings see in the sky.

JJ: In *Free Live Free* were you pointing to inner moral freedom as the true freedom that the characters come to in a society that seems to have mysterious conspiratorial forces operating in the background of it? Or were you getting something else?

GW: I suppose in a way. One of the things that I was trying to say was that America is not free and is becoming less so. And that we have to realize it and we have to resolve within ourselves to be free and to oppose the forces that are enslaving us.

JJ: So this is really a follow on, a more mature version of *Operation Ares*?

GW: I suppose, yes. Somewhat the same concern. I tried to give the four boarders each a besetting sin. Madame Serpentina, it's pride. Candy, it's gluttony. Stubb, I forget now. Osgood Barnes, sexuality of course. Envy, envy I think is Stubbs's. And I wasn't trying to write allegory. I wasn't saying he was a personification of envy. I wanted to show men and women who were actually beset by these sins, given an opportunity to become something bigger and better than they had been by defeating the sin to some degree. Candy of course gets what she wants. She stuffs herself to the point that she can stuff herself no more, and finds that this is not really paradise, it is not heaven even though she has achieved it. Osgood Barnes comes to see sex as something more than the physical act. He comes to see the possibilities of love and sacrifice and so on. That is what I tried to do at least.

JJ: I don't want to keep you too much longer. I wanted to ask you a few questions about the Severian novels. I have tried very hard to find out, find the meaning of the word Ushas but I haven't succeeded, so would you explain. You didn't make up any words?

GW: No, but some of them are typos. Ushas is not one of them though. It is a Qabbalistic term for one of the circles of the Qabbala and I don't want to try to answer questions on the Qabbala. I never knew a great deal about it and I have forgotten most of what I knew. But to find out what it is that is the place to look. Read Qabbalic literature. I have the great disadvantage of not believing in it and so I can't get so caught up in it as Qabbalists really do. To me it was a place that I could steal ideas and names from.

I think it is a Qabbalist name for the new earth after it has been cleansed by God or some such thing, but check it out in Qabbalistic literature.

JJ: This universe that Yesod and Briah are part of: is that our universe. Or is that a universe that resurrected saints have set up in the world to come as part of the cities that they made?

GW: No. I thought of it as a long past universe. Something that we are repeating rather than something that we are.

JJ: It is a universe in which angel-like beings actually have physical control over the universal stars and suns. I noticed that you had scarabs in the great machine in Yesod. Severian goes through and sees them.

GW: Yes.

JJ: Scarabs push the suns. But that is a past world, you say.

GW: Yes, I was looking at what past universes might have been like. I began with the idea of what is going to happen to us if we just keep going the way we are going and continue to live on the continents of Earth without ever really going into the sea or going into space and we just wait for the money to run out – the do-nothing future – and thinking about what that would be like. And then I got into the idea of universal cycles. And decided that I would show that this might be a past cycle. Some physicists at least think that the Big Bang is eventually going to be followed by a Big gnaB in which the whole universe coalesces again, which will be followed by another Big Bang, sort of like a succession of universes as piston impulses in an internal combustion engine. I certainly don't have any great emotional investment in that idea, but I do think it is a useful idea to play around with. Physics is coming nearer and nearer and nearer to mysticism. It has been doing this now for over fifty years, and it seems to me that is a fascinating thing that much too little attention has been given to.

JJ: That poses something of a difficulty in terms of Christian eschatology if there is to be a time when there is a resurrection where the world comes to an end. Are you making an attempt to unify those two ideas or just to play with the idea of a 'gnostic' universe?

GW: I was toying with those ideas, I think, rather than trying to make sense of them. Is our resurrection going to be in another universal cycle? Well, yes, maybe it is. I don't know. We don't know what is really meant by the world coming to an end, and God rolling up the sky like a carpet and all that. It is all picturesque language, figurative language to try to give a general idea to an audience that would not be capable of understanding the actuality. And I am not sure we are more capable of understanding that actuality than they were. It is like the Genesis story. I don't believe in a literal 'apple' and I don't believe that literally biting into the fruit had this effect, but if you have to explain to a bunch of primitives how men differ from animals and where men went wrong in differing from animals, this is a pretty good way to do it.

JJ: Who is on trial in *The Urth of the New Sun*? Severian or Tzadkiel?

GW: Severian is really on trial. Tzadkiel is pretending to be on trial as a part of Severian's trial as I remember.

JJ: Tzadkiel means 'Righteousness of God'.

GW: He is an angel of justice.

JJ: He passes judgement there. Apheta, that would mean apheta with
an *eta* that is 'speechless'. Was that your idea? Apheta with an *epsilon*
could mean 'forgiveness'.

GW: No, it is 'speechless'. They talk by centering the sounds that you hear
so that you think that you are hearing a voice, but they are actually speechless. In a completely silent atmosphere they would be unable to speak. It
was just a physical idea that I decided to play with and it has certain philosophical resonances to it.

JJ: As if the universe of words is at one level and there is something
higher or above that?

GW: Well, the idea of selection, that we can make ourselves clear to somebody else by selecting things to which they pay attention.

JJ: Okay. Severian's sexual relationship with her. What is the purpose
of that? He is a married man so at one level he is cheating on his wife. He
gets aboard ship and immediately takes a cabin near Gunnie and the way
you have it written he thinks to himself well it has been ten years since I
have had anybody since Valeria. It seems to be one of his lapses in virtue
at that point.

GW: Yes, I was not trying to show him as being that virtuous a man.

JJ: But here you have an angelic being take him for the night. What is
going on there? Is that an idea of a celestial marriage between heaven and
earth?

GW: I think that the idea was of the higher being trying to raise the lower
being to a greater height, perhaps. And also the attraction that the lower
being at least properly should feel toward the higher being.

JJ: So we could interpret that more on a symbolic than a moral level?

GW: Oh yes, yes. Well, he is there to be morally judged but the fact that
he is acquitted doesn't mean that everything that he does or will do is
right. If that is the criteria then none of us are going to make it. None of us
are without sin, which I realize is a platitude, but it is also truth and it is
very important truth – you have a spider on you. If that is what we mean
by good people then there are no good people. What we have to mean by
good people is people who are bad but are trying at times to be good with
mixed success because that is the closest that we get.

JJ: The holy slaves, Famulimus or one of them, tells Severian that he is
the center of his race, the savior of his race. That is so Christ-like language
you can see why interpreters would say that Severian is a Christ figure.
But is there a Christ figure in the book, or is He simply for this universe?

GW: In so far as there is a Christ figure it is Severian. That doesn't mean
he has to be identified with Christ. He is in a position similar to that of
Christ. But really it is a different position because Christ really is both God
and man. Severian is not. Severian is a Christian rather than a Christ. But

he has been taken as the representative of humanity by whom humanity is to be judged. This I think is what happened perhaps with the actual human Jesus. He is as fully human as you or I and we are saved by Him, by the fact that He passed. That the corruption did not destroy Him. I think that St Paul is absolutely correct when he says that Jesus was tempted in all the ways that we are tempted. I think that Jesus was tempted to commit murder or any other sin that you want to name just as the rest of us are. And the difference is that He did not sin.

JJ: Well, it's been two hours, and so let's leave this garden to the bugs. Thank you very much.

10

Gene Wolfe Interview

Brendan Baber

Baber's interview is perhaps the most unusual in this collection as the interviewer does not discuss any of Wolfe's fiction directly. As such it provides an insight into Wolfe's general thinking about genre writing, materialist philosophy and Chicago.

BB: What is the difference between science fiction and fantasy?
GW: Plausibility, really. Science fiction is what you can make people believe; fantasy is what people have to suspend disbelief for. Many physicists believe that there will never be a faster-than-light drive – it's impossible. But you can make people believe in one, since they don't know much physics. And there are some physicists who believe it is possible. If you talk about somebody genetically engineering unicorns, it's probably fantasy, because people don't believe in it. But it's so close that you can almost touch it; we're almost at the point where we can make a unicorn.

So it's all a matter of plausibility. Do people think, 'The future might be like this?' If so, it's science fiction. If they think, 'This could never happen', that's fantasy.
BB: Magic realism?
GW: Magic realism is fantasy written by people who speak Spanish.
BB: Horror?
GW: Horror is all over the map. It's one of those umbrella things, where you can write any type of material with 'horrific' elements, call it horror and sell it as horror. Read the complete works of Stephen King, and you'll find fantasy written as horror, science fiction written as horror, horror written as horror, autobiography written as horror, and so forth.
BB: Why write books at all?
GW: The easy, cheap answer is, 'To make money.'
BB: There are better ways to make money.
GW: Yes. If you're trying to make money you shouldn't do anything as chancy and hard as writing books.

The only real answer is that you can't help it. A real writer writes for the same reason a real songbird sings. Somehow it's in them to do it, so they do it. A human singer, for that matter, who can't make a dime singing, will sing in the church choir, sing at parties and sing every chance he or she gets. They like doing it.

I like writing. It's hard work. I get tired doing it. I've been writing five pages a day, and that is a lot; it takes a lot out of me. But I can come back to it the next day and still like it.

BB: How have you contributed to or changed science fiction?

GW: Oh lord, I don't know that I have. That's the kind of thing you ought to ask John Clute, for example. I've tried to do things that seemed to me should be done and nobody had done yet. But everybody who's worth reading is trying to do exactly that.

BB: What are those things that you've tried to do?

GW: Oh for heaven's sake – I had to lead with my chin like that. I've tried to use a lot of standard scenery and props of science fiction in a new way, and I have tried to rip off a lot of rubbish we inherited from the utopian and dystopian novels.

BB: Rip off?

GW: I don't mean steal; I mean tear it off and throw it away. Utopias in the utopian novels work because everyone is good and reasonable. But everybody is never going to be good and reasonable and want utopia to work.

BB: Except on *Star Trek*.

GW: There you are. The dystopian novel is just the other side of that: everybody is lousy and rotten in all their relationships, and they're lousy and rotten to everyone they know. There are probably some people who really are that bad, but there aren't very many of them, and most rotten people are only rotten selectively. They're not lousy and rotten to their kids, or they are, but they're nice to their drinking buddies.

BB: So the goal is to make complex character? How would you describe that?

GW: I think that's what real human character is. I used to argue this with Damon Knight when we were still friends. Damon felt that you should write science fiction primarily by reading other science fiction and thinking about how the author should have done it. I felt that you should write science fiction primarily by sitting in a place like this and looking out in the street – looking at the real world and saying, 'What's going to happen, what might happen, what would happen if.'

Both approaches can produce good stories, and I honestly think that Damon was using my approach some and I used Damon's some. There were some instances where I had read a story, and I said, 'Gee, that's a great story, but what he should have done is … ' And then I sit down and write that story. Why not? And of course the other people are doing that to me. Why not? That's the way we play the game. I hit the ball over the net and they hit it back.

BB: But you're specifically interested in cross-pollination?

GW: Oh yeah – to my detriment, at times. I wrote a book called *Free Live Free*; it's a science fiction novel, a time-travel novel, and there's a private eye. People say, 'You can't do that. This is a science fiction novel! You can't have a private eye.'

So I say, 'Look, there are real private eyes. Look in the phone book.' My father used to have a business partner who was a private eye. This is a real business; it isn't just in the novels of Dashiell Hammett. As a matter of fact, Hammett was a former private eye – he was a Pinkerton.

And they say, 'Well, you can't. And there's a witch in here! You can't have a witch in a science fiction novel!'

And I say, 'Yeah, well I've had witches give me their business cards.' They're real people. They're around here. Go to the nearest occult book-store, strike up conversations with the customers. I'll bet you hit a witch within the first ten conversations. Okay, so I've got one in my story.

And they say, 'Oh, you can't do that. You're mixing genres.'

I'm not trying to write genres, I'm trying to write a book.

BB: And yet the genre of science fiction has been good to you.

GW: Oh sure. Absolutely. So what? I write a book or a story, and I write it the way I think it ought to be written. Then I say, 'Where can I sell this?'

BB: What's available to an adult, adventurous reader in science fiction? Why should they read that genre? Why should they move past realism?

GW: The adventurous reader has probably already moved past realism. I realise that sounds like a smart remark, but I mean past the kind of fiction that is called 'realism' as a literary genre, and that's what it is: a literary genre. It is archetypically the story about the college professor who is married to the other college professor.

Did you read Ursula K. LeGuin's novel, *The Dispossessed*? It was about the college professor who's married to a college professor, only science fiction, and this planet is Russia and this planet is the United States. When I read it I was so disappointed. I'd had a dozen people tell me how won-derful it was.

BB: Yeah, I heard that too. Then I read it.

GW: I've read that book before; I've read it as realism many a time. It's a John Updike kind of book. I've read that story so many times ... now I read a book until I can recognize the story, and say, 'This is what it is', and that's as far as it goes, since I have no urge to finish it. I'm long past feeling so guilty that I have to finish everything I start. I don't finish ninety per-cent of what I start.

Look, the reason someone should go past that sort of realism is that it is narrow, stultifying and ultimately false.

BB: And the fantastic genres aren't?

GW: No, not the better stuff. We're dealing with the truth of the human experience, as opposed to what we are willing to accept from other people.

BB: Wait, I don't see that distinction. The truth of experiences versus other people's experiences?

GW: That you are willing to accept.

BB: You must forgive me; I don't follow that.

GW: I mean that if you were to tell me the pivotal events of your life, as they actually occurred, I wouldn't believe you. And vice-versa.

BB: [*Laughs.*] That's a pretty radical viewpoint!

GW: I think it's the truth. Have you ever tried telling people the pivotal events of your life, as they actually occurred?

BB: Usually edited down so they'll believe it.

GW: See? See? Okay.

BB: But that's a pretty radical point.

GW: You're dumbing it down for the audience! Let's write literature in which we don't dumb it down. Let's 'smart' it up.

BB: That's a wild spin on reality …

GW: Yeah. There's a great scene in one of [Neil Gaiman's] *Sandman* books. Do you remember the Emperor of America?

BB: Emperor Norton the First.

GW: Yes. And there's a scene in one of the *Sandman* books where he and Death are walking off into the sunset, and she's wearing his hat. That's real. Yeah.

BB: So realism is dumbed-down reality?

GW: It's a dumbed-down part of reality – an acceptable part. It's mid-twentieth century upper-middle-class reality.

BB: Would you call it 'materialism'?

GW: It is materialistic, but it's not materialism. Materialism is one of those things that's so barren you can't do much with it.

There was a materialist philosophy student who used to write to me, and would argue all of this stuff. He'd get enormously mad. (Do you know Tree's Law? Sir Tree, the famous British actor, coined the law, 'Madmen write eight-page letters.') So this guy would send me these philosophical tracts, and they were full of outrageous pieces of bullshit, like, 'Everybody wants to live!'

And I would say, 'A guy jumps off an eighteen-storey building. What could he do to convince you that he wants to die?' I tried to get him to answer that question, and of course he wouldn't. He'd dodge around, and he'd get madder and madder.

So he'd say, 'A piece of paper is really just hydrogen and oxygen and six other elements, and that's all it is.'

And I said, 'I believe it's actually a piece of paper.'

And he'd say, 'No no no, it's a bunch of elements!'

So I wrote him, and said, 'Okay, but remember now, every day of your life you'll have to adopt my viewpoint to live, to go down to the store and buy a ream of paper.'

Then he said, 'We cannot get along without logic.'

Hell, half the people I know are getting along without logic! Most of 'em are doing just fine! All of the animals do it, except on a very basic level. No, the one thing that we really can't get along without is the realisation that a piece of paper is a piece of paper. If you're a mouse you've got to say, 'That's cheese. Nobody's fooling me about that. That's not chemicals, it's not gas, it's not some sort of fake cheese. I know cheese.'

That's what you've got to do to live on the animal level.

BB: Identifying things in their relationships? On a 'thing' level? Knowing what's useful, what's functional, what you need?

GW: Knowing what it is. It is paper. It is cheese.

What I realized – years after this correspondence was over – the thing that made him the way he was, was that he had never tried to take the piece of paper, and reduce it into carbon and hydrogen and whatever. If he had done that he would have learned that it was really a piece of paper, because he would have found out how resistant it was to being broken down.

Go into a laboratory, start working on it with reagents or heat or whatever, and break it down into its constituent elements. That's how you learn that the theoretical stuff is all very well, but you're going to get an awful lot of glassware dirty.

It's a thing garage mechanics know. It's the difference between them and politicians.

BB: Who's exciting in science fiction right now?

GW: You're asking the worst person in the world. Just possibly, Robert Devaroux. He's written a kind of pornographic horror novel, and a wonderful story about a divorce between two clowns. The clown story is perfect as it stands, a monument for all time. The horror novel has all sorts of stuff wrong with it, but it's the kind of stuff you get when somebody has so much talent that they get published before he really ought to be. You know what I mean? Things are going too easy for him. Sometimes that's fatal, of course, but I hope not. He has an enormous amount of talent.

BB: Who are the science fiction authors living in Chicago?

GW: Phyllis Eisenstein is here. Algis Budrys is here. He's editing his own magazine now – *Tomorrow* – and I've been told that many of the stories are Budrys writing under pseudonyms. I don't know it for a fact, but when I look at the table of contents there are a lot of names I don't recognize. Budrys was involved in the Writers of the Future Contest for years and years.

BB: So he'd have the resources.

GW: He's in contact with tons of people who won prizes in it and never made a mark since.

BB: That's too bad.

GW: In most cases it's simple justice. The stuff they were writing and sending around wasn't that good. People do that, and they do it for years. Sometimes they make a breakthrough, and they do a good deal better.

BB: You had that period, didn't you?

GW: Oh sure, absolutely – something like six years between the time I started writing and the time I sold anything. For one thing, I was sending stuff to markets where I had absolutely no chance. You know, I was sending fantasy and science fiction stories to *Atlantic Monthly*. With new writers, you're so close to the material that you can't see it for what it is.

BB: Seeing it for what it is ... that goes back to the point you were making earlier.

GW: Oh, yes, it does. You see it as hydrogen or something – floats right off the table!

BB: [*Laughs.*] Hmmm ... what do you think of Chicago? Do you like the place? Does being a writer in Chicago do anything for you?

GW: I like it as much as any city I know. I have an urge to get away from it and be a rural writer, but that's not Chicago's fault; that's something in me. *The Tribune* shines and stinks. It may be the worst thing about Chicago, but Dan Rostenkowski is a runner-up.

BB: He got re-elected, you know.

GW: Oh yes, I know he did. But Chicago has a great deal going for it. A lot. All you have to do is visit St Louis and you realize what Chicago has going for it. You know? It's paradisiacal!

We used to have the most wonderful supermarket in the world in Barrington. It was called Bockwinkles, and I'm sure you never heard of it. It was like you had stepped into a higher order of reality. It was absolutely incredible – unbelievable. They moved in a baby grand piano and had a man in evening clothes playing Christmas carols. They had a waterfall – and this is a supermarket. Everybody who worked there was good-looking.

BB: They only hired beautiful people?

GW: Yeah! Absolutely! The box-boy was handsome; the check-out girls looked like they could be models or actresses! It closed, of course. It was too good for the area it was in.

So Chicago is probably as good as it can be without going the way of Bockwinkles. You've got to have a certain amount of dirt and noise and so forth or else people are going to say, 'This is fake.' People would look at that store, and say, 'This is very high-priced', but it wasn't. It wasn't any more expensive than anyplace else. But it was too good for them to shop there.

Chicago is about as good as it can be without being so good that something in us – the thing that hates things that are extraordinarily good –

destroys it. The same thing is true of Sydney, Australia, which is a beautiful city. I can't think of another American city that compares. Seattle,
perhaps.

BB: The thing in us that destroys the exceptionally good?

GW: Sure. It's a part of original sin. It's the desire for ugliness and evil in
human beings. Who was it that said, 'Sex is only dirty if you do it right?'

BB: Woody Allen.

GW: Ah! I didn't know who said it, but it's a great line. And it embodies
that entity. I wonder what Mia Farrow has to say about that.

What are the movies worth seeing?

BB: Hmmm … I've missed most of the first-run films. I should make it
out to see them. *Schindler's List* is supposed to be very good.

GW: It's supposed to be great.

BB: *The Piano* is supposed to be very good.

GW: It's a very good romance novel done as cinema. If you're familiar
with the romance novel genre, you'll recognize all sorts of genre mechanisms in it. It's very much a genre piece of writing. But people who aren't
familiar with the genre don't recognize it.

It's like the revenge play. *Hamlet* is a revenge play, but nobody knows
revenge plays. It's a genre work.

11

Peter and the Wolfe:
Gene Wolfe in Conversation

Peter Wright

In 1993 and 1997, I had the privilege of staying with Gene and Rosemary Wolfe as their houseguest. During my second visit, Gene agreed to be interviewed. The following is a transcript of the conversation we had in the basement of his home, a red brick bungalow set, like some latterday gingerbread cottage, beneath a canopy of arching trees on a quiet suburban street in Barrington, Illinois. We sat opposite one another beneath a ceiling papered with promotional posters for a variety of science fiction and fantasy works. The air was saturated with the scent and sense of books. We took the opportunity to reflect back on Wolfe's writing to date.

PW: With a professional writing career that now spans over thirty years, what have been the high points for you as a writer? Which stories or novels do you find particularly pleasing or satisfying to you as a creative artist?

GW: That's really very difficult to say, very difficult. The obvious one, and it was a very high point, was last November 3rd [1996] when I got the Life Achievement Award from the World Fantasy Convention. It's a high point, but also sort of a low point because you know they are telling you to lie down and let the dirt be shovelled into your face. I have no intention of lying down and letting the dirt be shovelled anywhere. The more people tell me to shut up, the more I talk is what it comes down to. But I'm sure that they meant well, and so that was a high point. The publication of my first book, *Operation Ares*, was an enormous high point, and I think that it is greatly inferior to most of my work. I try to keep it from being reprinted, actually.

PW: But it was published several years after it was written, wasn't it?

GW: Three or four years after it was written, something like that.

PW: And only two years before *The Fifth Head of Cerberus*. It seems to me that it looks worse in your canon because it should have been published much earlier. Your style and techniques developed very quickly between the writing of *Operation Ares* and *The Fifth Head of Cerberus* so it appeared at a time when you were writing far better fiction.

GW: Well, that and the fact it was cut with an axe. Berkley Books had not told me that they wanted an upper limit of sixty thousand words and

I wrote them a hundred and three thousand-word novel. After it was held and held and held and never published, they came back and said, 'Well you'll have to cut it.' I cut the front of it to the best of my ability. I was cutting very meticulously, rewriting sentences, taking out words, when Don Benson at Berkley said, 'We need it right away so I'm going to cut the remaining two thirds, or three quarters of it.' And he cut it by striking paragraphs, and so it got very choppy, and at the same time the paragraphs that remained were rather slack because they were too loosely written, they were too wordy. The whole thing needed tightening up, but at that point I wasn't experienced enough to tighten it up terribly well, and it was taking me a long time to do it.

PW: But you still admit that its publication was one of the high points.

GW: Oh yes. You know, I prayed that I would live to see that book published and promised God that if he would grant me that I would not ask for it again, so I haven't – although I would like to see the books that I am working on now published, if that's all right with everybody. I would like to be around for that.

PW: After publishing *The Fifth Head of Cerberus* you won extravagant praise and several major awards, particularly for *The Book of the New Sun*.

GW: Well, yes. I was well known as a writer's writer before *The Book of the New Sun* ever started to come out, but I wasn't well known with the reading public – even the reading public that reads the sort of thing that I write. I was well known with other writers by then, though. The publication of 'The Fifth Head of Cerberus', the first story in *The Fifth Head of Cerberus*: *Three Novellas*, really did that for me. Other writers started paying a lot of attention to what I was doing, which was enormously flattering – and still is.

I wrote 'The Fifth Head of Cerberus' for the Milford Science Fiction Writers' Conference and it was too long. Damon Knight, who was the conference director, didn't feel that he should oblige everybody in the workshop to read that much. He put a notice in the middle of the story: 'You have now read the first ten thousand words and that is all that you will be required to read for the discussion. You can stop reading now if you wish.' I don't think anybody did. I think everybody read it right though to the end. That seems to me to be as good, as fine, a compliment as a writer can get.

You know, I start about a dozen books and stories for every one I finish, because I read into them far enough that I realise that this is not something that I want to spend time and effort on. There may be – there are, in fact – some books and stories that start badly and get much better as you get deeper into them. But they are very rare. Usually, you are soon aware that you are on an uphill slope, that the thing is improving. But, if you read the first ten pages, or the first twenty pages, and there is no sense that things are getting better, I usually don't have the patience to go on. I have no desire to do it.

I hate to read things that I want constantly to rewrite, because it is so distracting. I want to read things and say what a marvellous paragraph, how did he do that? And I look to see how he did it, and that's enlightening because you learn something from it. You also have a tremendous – well, tremendous is too big a word – but you have a very fine reading experience reading that paragraph. It gleams. It glistens. How did he do that, I ask? But I don't get that feeling nearly as much as I'd like to.

PW: You say you start about a dozen books and stories for every one you finish, yet you have finished over a hundred short stories and almost twenty novels, to date. That begs the inevitable – and terrible – question, where do you get your ideas – a question I was determined not to ask.

GW: Well I can talk on that as long as you want to hear it. It probably is a terrible question. The real answers are everywhere. I don't find television a fertile source of ideas, but I find almost everything else under the sun a fertile source of ideas. I get a lot of them by reading; I've gotten ideas by misreading, by misreading what's actually on the page and thinking, 'My, that looks interesting', and when I go back it's not there at all. But what I thought I saw was interesting. There are many things, people you meet, things that you see, things you remember, dreams. I've written several dream stories.

PW: Do you ever get ideas for stories from single words?

GW: Yes. Yes, I have done that. It's kind of odd because it can be a very common word but you see it new. It's almost like religious revelation, at least as far as I know anything about it. It isn't that you learn some new fact really, it's that you come to understand a deeper significance of some fact you already know. It's like a drug experience. I remember reading about some man that had taken LSD. He saw his shoes, and he realised that shoes were for feet. Now, it's a very ordinary thought, but he realised it at a much deeper level. He saw the profundity of it, and there's profundity in almost everything. If you find a word or a phrase – I don't think that there's really any difference between the two – which you suddenly see the depths to, you don't have to take the drug.

I think the difference between not using the drug and using the drug is that when you use the drug you don't seem to be able to do anything with the revelation, or you can rarely do anything with the revelation. When it happens in a normal mental state, there really is a sort of permanent change. One of the things you can do with this permanent change is to tell a story about it. It may even be the best thing that you can do, because you are trying to put a little bit of the enlightenment that you got down on paper in such a way that the reader can share it. The difference between the revelation and the written story is like the difference between the digest of a story and the story itself. It's very easy to write a digest of a story (and this is what we all have to do because people come up and say what is your new book about?) but to really understand the new story they have to read it. Sometimes they have to read it more than once, particularly if they read it rapidly and carelessly the first time.

PW: Can you think of any particular stories that have been influenced by a single word or a single phrase or a single image?

GW: A single phrase … The one that I always remember is 'When I was Ming the Merciless'. Of course, Ming was the Emperor of Mongo, the villain in *Flash Gordon*. I have no idea where that phrase flashed into my consciousness, but it did and I thought it was a very telling phrase. I wrote it down on a 3" by 5" index card, which I call 'dumb idea cards' because when I get dumb ideas I write them down on these cards and usually they go no further than that. Well, I had it for about a year and several times tried to write it as a story. I thought it was the first line, the beginning of the story: 'When I was Ming the Merciless … ' This absolutely would not work for me. I could not get anything out of it. After about a year, I realised that it wasn't the beginning of the story, it was the end of the story. When I realised it was the end of the story I just sat down and bang, bang, bang, there was the story, and it ends with the words 'and that's how things were, when I was Ming the Merciless.'

Early on I wrote a story called 'The Mountains Are Mice' and that was a misreading from a book. I thought I had read the phrase 'the mountains were mice', but that wasn't it at all. It was something much more ordinary, but it struck me as another telling phrase. So I thought, what would that mean? I decided that what it meant was that on this world the mountains were a sort of laboratory area in which things were being tried out, as you test new drugs and so forth on mice in the laboratory. I wrote this story and sent it to Fred Pohl, who at that time was the editor of *Galaxy*, and I got it back. I didn't know I was sending it to Fred Pohl. I didn't know Fred Pohl, or I knew very little about him at that time. I got it back with a rejection slip – which was how I got all my stories back in those days. I was working from an alphabetised list of science fiction markets, and the one after *Galaxy* was *If*. I didn't know that Fred was also the editor of *If*. So, I put it in an envelope and wrote a cover letter for it and sent it off. I got a nice letter back from Fred saying, 'I'm glad you let me see this again. I think that the changes have improved it and if you're willing to accept – I think it was two cents a word (it was a fairly low rate of pay) – I'll take it.' And, I took it.

But you asked about images. I had a nightmare one time in which the ending image was extremely horrible. It was a room rather like a private library that had big French windows, which were open, and the curtains were billowing in the wind. I took little scraps of that dream and wove a story from them called 'Kevin Malone'. It was about a young couple, very well bred, very well educated, with very little character, who have no money. The man has lost his job in a brokerage office because he wasn't a terribly good broker, and the woman has been disinherited by her wealthy family. They see an advertisement for a well bred, well educated, nice-looking young couple, to come and live in a mansion. They answer the ad, and it turns out that the mansion belongs to a man who is being haunted, or being possessed, by the spirit of Kevin Malone, who was a servant, I believe, a gardener or stableman, in the mansion. Malone has a tremendous desire to live as a servant in this mansion with a young couple occupying it as it was in the 1920s when Kevin Malone was killed there, or committed suicide there. The story goes on from there. As you can see, I don't remember it as well as I would like to, but I do remember that it's a wonderful story. Fortunately, all my stories are wonderful stories.

PW: Of your most recent work, which of your single novels, or stories, or series of novels, have you found to be the most satisfying, the most 'wonderful', when you saw them published?

GW: Although a great many people dislike it, probably the singly most satisfying was the novel *There Are Doors*, because that came out about as close to the way I had conceived of it as anything that I have done. I felt that I had really achieved what I set out to achieve when I started to write the novel. Patrick O'Leary says that he dislikes it bitterly, but I haven't been able to find out why. That is something that I find maddening: people who come out and say, 'Oh, this is wonderful', and you say, 'What did you like about it?' and they say, 'Oh, I don't know. It's just wonderful.' Or they come up and say, 'This stinks', and you say, 'Where do you think that it failed?' and they say, 'I don't know, but it stinks.' It's not very helpful. You don't know whether they are reacting to what is on the page, or what they expected to find on the page, and didn't find, or the colour of the binding, or the picture on the dust jacket.

PW: *There Are Doors* is quite a strange synthesis of ideas, isn't it? You have elements of Kafka's *The Castle*, the myth of Atys and Cybele, and a story of obsessive love in an alternate reality.

GW: That's fundamentally what is it, a story of obsessive love. I wanted to write a story about a man who was very ordinary and perhaps even just slightly inferior to the average person – not morally, because morally he is rather a good person – but he has very little intellect. He's not athletic, he has no great talent for anything, but he is a good employee at a department store, and that's about as good as he is ever going to get. If you want a man to sell furniture, or sell hardware, or power tools in a department store, he's fine. He will do it. He will come in every day and talk to the customers in a decent and sane fashion, sell them what they want, but there is nothing extraordinary about him. Normally, when we write stories, when we write a book, we're writing about extraordinary people, which I think is right. But I don't think that we ought to write always about extraordinary people and never about anyone else. So I took this man, whose name is Green, and had him fall in love with a goddess from an alternate universe. I asked, what would happen to this man who was desperately in love with a woman who was in fact a sort of minor divinity, which is similar to the Atys story? As I wrote it, I realised that some ancient Greek, as is so often the case, had anticipated me by two or three thousand years.

PW: Why did you synthesise it with elements from *The Castle*?

GW: Because that is a rather similar story again. K – in *The Castle* – is really trying to get to Heaven. Not so much to reach God as to reach Heaven, as to reach the glowing place were God is. And he doesn't know that's what's going on. I thought that I owed Kafka a bow in that. It was also fun. It was fun to do it. The Head of the Secret Police with the big moustache is a Kafka character that I lifted from *The Castle* and inserted into my own book. It was a way of giving Franz Kafka a little salute.

PW: There's also the implication, though, that the Goddess has visited the world of Kafka's *The Castle* and recruited the Head of the Secret Police.

GW: Oh yes. That's where she got the man. She does that.

PW: *There Are Doors* also problematises the whole notion of reality, too. Since we know from his visits to the mental clinic in his own world that Green has certain psychological problems, we can never be certain whether Green is visiting alternate realities or not. Where does that uncertainty factor, which appears in so many of your books, including *The Fifth Head of Cerberus* and *The Book of the New Sun*, come from?

GW: Well, I suppose I would have to find a root idea for all of them because, as you say, it's an idea that I go back to again and again and again. It's the unreliability of memory. The pages that I was writing yesterday were back to that again because this very blunt, down to Earth, honest sea captain has had a strange and a nightmarish experience. The narrator realises that he is in the early stages of convincing himself that it didn't really happen. We all do that to some extent. I don't know if you read about the experiment in Britain about the ghost in the graveyard?

PW: No, I didn't.

GW: The English researchers found two little villages. One village was so small that there wasn't a pub. As a result there was a nice footpath going from this village to a neighbouring village, which did have a pub. The footpath passed close to an old graveyard. The researchers arranged for people on their way to the pub to see a mysterious shrouded figure in the graveyard. Then, when they got to the pub, there were people planted there to overhear, to see if any of them talked about it, if any of them reported it. Very, very few people said they did. They had to run umpteen people through this before one of them even mentioned it to someone else, and he mentioned it only because he had been prompted by one of the experimenters. We try and censor that stuff.

The universe is far larger, far stranger, than we are ever going to be able to recognise. We live our lives mostly by deliberately disfiguring the bits we don't understand. We say, 'Well, this isn't a piece of the puzzle, at all.' Well, it is a piece of the puzzle – it's just that the puzzle is a lot more comfortable to work with when it's simple, if we push the things we don't understand to one side.

PW: So, with *There Are Doors*, you leave the reader with the option of doing that very thing. He, or she, can decide that it's all in Green's imagination, that Green is, perhaps, somehow disturbed, or else the reader can believe in the veracity of Green's experiences.

GW: The thing is, Green is 'somehow disturbed'. Just about everybody is 'somehow disturbed'. If they are not now, they will be later, or they have been earlier, or whatever. The question is: are you going to trust your eyes? Are you going to trust your senses? I had a man who was dying of cancer who used to write me letters – I'm sure he's dead now, after about the fifth letter, there weren't any more. He said, 'If only I could experience the supernatural in some way, then I would die comfortably, in peace.' I wrote back and said, 'You wouldn't, because you wouldn't be sure that it really happened. As soon as it was thought, as soon as it was experienced, you'd dismiss it.' He was talking about deer in his front yard – he lived out in the country in California – and I said, 'Suppose one of the deer spoke to you. As soon as the deer stopped speaking and ran off into the woods, you would wonder if it really happened.' You go into town, or go and get your wife, or whatever it is, and you say, the deer just spoke to me. And the villagers or your wife say, 'Where is it? Make it talk for us.' You can't do that.

James Thurber wrote a wonderful story called 'The Unicorn in the Garden.' A man goes into a garden and there's a beautiful, beautiful unicorn. And he talks to the unicorn. It doesn't talk back but it comes up to him in a friendly, horsey fashion, and he strokes its nose a little bit. They decide that they are friends and the unicorn runs off, jumps over the garden wall, and is gone. He goes back into the house and he says, 'There was a unicorn in our garden.' He tells his wife all about it. His wife, who hates him – wives in Thurber's stories always hate their husbands, and vice versa generally – and his wife calls up the booby hatch and says, 'Booby hatch? My husband has gone insane. He thinks that there's a unicorn in our garden. Come and get him and put him in the booby hatch.' So the booby hatch men come with their white suits and the big net. And they go to the man and they say, 'Do you think there's a unicorn in the garden?' And the man says, 'Don't be ridiculous. Unicorns are fantasy figures. There's no such thing as unicorns. What are you talking about?' And the wife says, 'He does! He does! He does! He thinks there's a unicorn in the garden.' And they put that net over her and they take her away.'

PW: You believe that we cut ourselves off from the extraordinary to be accepted?

GW: Absolutely.

PW: Fear of ridicule?

GW: Absolutely. I've been doing that all my life. I've gotten very good at it. I can pass as an ordinary person. In elementary school I wasn't nearly this good, and it was living hell; I was held down in the fire ants' nest by the other children. But after a while, you learn to take on a protective colouring and talk about baseball, or something like that.

PW: So, we deceive ourselves.

GW: We also like to deceive others, or at least a lot of us do.

PW: Do you think that happens at the same time? We deceive other people and we begin to believe that deception, and in so doing we deceive ourselves.

GW: I think it's part of the desire not to be seen as some strange, different kind of person. But I can't prove it. Moses can't go back to Egypt and show them the burning bush. He can't do that. It's not there any more. All he can say is, 'I saw this bush and it was on fire and an angel of the Lord spoke to me out of the bush.' And he knows it happened. At least, he's pretty sure it really happened, but he can't prove it.

PW: From where does your fascination for the subjectivity of perception, for the notion that we all live in our own discrete worlds, arise?

GW: It's simply what seems to me to be one of the things we don't think about and we should. And there are an awful lot of them. Beyond that, I think, I'm fascinated with a lot of things most people are fascinated with, but this is something most people don't seem to deal with to that degree.

PW: What are your principal concerns as a writer? What themes fascinate you most?

GW: Memory, I think, memory. The business of returning to a remembered place, that sort of thing.

PW: Why does memory fascinate you?

GW: I don't know. I think that a lot of it may be that I was an only child, and I am the only survivor of that little family. We lived a long way from the few relatives my father had. We lived in Texas, they lived in Ohio; from Texas to Ohio was much longer when I was a kid than it is now. My father's parents were divorced when he was very young. He had very little to do with his father, so his family, for practical purposes, consisted of his mother and his sister, and they lived in Ohio. My mother had been virtually rejected, cut off, from her family. She was the favourite child of a tyrannical father whom the rest of the family hated. He was the kind of man who came home drunk and beat up his wife and beat his children, except for his favourite child, Mary. And Mary was my mother. When he died, the rest of the family wanted nothing more to do with Mary because she had been the favourite. She was a strikingly beautiful woman and could have been the model for Maxfield Parish's 'The Lute Players.' Red-haired, blue eyed, marvellous profile, marvellous face, very slender because she had an ulcer. If she ate more than three of four bites of food she was in pain. When I was a child, she was frequently struggling to keep her weight up because when her weight got below about eighty pounds she started to get weak and she would try to make an effort to eat more. Anyway, my family consisted of my mother, my father, the dog and me. All the others are dead, and there is nobody else who remembers what it was like. Rosemary had two brothers, Richard and Robert – Robert is dead now, but Richard is still alive so it's not the same for her. They can get together and they can talk and share. She knows that Richard remembers those things, remembers what home was like, what their family life was like, and he knows that she does. For me there's nobody. I'm the only survivor. I'm Ishmael at the end of *Moby Dick* who quotes the line from Job: 'Only I am left to tell you.'

PW: So, really, memory for you is a form of individual validation?

GW: That's certainly a big part of it.

PW: And also an internalised fantasy, perhaps? After all there is nobody left to disagree with you?

GW: I won't argue with that.

PW: Is this what drives your interest in subjectivity, too?

GW: Yes, and the strong realisation that most people don't seem to recognise that it's *all* subjective perception. I think that God can see reality, as it is, actual, objective reality. We cannot. I know that we cannot.

PW: In many of your books and stories, there seems to be a contextualising reality somewhere beyond the evidence of the story that the reader can piece together, although the characters or the narrator cannot. The reader seems to be able to actually determine the world system that forms the basis of a particular text even though the protagonists may not be able to do so. I'm thinking particularly of *The Book of the New Sun* where Severian really doesn't understand what the Hierogrammates are acting towards and yet the reader, with careful reading and rereading, can actually work it out. Do you think that by allowing the reader to determine what is occurring at a higher level than the characters you are undermining or betraying your commitment to the subjectivity of perception?

GW: No. I think that what I'm saying to the reader is that this is how life is and if we were to think about it more than we do, we would see deeper into it than we do. We would have a better grasp of what you call 'the contextualising reality' of our own lives, of our own society. The problem is we don't look at things that we take for granted and as a result we generally don't look very deeply at the facts. The best way, I think, to get people to look more deeply into them is to show them some other reality, some other system, other kinds of lives, so that they can see into theirs to some extent.

PW: One other recurring theme that's interested me in your fiction is the manipulation of individuals by godlike beings or powers. Where does that notion derive from?

GW: I suppose it comes from the idea that we are in fact manipulated – and we all are. Some of us are willing to acknowledge God as the god-like power in our lives. Even those who are not – and probably even more those who are not willing to acknowledge that sort of thing – are manipulated, not only by God but a whole host of subsidiary powers, political, economic, and so on. We tend to think that we have free will and so on. In the mass we're very predictable. There's very little difference between traffic flowing on a highway and a liquid flowing through a pipe. They act in about the same way.

PW: You see predictability as the basis for exploitation.

GW: Certainly it is part of the basis, yes.

PW: Where does that interest in manipulation come from?

GW: Because I have to live in this world, as we all do. When we write fiction – if we're trying to do anything that's worthwhile as opposed to providing wish-fulfilment fantasies (which, frankly, most people can do for themselves pretty well) – we try and pass on what we have learned, or what we think we've learned, to others so that they go away wiser than they came in. Wiser is one of those loaded words that people get heavily criticised for using, and yet wisdom does exist. Wisdom is, to some degree, attainable, even if none of us can ever attain all of it.

PW: What are your principal artistic concerns when you conceive of a story and attempt to express these insights?

GW: I think the bedrock of it is to write good, smooth, tight prose that is visual. Visual is really the wrong word. Sensual again carries a bunch of connections that you don't really want because it is used too often with sexual connotations. You want the reader to see the world, to feel that he knows the people, to hear certain sounds, to smell certain odours, to feel the texture of rich leather upholstery or the burlap rags worn by a deformed character that I was writing about not terribly long ago.

PW: World building?

GW: World building if you want to call it that but world building has been so confused with planet building which means, what is a planet going to be like? If it has a gravitational field ten percent greater than our own, would it be habitable? How is the world going to be affected by glaciation, et cetera? That type of thing. This is an interesting little field but really is a very different sort of thing. It's something that we should get right if we're going to write about worlds other than our own, but the terrible thing is that we so often get it wrong when we are writing about the world we actually live in. There are people who seem scarcely to realise that the length of daylight isn't always twelve hours here. If you live on the equator that's pretty good, because it generally is just about twelve hours all year round. If you live in high latitudes it becomes less and less true until you get up into northern Alaska where the sun doesn't set in the summer and doesn't rise in the winter.

PW: Complex characterisation is also a major concern of yours.

GW: Character is one of the main things that has to be done. It's easy to do, as I explain in 'Balding, Avuncular Gene's Quick and Dirty Guide to Creating Memorable Characters', but so often it isn't done at all. The fact that something is easy to do doesn't mean that it's going to do itself. It does have to be done. If it's missing then you're missing a large part of the story that you're trying to tell. In a synopsis of a story, characterisation is one of the principal things that is omitted and this is why reading a synopsis, reading a digest, is so much less satisfying than reading the actual work. Character is a big part of writing because it's not just the character of people, it's the character of animals, of houses, of landscapes, what have you.

I could write a story in the first part of which the people are manning one spaceship and in the second part of which they are manning another spaceship. The spaceships would be very different places. If you think of sailors being at sea, they get their money and they leave one ship and they sign aboard another ship and these ships are very different. The captain is different; the ship is different. One ship answers well, the other does not. I'm beating this to death – I tend to beat these things to death because I think they're important and maybe if I can find enough new ways to say it will be different. A ship, without being alive in any genuine sense, without being able to speak words to characters, has its own character. When Ulysses goes from island to island, he finds that the islands are rather different.

PW: This has been a problem of a lot of science fiction. You have standard worlds that are the same wherever a character travels.

GW: Absolutely. The thing that really bothers me that we do in science fiction again and again and again – and I'm probably guilty of doing it myself – is the world in which everything is the same all over the world. No matter where you go in this world you find the same type of people living in the same type of society, dealing with the same type of flora and fauna, and weather, and it's simply not true.

PW: As you show in *The Book of the New Sun*, for example.

GW: I'd like to think so.

PW: Do you think that this meticulous treatment of character and the process of writing is what led you to be described as 'an author's author'? Do you still consider yourself as such and, if so, to what degree?

GW: Well, an author's author is an author who is read carefully by other authors, although the reading public doesn't pay much attention to him or her. I think, to some degree, it is probably still true.

PW: How would you consider yourself as a writer? Do you see yourself as an author's author or a reader's author? In 'Sun of Helioscope' in *Castle of the Otter* [now reprinted in *Castle of Days*], you call the reader 'master'. Is that truly how you feel?

GW: Of course. I try to write for the reader, absolutely, every time. Writers are all descended from Homer, who was a blind man who wandered from one great house to another to tell his stories. He told them in the Greek form of metered verse because that made them easier to remember for one thing, and also because his audiences liked it. If he succeeded in entertaining them he got bread and soup that night. If he didn't he very likely got kicked out of the great house. We are his children. I may write a book and Tor or somebody may publish it, but if nobody buys it, we're finished.

I think that one of the big mistakes that people make occurs when they are trying to write for someone other than the reader: for themselves, for the editor (usually they don't have nearly enough knowledge of who the editor is to write for that person, but they think they do), for their mothers, or whatever. All of these are wrong. You have to write for the reader, or you ought to write for the reader. I think your chances are far better of achieving what you are trying to achieve if this is the case.

The problem of writing children's books is that there are extra and unnecessary barriers set up to prevent the author from writing for the child. The author also has to write for the children's librarian, for the parent who will actually buy the book, and so on and so forth. You wish you could eliminate these middle persons and write directly to the child, the kind of thing Lewis Carroll did. He was writing for Alice Liddell and he began his story with the idea simply that he would read this story to Alice Liddell, who was a child friend of his. That's what we all ought to do, but the publishing set up is such that it's very difficult.

PW: I heard somebody recently describe *The Devil in a Forest* as a 'dangerous' children's book. How do you feel about that?

GW: I would certainly be happy if dangerous children read my book. I'm also happy when rather safe children read it. I certainly did not set out to write specifically for the dangerous child.

PW: All puns aside, I think the commentator meant that it is a dangerous book for children to read in the sense that there are moments within the novel when the evil character, Wat, is quite attractive.

GW: And that's the thing that makes him so dangerous. That's the thing that makes the Wats of this world so dangerous. If vice, to use the old fashioned term, were always a hideous monster, it would do very little harm. The problem is that vice is so often attractive. For Heaven's sake, the greatest example of this is *Treasure Island*. You like Long John Silver. He's a pirate, he's a cut-throat, but you like him, and Jim Hawkins likes him. This is the thing that everyone, including children, have to deal with: the fact that your mother's new boyfriend, who seems like such a nice, exciting person, may be taking you down a path that's going to land you in prison in another two or three years, for example. That happens a lot.

PW: The observation about *The Devil in a Forest* derives, I think, from the fact that it is not a simple-minded book, which is one of its greatest qualities. Too many modern children's books are simple-minded. The distinction between good and evil found in them is an obvious one.

GW: This is the kind of thing that my publisher tells me I ought to write: 'These guys are in white hats, these guys are in black hats.' It should be obvious that the Americans and the English are good and it's obvious that the Nazis are bad. But that's not a very difficult situation to deal with. If you know that the people on the other side are shoving little children into gas chambers, you don't have to think much about it.

The problems that most of us get into in life are that people are not wholly good, people are not wholly bad, and some of the worst ones are very attractive. You have to look at what they do as well as what they say. You have to look beyond the way they themselves look and realise what you are seeing. This might be a lovely looking reptile, but if you pick it up it will bite you and your arm will swell up and turn black. It may look like a very pretty piece of Bolivian jewellery, but it looks like that because it has evolved so that other animals don't mistake it for something harmless and leave it alone. You'd better not mistake it for something harmless either.

PW: This shades into one of the best pieces of advice you gave to a beginning writer when you said that you should always make your evil characters consider themselves to be good.

GW: Because they do, they do. Evil people don't think that they're evil people. Milton has someone saying, 'Evil, be thou my good.' Real people don't say that. Real people say, 'He was asking for it. I had to do it.'

PW: We're back to that excuse response again.

GW: Of course, of course. We all do that to some degree. Angels and devils are idealisations. In the real range of human beings, everybody arrives along the curve somewhere.

PW: The angels – if we want to call them that – in *The Urth of the New Sun*, the Hierogrammates, are of that nature. They are not simply good angels, despite appearances.

GW: They are certainly not simple good angels. If you are not wholly and totally good and pure yourself, and you're not, an angel may be a very dangerous person for you to deal with, because he is.

PW: Do you ever despair that many readers buy simplistic, unimaginative or unchallenging books?

GW: No, I don't despair. Many people read bad books. I wish that there were fewer bad books around, not including my own. But the more people read the better their taste becomes, usually. God knows I have met some horrible exceptions to that. There are people who begin by reading junk, and really like junk, and forty years later are still reading junk. But there aren't very many. They tend to go along to something better and you do need the simple stories, you do need stories for people who can't really understand what's going on unless the good guys all wear white hats and the bad guys all wear black hats.

I want to write 'The Three Little Pigs' from the standpoint of the wolf. That kind of thing. The original author sympathised entirely with the pigs. The wolf sympathises with the other wolves and their children and he says, 'Somebody is going to eat these pigs – might as well be me.'

PW: Again, you've got an 'evil' character justifying his actions.

GW: He's not an evil character, is he?

PW: No.

GW: Or is he?

PW: Well …

GW: Yeah.

PW: Well, he's just following his instincts. But the thing about fairy tales is that many of the animals found in them are anthropomorphised and they become classified as good and evil.

GW: Exactly. And it's rather unfair to the ones we generally characterise as evil.

PW: In 'Sun of Helioscope', you refer to a cultivated reader. Just how do you define that kind of reader?

GW: Oh, that's difficult. That's very difficult. Someone with some mental sophistication, I guess. Perhaps as you would define a cultivated garden, I suppose, if the garden were able to some extent at least to weed itself. It's likely to be a reader of some good education who has continued to improve his own taste and sample work that others have told him is worthy and from his own opinions of what he prefers to read.

PW: Do you write for that kind of reader?

GW: I certainly try to. I'm very conscious that reading is done in isolation. I may hope for thousands upon thousands of readers – in fact I hoped for millions, I just never got them – but each of those readers is going to be reading me alone and I'm very conscious of that.

PW: You say at one point that some of your readers are actually angry with you.

GW: Oh, sure.

PW: For what reasons?

GW: Oh, for all sorts of reasons. The one that I liked best was a little boy who was angry because the sword *Terminus Est* was destroyed in *The Sword of the Lictor*. You would think that a small boy wouldn't read that sort of book but he was a bright small boy. He said it was such a nice sword, why did you have to break it?

I got not dissimilar reactions from a chemist in the Philippines who was just terribly, terribly hurt that Shields dies at the end of *Castleview*. It came as a heavy emotional blow to him. He was to some degree angry and sorrowing. He felt that he had lost a friend. He had really associated very, very deeply with Will Shields and at the end Will Shields has to fight the Doctor who is in fact a sort of a werewolf and he's killed. And this man was devastated. So, you get those.

There used to be a man who published a very influential fanzine, a reviewzine, and he always gave me very bad reviews. The thing that he really hated about my work was that it was different from other works and it wasn't the kind of thing that he was used to reading. He really resented that. I would write him and say, 'There are thousands of books of the kind that you want, which are simple straightforward stories along story-lines that you have explored often before. The shelves in every book-store in the world are groaning under these books. There are tons of them. Why does everything have to fit that?' He wouldn't tell me, but eventually I realised that as long as there was one book that didn't fit, he felt threatened by that. Not all books were familiar comfortable things. There were these strange pseudo-books that might leap out at you and bite and suddenly make you think of things that you had never thought of before, regret a missed opportunity from thirty years ago, or whatever. He was very disturbed by that and very angry at me because I try and write that kind of book.

PW: It seems strange that anyone would object to novels that challenge both conventions and the reader.

GW: Well, it seemed to me strange at that time but I learned that it does happen and the fact that you tell people you shouldn't do this, you shouldn't feel this way, doesn't have any effect. They continue to do it and they continue to feel as they feel.

PW: I remember reading a review of *Castleview* in which the reviewer felt compelled to go away and look up every allusion and every reference within the book to gain a better understanding of it – which I think we've all done at some point. Yet, having done all that, and clearly expanded her knowledge of Arthurian myth and legend significantly, she confessed to feeling stupid, or feeling cheated, and that is something I don't understand. The book educates you, or you feel you should educate yourself to understand the book better.

GW: I don't understand why she felt cheated. Too often the reviewer dislikes the work and either is floundering around and trying to find out why, which at least is honest, or creates some reason to condemn the work that is thoroughly dishonest. I bitterly resent that when I come up against it, as I do from time to time.

A great fuss was made a while back in this country about a little children's book that was about a black rabbit and a white rabbit and they were both perfectly nice rabbits and they became friends in the course of the book. The whole thing was felt to be racist and you realise arguments like that show a determination to be displeased. You cannot write so well – I don't think you can write so well – as to please someone who sets out to be displeased, who sets out saying that I know this is going to be a bad book and a dishonest book and I hate it. No matter how good or how honest the book is, you can't ever get past that.

PW: Some of the angry letters you get, if you want to call them angry letters, are quite comforting in their way, if the reader has identified so much with the characters or fallen in love with a sword.

GW: I got a letter from a man in Georgia or Alabama, and he said that 'in "The Tale of the Boy Called Frog" [in *The Sword of the Lictor*] you are ripping off Kipling. Nobody else saw that, but I recognised that you were ripping off Kipling.' I wrote back and said that I thanked him very much, I'm glad that you saw what was going on. And he wrote back to me and said, 'never do it again'.

PW: The notion of synthesis behind that story, and others in *The Book of the New Sun*, the weaving together of different elements from myth and story, was very much a Borgesian idea. Borges' essay, 'The First Wells', suggests that, like the myth of Theseus and the legend of the Wandering Jew, Wells' early scientific romances will cease to be identified with their author and pass into a general currency of story and fable that will be drawn upon and endlessly reconstituted. I think that's an interesting notion and one expressed very well in *The Book of the New Sun*.

GW: Someone once said that the greatest honour that can befall a poet is to become anonymous in his own lifetime. You know, the poet is quoted so much that everybody has heard his work but most people don't know who wrote it.

PW: From your own career, what are the most important things you've learned about writing?

GW: The first thing is, forget yourself. What matters is the story. Many, many writers are much too concerned with how you, the reader, will perceive me, the writer. You need to toss all that out the window. You need to toss all concern for how husbands, wives, mothers, daughters, brothers, sisters, friends, et cetera, will react to the written piece. The thing no one thinks about is how hard it's going to be to get them to read it anyway. If there's something in there you don't want them to see, all that you have to do is not ask them to read the work. Don't worry about that.

Great writers are afraid of boring the reader. Beginners are afraid of shocking the reader. Stephen King is not afraid of shocking the reader, neither is Clive Barker, I guarantee you. Name any decent writer you want – they're not afraid of shocking the reader. You also have to armour yourself against the feeling of superiority that you get from publishers. Publishers tend to think first of all that they are immensely superior to their writers and secondly that their readers are dolts. Neither one is true. Publishers are people who, at the moment, happen to be in positions of power. There is no innate superiority that put them in those positions of power. You, as the writer, are also in a position of power, but have no innate superiority. Neither are you inspired. There are people who are as intelligent, if not more intelligent, than you are. Starting from a position of humility is extremely valuable. Humility does not mean saying I am not good to enough write, humility means saying I am bad enough that I must be very, very careful about the way that I write or my writing is going to be bad, too.

PW: You say that writers are in a position of power, in what sense?

GW: Well, they control the written word, they control what we read. Who said that for a country to have a great writer is to have second government? That's overstated. That's hyperbole. But there is a strong grain of truth in there. What writers write determines, to some extent, what their society thinks about things. In the immediate, in their present, they're about as colourless as anybody can get. But in the long run they're having an enormous amount of influence. This worries me: 'the hand that rocks the cradle rules the world'. Writers can't direct the government into making decisions to declare war on someone and so on and so forth but they have a lot of responsibility.

PW: Surely some publishers have, or have had, good editors working for them – Damon Knight for example?

GW: Absolutely. When I sent 'Trip, Trap' to Damon Knight I set it out in two columns, one showing how each of the characters saw things from their perspective. He couldn't reproduce it as two columns so he sent it back to me marked with the breaks that he thought would be the best places for the Earthman to speak and for the alien to speak. I spent an evening going through it and trying to improve on what he had done, and found out that I couldn't. He had gotten the whole thing right. All the breaks were right. When I got through that evening I felt that I had learned a great deal just by going over his work and seeing why it was right and why it worked to break it in those places. And why the other places where I tried to break it did not work. Then I realised that I had matured in a certain sense. I was no longer an apprentice. I was a journeyman. Of course, at that time, I was not a relatively unknown writer, you understand, I was a *very* unknown writer. Subsequently, Damon Knight wrote back and said, 'I feel as though I'd grown you from a bean', because I would continue to write stories and send them to him, and they got better as time passed.

PW: These were for the *Orbit* anthologies that Damon Knight was editing at the time?

GW: Yes. *Orbit* – or rather Damon Knight, who was making all the decisions for *Orbit* – was the first market that bought me regularly. It wasn't my first sale, it wasn't even my second sale. My second sale was 'Mountains Like Mice' to Frederick Pohl. But these were one-time things. Damon Knight bought about half the stories that I sent to him and no other market was even close to that. The others were buying at random. The percentage was so low and so occasional that you couldn't really do statistics on it.

PW: 'Trip, Trap' always seemed to me to be very much a foundation work. A lot of the essential themes that reappear in your later work – mainly subjectivity and perception – are there in 'Trip, Trap'.

GW: Probably. That's probably very true. The alien troll under the bridge, of course, is quite mad. He has marvellous powers; he's a relic of a marvellous civilisation, and he's crazy. He is the last of his race and he's gone into denial; he refuses to accept the fact that he is the last of his race and that the civilisation that his race built is finished.

PW: It's quite an ironic story then, inasmuch as the traki, the troll, remarks to the human narrator, that your race is 'without objective perception'. Yet the traki, too, has lost his objectivity. All three characters, Garth, Carson and the traki, offer the reader intensely subjective interpretations of what is occurring within the story.

GW: Yes, yes. Of course. We always see the faults we have, but we see them in others. That's what the traki is doing.

PW: In a sense, though, in its madness, the traki makes quite a sensible observation. He simply does not see the irony inherent within that observation.

GW: Yes, yes. You know the story of the man whose tyre blows out and he has to stop the car to change the tyre. There's a fence beside him, and there's an insane asylum beyond the fence. A patient is watching him change the tyre through the fence. So the man takes off the lug nuts and he puts them in the hubcap the way that you do. As he's fooling around to get something, his foot brushes the hubcap and the lug nuts fall out of it and down into a storm sewer. The man is standing there nonplussed and the patient says, 'Take a lug nut off each of the other three wheels, put them on this wheel, and you'll be able to get to a gasoline station.' The driver looks at him and the patient says, 'I'm crazy, I'm not stupid.' And he's right, he's right.

PW: Do you have a rigorous routine for writing?

GW: No, not really. Fundamentally I start writing after breakfast and finish writing sometime after lunch. That's pretty well normal for me. Occasionally I violate it, particularly on Sunday because I like to write a little on Sunday and my wife and I go to Mass and then we go to brunch. By the time we've done that it's after noon already. By the time that I start writing it may be three o'clock. I won't write very long, but I will write a little bit of something.

PW: Do you think it's important to write something each day?

GW: I think it's helpful. You need to stay focused on the story that you're trying to tell. You need to keep the project active so it isn't 'something I tried to do awhile back and put aside'. I do that constantly with projects around the house. I'm supposed to be putting in a new ceiling in the 'east wing'. I don't know how long it's been since I worked on it but it's been several years, back before Becca, my granddaughter, was born. Other jobs come up and other things come and we go away and we come back. I start a book, I read it and I'm interested in it and then I have to stop reading it because I have to read something else – somebody's novel in manuscript or galleys. I suppose we all do that sort of thing. But, if you're trying seriously to write you can't allow the story or novel that you yourself are writing to become a past project. By working a little bit every day you keep it from doing that. It remains a current project.

PW: Have you ever been working on a short story or novel and had a new idea and set the story you're working on aside, to work on that new idea? Or do you put the new idea aside and finish the story you're working on?

GW: Usually I put the new idea aside and finish the story I'm working on. Sometimes I continue to work on the same story but also work some on the new idea, particularly if one of the two things is short. I can't remember ever trying to write two books in tandem, unless they were part of a series, in which case I had the whole thing in manuscript before I started revising each volume.

PW: Do you have a routine or a procedure for writing a story once you have the initial idea? Is there a process that it goes through?

GW: What usually happens is that I hook it up with several other ideas. There are very few ideas that are strong enough to carry a story by themselves. There are some, but not many. But usually it's a good principle, to combine several ideas in the same story so that one of them doesn't have to carry the entire load. So, the first thing that really happens is for me to shake it up in my head. I think, 'That idea would go with this person', or 'I'm not writing about this person' or 'This is a nice person, though I can't use her now, but I still like her and I can pull her back out and use her again in this.'

The next thing to think about is where the story should begin and how it should be told, whether it should be a first person story or a third person story. Those things come almost automatically in most cases, if you've written enough. Occasionally you realise you've started a story in the wrong place or that the story should be third person instead of first person or something like that. But, with some writing experience, that rarely happens.

PW: So it's largely a process of synthesis, as we were talking about previously with *There Are Doors*?

GW: Yes, it's all synthesis.

PW: Before you begin a story, do you have a clear idea of where it's going to end?

GW: Yes. That idea is not always correct, but I do have a clear idea at the time that I begin. If I think of a better ending, then I use that. Often I take several ending ideas and try to use them all. If you can stack them all in the correct order, then you may be able to do more than any one of them will do. You really need to have a feeling for where a story is going in order to do the early part of the trip right.

If I were to leave this house and wander at random, literally at random, I wouldn't get very far from it. A month from now I would probably be less than a hundred miles away. You don't want a story to do that. A much more common problem is that you think you are going here, and you end up going there. You then have to go back and revise and point the story in the direction that you now know it is going to go.

PW: You see writing as very much a travelling process, then? That's what provides you with the structure?

GW: That's an obvious metaphor. And, of course, so many stories are really journey stories. It's how Galahad went out searching for the Grail or whoever and whatever. In some cases, the journey may be mental or moral or what have you. Nevertheless, it is just a journey. I recently wrote a story called 'Wolfer', to take a specific instance. It is about a woman who is recruited to free wild wolves in a national park by people who feel that there should be wild wolves in our wildernesses. In a sense, it is a journey story because she has to go and get the wolves and she has to take them to the park where they are to be freed. Then, it turns out she thinks she is going to turn them over to someone else who'll do the actual freeing, but then she has to free them herself. I knew from the beginning how the story was going to end. Before the story begins, she is already taking care of two Scotty dogs for a couple who are on vacation in Europe. At the end of the story she is going to realise that she has been taking care of God's dogs for God, and that is fundamentally the ending of it. Then I got to play around with, 'What is she going to do next?' and 'What are the two dogs who are still with her going to have to say about what happened?' And so on. I got a second ending out of that and I stacked the two endings. There is moment when she is kneeling in the snow and saying, 'It was a great pleasure, and a great honour, Lord, to look after your dogs for you, even if it was only for about a day. I'd be happy to do it again, anytime.' And then she realises that God wants something more. She has to do more than that. Then the dogs come in and they affirm or validate this additional feeling that this part of the job is done, has been prepared for.

PW: Have you ever been tempted to imitate John Fowles and provide alternative endings?

GW: Yes I have been tempted. I'm not sure that I've ever actually done it. I'm kind of uncomfortable with the idea myself. I may do it some time. I can't think of an instance when I have done. If I see two paths, I tend to go down them both, rather than saying to the reader at the end, 'Well, if we go down this one, this one is going to the carnival, and if we go down this one, this one is going to the sea.' I tend to go to the carnival *and* go to the sea.

PW: In 'The Rewards of Authorship' in *The Castle of the Otter*, you make a distinction between academics and novelists, and quite a stark distinction, and it seems to me that you have little respect for academics.

GW: I have great respect for the thing that academics are supposed to be trying to do. I think that many of them are cheats and pretenders and essentially well dressed, well paid, confidence men of one sort or another. I really dislike that because the thing that they are there to do and the thing that they should be doing is enormously important. The pretenders, the fakes, and so on, are poisoning the well. And it's a well that we desperately need.

PW: What do you conceive of as their mission? What are they supposed to be doing?

GW: In the first place they should be reading and commenting with great intelligence and insight and respect on the best English Literature available and fundamentally making it available to people who have difficulty in getting into it. And they're not doing it. I've sat in classrooms and listened to academics patronising Shakespeare. They could not – with all of Shakespeare before them to study – add one decent scene to a Shakespearian comedy, to the least of Shakespeare's comedies. They have no business patronising him.

One thing I get into with reviewers, and particularly fan reviewers, is that they are acclimated to dealing with only dead writers because the dead writers can't defend themselves. You get some of this frankly from academics, too. They say all these awful things and then they are shocked to the marrow when the writer says, 'That isn't true, it isn't there, that isn't what I was saying' and starts to argue with them. They have this deeply ingrained belief that they themselves are completely beyond criticism and I don't think they should be. I think that their writings are as legitimate an object for criticism as any other writing. If somebody can write criticism of a novel, it seems to me that somebody else can write criticism of the criticism that has been written.

I have a book on criticism written by some academic or other, and in the book the academic says that Proust never makes it clear why Swann marries Odette after he has fallen out of love with her. If you know Proust, you know that Odette was a loose woman, a woman of low moral character. She wants Swann to marry her (Swann is a very wealthy French Jew). Swann, who loves her desperately, refuses to marry her, because he knows that his family is going to virtually disown him if he marries this woman who is not only a gentile, but is also not a very nice gentile at all. And then, when he gets over his infatuation with her he does, in fact, marry her. The reason that he does this is that she has had an illegitimate child by him and he feels compelled to legitimatise his daughter, and Proust tells you all that.

Well, here's an academic writing a book about Proust and he's missed that. He didn't read those pages, or something, and he doesn't understand why Swann married Odette, which I think is … A GOOD BIT. You say, 'Oh yes, this could happen, Swann is this kind of a man; he could do this under these circumstances.' Proust is right, he got it right here. Okay, I think I'm entitled to criticise this book of criticism. Proust isn't around to defend himself and when Proust isn't around to defend himself the rest of us have a sort of obligation to defend him in a case like this, in which he is falsely accused.

PW: Whilst Proust is busy showing rather telling, the academic is complaining that he is not being told, and doesn't see the show.

GW: You get this from readers constantly. You get readers who cannot understand that a character is a liar simply because he is shown lying a lot. The writer has never said so-and-so is a liar and so it never gets through to some readers that the character is lying. They say, why is he saying that? That isn't the way it happened. Well, he's saying that because it's to his advantage. That's why.

PW: That makes me think of Severian's conversation with Valeria in *The Shadow of the Torturer*, in which Valeria enquires about a tower of pain and torment where everyone who enters dies in agony. Severian answers her question literally, and says that there is no such place, that it is a myth. Because he takes her question literally, he is correct to say that not everyone who enters the Matachin Tower does die; some are released, some are never released and go mad, but Severian's answer indicates that he speaks to his advantage. The reader is left to assume that he writes to his own advantage, too.

GW: Yes, but he's not doing it in that instance because it is to his advantage. He is doing it because she is seeing the Matachin Tower from her viewpoint, that of a prospective client. He is seeing it from his viewpoint, that of one of the torturers employed in the Matachin Tower. Chesterton says somewhere that the judge cannot see the great and terrible courtroom, the judge sees his workshop, his office.

PW: We're back to subjectivity again. Two people perceiving the same thing from different perspectives.

GW: Absolutely. But, of course, Severian does talk to his own advantage at times as well.

PW: Having said what you've said about academics, and the best kind of academics being conduits for understanding, how do you feel about the academic study of your own work? It's received some, and hopefully it will receive more.

GW: I'm rather embarrassed by a lot of it. I'm not sure I'm up to bearing the kind of scrutiny that people like you give my work. It's humbling, and I suppose none of us likes to be humbled.

PW: I don't think any of us set out to humble you.

GW: Well, I don't mean that they intend to do it, but if you're sitting around a table amusing yourself by making sketches, and someone starts picking up all the discarded sheets and saying this is great art, look at this, look at that, you feel a little strange.

PW: I can understand that. The academic criticism of science and speculative fiction in general is increasing now, particularly in Britain. The University of Liverpool has an MA programme in place, and I was wondering if you see this as a good thing, or should sf be left alone, as once it was?

GW: If I could choose, and obviously I can't, I would have it left alone. It seems to me that the danger of bad academic work is much greater than the benefit to be gained from good academic work at this time. Later, things may change. Since it is being done, all I can do to some very small extent is try and steer things a little bit so that it's good academic work. If it is good, it will do very little harm and a great deal of good, which is what we want. There is always a good deal of danger that sf criticism will go off in some other way.

So much academic work is done not because the academic in question likes or sympathises with the work but because this is what he or she is paid to do. The book gets an unsympathetic and rather superficial reading followed by condemnation that it doesn't really deserve, or at least that I don't think it deserves. It's very easy to pick up a book and say this is what the book should be doing and it isn't doing that and that's wrong. Well, maybe the author had some other idea in mind.

PW: If you had the authority to shape sf criticism, what would you do?

GW: I would get rid of the notion that all science fiction or all fantasy or all whatever you want to put in here, has to be written with reference to present social conditions, that every ship that lands on Mars has to be a metaphor for something that's going on on Earth now. It can be a metaphor, but it doesn't have to be. It can be a lot of other things, including a ship landing on Mars.

PW: I think there is perhaps an out-dated obsession for that kind of metaphorical reading in sf studies.

GW: Absolutely. And you get people who try obsessively to apply that sort of reading to everything that they read and sometimes it fits, but very often it doesn't.

PW: In connection with academic study, you show scepticism towards university and college writing courses, too. Do you believe that people can be taught to write?

GW: Yes, to some degree. They can be taught to write in the same sense that they can be taught to play the violin or to play basketball. Obviously, there has to be initial desire and motivation. There had better be some sort of talent, slant, ability, whatever, toward it. If your co-ordination is much worse than the average, you're not likely ever to become a very good violinist or a very good basketball player, although you may become a superb mathematician because that doesn't require co-ordination. But in the sense that these things are taught, then writing can be taught.

There is, though, a massive wall between teaching someone about something and teaching someone to do something. If you are teaching medieval history, then you are teaching the students about the Middle Ages. The man who had to teach a young man how to manage his horse, how to manage his shield, all the things that could be done with a lance and so on, was teaching something else. This is the kind of thing you're teaching when you're trying to help people learn to write. It's like swimming. You don't really teach people to swim, you help them learn to swim for themselves.

I think I have nothing against writing courses except that so often they are taught by those who can't do the thing themselves. It's pretty well worthless if they can't. The medieval historian does not really have to know how to use a crossbow in the sense the medieval crossbowman did, but someone who is teaching writing has to know how to at least write the kind of material that he's teaching. If he's teaching novelists and short story writers, he should be able to write novels and short stories himself. Too often, it's somebody who is already on the payroll and who doesn't have a class to teach at that hour.

PW: In your opinion, then, what is the function of a good writing class?

GW: Boy, that is really very difficult. It has to do so many different things. In the first place it has to deal with the psychological needs of the students. Many of them really need encouragement, many of them need to

be freed from moral hang-ups, convinced that it's all right to 'tell lies' on
paper if that's what you want to do, that you're not doing any harm by
lying in that way. These are not really lies. If you get into moral theology
you learn that a lie is an untruth told with the intent to deceive. Untruths
that are told without the intent to deceive are not lies. They are stories, or
jokes, or whatever. They are not morally wrong and, as far as that goes,
lies themselves are not always morally wrong, although they usually are.
So you have to deal with that end of it.

   You have show the students, or at least try to show the students, what
their own strengths are and what their own weaknesses are; how to ex-
ploit their strengths, how to improve the areas they are weak in. You need
to give them some grounding in the process of publication – the business
aspects of writing, if you will. There's a whole lot there to be done. And
you try, if you're doing a decent job, you try. With some you succeed to an
extent, and that's about the best that can be said for it. The problem is that
they become much too oriented by criticism, and by criticism I mean criticism in the street sense of it, rather than the academic sense. It's of very
little help to say this is wrong, don't do this, this is wrong, don't do that.
You have to do some of it, but you have to keep it to a minimum. The
student learns to write better not by being told that he's writing badly but
by being encouraged to write more. The beginning swimmer has to be
encouraged to swim. If you don't go to the pool today, you're not going to
learn anything more about swimming. If you do the thing right, the student wants to come to the pool. And if he can't come to the pool today,
he's unhappy because he couldn't come to the pool. That's the attitude
that you need to foster insofar as you can.

PW: Do you think that literary studies aid or hinder the novice writer?

GW: It depends on how well they're done. That's the thing. Good criticism aids, bad criticism hinders. So it's not the thing in itself that's good or
bad, it's how it's used, as is true with twenty other things. It also depends
on how students are taught to analyse texts. Are they taught to see
strengths, see what's good in this story, see why it's good, and how it's
been done, or are they taught to pick flaws? If they are taught to pick
flaws, I don't think it's helpful at all, frankly. If it is helpful at all, it is
helpful to only a very minor degree. If they are taught to see what's good,
what's strong, then that may be of genuine help provided that there isn't
– let's put it this way – such a concentration upon works of genius that
they expect genius from themselves and quit in disgust when they don't
get it. The works of genius, with very few exceptions, were not the first
works to come from the author's pen.

PW: So, as an apprentice writer you should be looking at first novels,
first short stories?

GW: No, you should be looking at short stories and novels that are not

exclusively the very best to be found. You should teach the students that there are worthwhile things in these stories even though they are not perhaps particularly memorable. Yet, there are certain things in them that are done well and they can be read with pleasure by a great many people.
PW: From your experiences as a writing instructor – you've taught at Clarion East and Clarion West and at Columbia College in Chicago – what have you learned?
GW: I've learned that it's fairly easy to tell students how to write. That is what you are doing initially: 'this is what's good, this is what's bad, you're starting the story about the middle of page three, in fact you're starting right here. Page one and two and down this far to page three are all things that you yourself had to know to begin the story but that you did not need to set down on paper for the reader', and so on, and so on. All that stuff is easy. But it's difficult to make the students, or get the students, to realise that you are right.

I told my students the Simon story. I used the name Simon because I'm sure the man's name was not Simon. Before you go to Clarion to teach, they send you the student's application story, the story that was submitted with the application, and which really, more than anything else, determines whether or not the student is admitted to the course. In other words, the people who are doing the screening, doing the sign-up, read through these stories and they say well, this person seems like he might have talent, she seems like she might have talent, so we'll accept them. So, you go through these students' stories, and you go through the applications, and I did this and Simon seemed like he should be one of the leading students in the class.

He was an American who had lived for a time in Britain. He had written several radio plays, which had been produced by the BBC. He had written a fair amount of non-fiction. This was Clarion West, by the way. Amazingly, he had gone completely through Clarion East already; he was a graduate of Clarion East, and I thought Simon was going to be one of the leading lights of the class, no question about it. And I got there, and he wasn't. He had a bad writing habit, which I will not give to you in too much detail. The habit was stopping dead and throwing in large quantities of material that were of little or no interest, and starting the story again. I knew, both because I knew that the instructors who had been at Clarion before me were competent and because the other students told me so, that he had been roundly criticised for doing this in various styles in various summaries. Instructors all have their own styles. There's the woman who says, 'Well, Simon, I really don't think this belongs where you've got it.' And there's the man who says, 'Rubbish! What are you doing here?' But they're all saying the same thing, basically. He'd been getting this from all of us, and he got it more from me. I tried to explain to him that it was pointless to tell us things about the characters that we weren't interested in. We must be interested in the character before we are interested in what sort of food this character is prone to order in restaurants. And Simon would tell you this. Now, I won't care about what the character's tastes are in cufflinks until I care about the man. Then, I may care about his taste in cufflinks.

After Simon's very last piece of writing, which had all this stuff in, I called him in one-to-one. You have to be somewhat diplomatic when you talk to people in classes, but this was not in class, this was Simon and me alone in a room. I said, 'Simon, I've been telling you not to do this all week. I know that all these other instructors – I was the last of six instructors, the final guy, the capstone – must have been telling you the same thing and yet you're doing it. Look here, look. Practically the whole of the middle of page four is this stuff. Why are you doing it?' And he said, 'Well, I think we need that.'

Now, what is difficult is to make Simon realise that this is not helping the story. It is hurting the story. It's easy to say that. What is hard is making Simon realise that it's true, that you're right, that you know. You get people who believe that readers will never understand something unless it's explained in seven different ways and on almost every page. They are certain that some people will never realise that Jane hates your stepmother unless it is said repeatedly that Jane hates your stepmother. 'Mrs Wilcox was a truly detestable person', they say, and so on and so on and so on. And this is again and again and again in the story. It's very easy to laugh at that stuff but it's not easy to make the person who writes like that realise what harm they are doing to a story by doing it.

One of the problems that you get into with beginning writers is that they write their first draft and then they look at a published story, probably the third or fourth or fifth draft of somebody who has been writing for twenty years. They're honest critics and they say, 'Gee, mine is very inferior to this.' And they're right. But this person has had far more practice and this was the final draft.

My first drafts aren't as good as my final drafts – that's why I keep redrafting, going through and seeing that I said one thing on page twenty-three and there it is again on page thirty-eight. Which of them is better, which is the better position for it? Maybe I should take the wording from twenty-three and put it over on page thirty-eight. And if that's what I decide, then that's what I do. Now we have marvellous computer-style things that enable us to do this with electronic magic. We used to do the same darn thing by cutting it out and pasting and then re-typing. The process hasn't changed; it's become a little more convenient. But you read Rudyard Kipling's advice to writers and he talks about having a brush so that you can dip the brush in India Ink and use it to line out things. That sounds like the Stone Age to us, but we're still doing the process.

PW: Until we get it right.

GW: Absolutely.

PW: Thank you.

12
Suns New, Long, and Short:
An Interview with Gene Wolfe

Lawrence Person

Wolfe's *Nightside the Long Sun* (1993), the first volume of *The Book of the Long Sun* (which continued through *Lake of the Long Sun* (1994), *Caldé of the Long Sun* (1994) and *Exodus from the Long Sun* (1996)) not only marked his return to writing multi-volume fiction but also saw him revisit the universe of *The Book of the New Sun*. In 1999, he continued the series with *The Book of the Short Sun* (*On Blue's Waters* (1999), *In Green's Jungles* (2000) and *Return to the Whorl* (2001)). Lawrence Person's interview from *Nova Express* (Fall/Winter 1998) questions Wolfe on the interrelations between the three parts of this 'solar trilogy'.

LP: I'm given to understand that there are going to be at least two more books in the *Long Sun* cycle. Is this true, and will they take place on Blue, the planet settlers reach at the end of *Exodus From the Long Sun*?

GW: Actually, I call it *The Book of the Short Sun*, and it will be three books. It takes up about 20 years from *Exodus from the Long Sun*. Most of the action takes place on Blue. Some of it takes place on Green, and some of it takes place back in the Long Sun world.

LP: In *The Book of the Long Sun*, Patera Silk is one of the most wholly good, in the sense of being truly moral, characters in recent science fiction. Do you find such characters are rare in modern science fiction, and did you find it refreshing to use him as your protagonist?

GW: Very much so. The idea of the clergyman hero was very popular back around the 1900s, and has gone completely out of style except for a few clergyman detectives. [Harry Kemelman's] Rabbi Small is the one that comes to mind immediately. G. K. Chesterton did a Catholic priest, Father Brown. But those are exceptions, and I thought to do something with that idea again. We were talking about war in my most recent panel, how easy it is and how dramatic it is. The same thing can be said about evil. A lot of people have the notion that evil is interesting and basically fun, and that good is dull and no fun, and I don't think that's true. If anything, the reverse is true, and I wanted to have a shot at proving that I was right.

LP: Even though Silk does his best to serve a religion that is in many ways a complete lie, he still does much good for the people of his manteion. Do you think that even false religions can serve salutary roles in people's lives?

GW: I think that that's obviously true, and I think that just about any religion that we care to name is going to have elements of falsehood. Jesus Christ lived 2,000 years ago. That gives us 2,000 years to attach extraneous elements onto the Christian religion, and some of them I think are false and wrong. The same thing could be said of Judaism. Moses lived, what, 1,200 BC or so? So 3,000 years or so ago. Yet you have people like Patera Silk, who are good people in bad religions, and they do a great deal of good despite the fact that many of the ideas they are serving are false. [*Pause*] I don't know it that's a satisfactory answer, but that's the best I can do.

LP: Just how do the religious values and theories Silk espouses in *Exodus from the Long Sun* accord with your own?

GW: They're generally pretty close. I've tried to avoid having Silk become a mouthpiece for ideas that are basically wrong. Obviously, Silk begins, at least, by considering Pas and Echidna and the other false gods of the Long Sun world as genuinely divine, and they are not. But his ideas of what divinity *means* of what divinity consists of, I think are fairly sound.

LP: You have literally dozens of characters in *The Book of the Long Sun*, yet many times you have scenes with a number of characters all speaking in turn without being identified, and yet their speech patterns are so clearly and cleverly differentiated that we're never confused about who's talking. Just how do you *do* that?

GW: [*Laughs.*] I'm certainly glad that you were never confused! There are two things. Obviously, you have the speech patterns. Spider does not talk like Maytera Mint. And if you understand speech patterns, you should be able to put in any statement Spider makes, certain characteristic phrases or mistakes, or whatever, that will identify him as the speaker. The other thing is, that if you're doing it right, the speech that, oh, let's say, Maytera Marble makes under a certain circumstance, is not the speech that Blood would make under that circumstance. When Maytera Marble talks, she is saying something that only Maytera Marble would say. When Blood speaks, he is saying something that only Blood would say. And so the reader, if the reader is intelligent, knows who said that from what was said.

LP: Early in your career, critics placed you both inside and outside the New Wave. How heavily did the New Wave influence your own work, and did you feel you were part of it?

GW: I don't think I was heavily influenced by the New Wave. If I was a part of it, I was only a very remote, peripheral person. I suppose the epicentre of the New Wave was J. G. Ballard, although you might dispute that, and I certainly was at a great distance from J. G. Ballard. But if I could sell a story because of that connection, I was happy to do it.

LP: Speaking of the New Wave, *The Fifth Head of Cerberus*, especially in book form, does utilise a lot of New Wave techniques, including non-linear narrative forms and unreliable narrators. Why did you feel you needed to tell those interlocked stories in that particular way?

GW: [*Pause.*] I don't really know at this point, except that they were the stories I thought to tell. I wrote the original novella 'The Fifth Head of Cerberus' to begin with. It always seems to me that if you have a narrator, if the narration is not by an all-knowing, all-seeing author, if you're going to say that this person in the story is going to tell the story, then the narrator is damn well going to be unreliable. Real people are unreliable narrators, even if they try to be reliable narrators. Ask any courtroom lawyer about examining five or six different witnesses to the same event. The five or six witnesses are all trying to tell the truth, but they have all seen different things, or in some cases think they have seen things that are not in fact there. Once I had done the original story, I wanted to do other related stories so that I could make a book, and the obvious thing seemed to be to do a prequel and a sequel, which is basically what I did. So they're non-linear, if you want to put it like that. Of course, I did do the rather tricky thing, which I suppose is New Wave, of having one of the characters in one of the other stories as the purported author of, a, aggh … .I'm sorry, I've lost the titles of my own stories.

LP: '"A Story" by John V. Marsch.'

GW: '"A Story" by John V. Marsch', yes, which is not actually written by John V. Marsch, but by the shadowchild who has *replaced* John V. Marsch. [*Laughs.*] *That's* New Wave. But belonging to a literary movement doesn't consist so much of using a certain set of techniques, as it consists in running with a certain set of people, and only to a very small degree did I run with that set of people. So as I said, I would be very peripheral as a New Wave writer.

LP: By contrast, the story in *The Book of the Long Sun*, though very complex, is told in a very straightforward and transparent narrative style. Do you think that the more complex the story, the more clear the narrative structure should be?

GW: It's almost that it has to be, or it isn't complex, it's simply confused. If you have a machine with three or four parts, you can shake them up in a box and it's still pretty clear what's there. If you have a machine with 10,000 parts and you shake them up in a box, what you have is a box of junk.

LP: I know a lot of people ask this, but is there a link between *The Book of the Long Sun* and the *Urth* cycle?

GW: Is there a connection? Oh yes, absolutely. In fact, in *The Book of the Short Sun*, we will come back to the world of Severian's childhood.

LP: A few years ago, Michael Andre Driussi published *Lexicon Urthus* about *The Book of the New Sun*. How did it make you feel that someone was writing an entire book about your work, even after you had provided a stab in that direction with *The Castle of the Otter*?

GW: Well, I was immensely flattered by it, and I've found Michael's work actually to be useful to me. I have those books (he's also done one on the *Long Sun*), and I use them for reference. This is what's called critical apparatus, and you get this when at least one person thinks what you've written is important, and I'm flattered that Michael Andre-Driussi thinks I'm important.

LP: Critics have made much of Severian as a Christ figure. Do you think that this interpretation is valid in view of the first four books?

GW: No. He is a Christian figure, which is different. He is trying to become Christ-like. He is basically what practically all of us who are men are, he is a bad man trying to be good. He makes progress as the books progress. He becomes a better person, and a larger person in a spiritual sense. But no, he is not a Christ figure. At least he never was to me.

LP: And did you feel you needed to write *The Urth of the New Sun* to make his spiritual progression clearer?

GW: No, I felt I needed to write *The Urth of the New Sun* to show what the ultimate outcome was. Really, David Hartwell said that I should put a paragraph in at the end that says 'Oh, Severian leaves Urth, and saves the sun, and everything is OK.' [*Laughs*.] And I said 'David, that's more than a paragraph.' It's really like the Acts of the Apostles, you read it to find out what happened to St Peter. Well, what happened to all these people, what happened to all these places? Did the sun in fact die? It was written to answer those questions.

LP: How heavy an influence was Jack Vance, and how much did you use *The Dying Earth* as a conscious template for *The Book of the New Sun*?

GW: It was very considerable. I did not try to write an imitation of *The Dying Earth*. I certainly took that idea from Jack Vance. I had read that years and years before and had been enormously impressed with it. So yeah, he was a very considerable influence. I'm sure that's where I got the basic idea that's behind *The Book of the New Sun*.

LP: Who are some current writers whose work you admire?

GW: I hate this question because I know I am going to leave out some people who I absolutely and positively should not leave out. Nancy Kress, Patrick O'Leary, Kathe Koja, Michael Swanick, Harlan Ellison.

LP: Let's jump back a bit. Who were some of the writers who influenced you in your youth?

GW: Vance was certainly one. G. K. Chesterton. Much earlier than either of those, L. Frank Baum and Ruth Plumly Thompson, who continued the Oz books, they certainly influenced me. The first science fiction story I ever read was by Theodore Sturgeon, and I think that was a major influence. I read *Alice in Wonderland*, and at least *tried* to be influenced by it.

Arthur Conan Doyle, H. G. Wells, Bram Stoker. I remember reading all those guys.

LP: You've won, if memory serves, two Nebulas. Yet, in a rather infamous incidence you *didn't* win a Nebula for 'The Island of Dr. Death and Other Stories', even though you had been told you had. How did this particular incident come about and what was your reaction to it?

GW: Well, superficially at least, it was a mistake by Isaac Asimov. In those days they gave the MC not only the name of the winners, but also the names of the runners-up, which he also announced. And in the case of whatever category that was, Isaac's eyes slipped over 'No Award' to the first actual name of the list, which was Gene Wolfe. In retrospect, it was kind of nice for me, since Joe Hensley told me that if I would now write 'The Death of Doctor Island', I would win on a sympathy vote. So I said 'Well, I'll try it.' [*laugh*] This guy obviously doesn't think I can write a story called 'The Death of Doctor Island', so I *will* write a story called 'The Death of Doctor Island' and we'll see. And so I did, and it won a Nebula. Of course, after that, fans kept coming up to me with new titles, until I wrote 'Island of the Death Doctor' and 'The Doctor of Death Island'. And after that I said 'I quit! I'm not going to do any more. They're confusing enough already!' The other confusing thing is I have both a story and a book called The Fifth Head of Cerberus, and my agent and I frequently get requests to reprint The Fifth Head of Cerberus that fail to make clear whether it is the book or the story they're talking about. It makes a great deal of difference because the legal situation is different as to who controls the rights, and we have to find out what it is. It's usually translation rights, someone in Norway or something. You have to find out which they want, to find out whether we can sell them to them, or whether we have to send them to Tor books.

LP: You've done some work with small presses, including Mark Ziesing and Cheap Street. How does working with a small press differ from working with a major publisher, and how vital do you think the small press is to the genre?

GW: It differs in that it's so much easier to pin down responsibility. With a major publisher, if they want to run you around in a circle, they can run you around forever. Jane says that Joe made her do it, but Joe says that Sam made him do it, and Sam says that it's company policy established by Bart, and blah blah blah blah blah blah, and what it all boils down to is 'We won't do what you want us to do.' With a small press publisher, there's an easily identifiable individual who is in charge, and if this person is saying no, you know damn well who it is who's saying no. And at least there's somebody who you can argue with and deal with and perhaps cut some kind of deal. One of the nice things about Tor is that you don't get this runaround to the extent you get from other publishers. When push comes to shove you can go to Tom Doherty and the buck stops here. He is the man. And if he tells them to do it, then by God they'll do it or lose their jobs. I think that small press publishing is the lifeblood of the genre. If we were to lose all of the small presses, which I don't think we're going to do, but if we were to do that I don't think the genre would survive indefinitely.

LP: Since you've worked at all three, which length are you most comfortable with: short fiction, stand-alone novels, or multi-volume works?

GW: I'm most comfortable with short fiction. After that, the multi-volume work. Short fiction gives something of nice size that you can deal with. The multi-volume work can give you all the room that you need. The stand-alone novel is quite tough because it has to be pretty darn long, but not *too* long, and I find it the most constricting of the bunch. To put it another way, I can write a 2,000 word short story, or I can write a 4,000 word short story. I cannot go from a 60,000 – well, I could go from a 60,000 – I couldn't go from an 80,000-word novel to a 160,000-word stand-alone novel. I would probably have something no publisher would want at that length. Come to think of it, all the books in *The Book of the Short Sun* are pushing it, so we'll see.

LP: Unless, of course, it's a big, big fantasy book, and they want the huge bugkillers for that.

GW: That may be. They want the bug crusher. I've seen some of those Robert Jordan novels. I haven't read them in their entirety, I've read pieces of them, and they are enormous novels.

LP: I for one don't have the time to read Robert Jordan. I just wonder who has.

GW: Well, you would have time if the story *seized* you sufficiently, and there are people that it does. They will devour the damn things over the space of a week and feel awful when it ends, because their book is now finished.

LP: Both the 'Sun' works feature worlds upon which multiple societies and cultures co-exist in different locales, and you have in the past criticised sf works that depict monocultured worlds and societies. Do you think it's too hard for modern science fiction writers to create multiple fictional cultures, or is it just sheer laziness on their parts?

GW: I think it's mostly laziness. Mental sloth more than anything else. We have no indication that we are ever going to get a homogenous, world-wide culture. A number of people seem to take that almost as a given, as communication becomes faster, as transportation becomes faster, everybody will speak the same language and everybody will go to the same movies and so on and so forth. I doubt it; I really, really doubt it. There is an awful lot of vitality in languages, there is an awful lot of vitality in cultures. If you look at a big city, you discover that, on various levels of society, people are talking in ways that are almost different languages already. Now, if you posit a city that would occupy, say, the eastern half of North America, which would be far bigger than anything we have, it seems to me highly likely that you would get a great deal of diversity among the neighbourhoods and social levels. If you haven't read *The Napoleon of Notting Hill* by G. K. Chesterton, you really should. It's a London in which each neighbourhood takes it upon itself to be its own little city-state with its own flag and its own sacred ceremony and so forth, and the balkanisation of London and what comes out of it.

LP: How do you go about researching a book? In particular I was wondering where you found the vast array of arcane and foreign words used in both of the Sun works.

GW: That's really tough as far as the words are concerned. I started out with the idea of not coining Tars Tarkas type names. I don't mean that I think that's something other people shouldn't do, I don't feel that way at all. But I felt in this book I am not going to do that, I don't think it's right for *this* book. What's right is using archaic names and archaic terms for things in connections in which it will be clear to the reader what is meant. Then I had to go looking for a whole bunch of them, which I did. I have the *Oxford Unabridged Dictionary* in the microtype thing that you have to read with a magnifying glass. Some book club was giving it out as a premium at one point, and I think every writer in the world joined to pick it up. I have found you can do a lot by looking up the Latin or Greek word that corresponds to something you need a word for, and then going back to unabridged dictionaries on the assumption that someone will have anglicised this term as a new word. And very often you find that somebody did indeed do that, and it crops up in the *Oxford* dictionary for a citation in the 18th century or whatever. Of course, I used the names of extinct animals, and I myself anglicised them to a certain degree. Avram Davidson did wonderful work like that, in using obsolete placenames, and he had these funny little European countries that don't actually exist, but if you look back, he's taking a place name from the third century AD, or something like that, and saying to himself: 'Suppose this place survived as an entity with that name? Here it is.' Davidson was a fine, fine writer.

LP: Who are the best editors you've worked with over the years?

GW: Oh, David Hartwell, obviously. He's been my principal editor over the years. Other than David Hartwell, Damon Knight would have to come in second. After Damon Knight, perhaps Kris Rusch.

LP: For quite a while you were the editor of *Plant Engineering* magazine. Do you think that doing so gave you any special insights into how the pace of technological change is reshaping society?

GW: Yes, I was *an* editor, actually, on the staff of *Plant Engineering* magazine. I was lucky enough to be the robot editor, so I got to work with modern, real world robotics. I actually have two diplomas from robotics schools I attended. So that was very nice. I guess I'm branching off into other things, but I also got to be the Letters to the Editor editor, which was good and fun and taught me a lot of stuff, and I was the cartoon editor. [*Laughs.*] Basically I had a *real* good job.

LP: Along those lines, is it true you invented the machine that makes Pringles potato chips?

GW: I developed it. I did not invent it. That was done by a German gentleman whose name I've forgotten for years. I developed the machine that cooks them. He had invented the basic idea, how to make the potato dough, pressing it between two forms, more or less as in a wrap-around, immersing them in hot cooking oil, and so forth and so on. And we were then called in. I was in the engineering development division, and asked to develop the mass production equipment to make these chips. And we divided the task into the dough making/dough rolling portion, which was done by Len Hooper, and the cooking portion, which was done by me, and then the pickoff and salting portion, which was done by someone else, and then the can filling/can sealing portion which was done by a man who was almost driven insane by the program because he would develop a machine, and he would have it almost ready to go, and they would say, 'Oh, instead of 300 cans a minute, make it 500 cans a minute.' And so he would have to throw out a bunch of stuff, and develop the new machine, and when he got that one about ready, they'd say 'Make it 700 cans a minute.' And they almost put him in a mental hospital. He took his job very seriously and he just about flipped out.

LP: I work for a semiconductor equipment manufacturing company as a technical writer, so I deal with the engineers who are building the machines that are building computer chips, so that story sounds fairly familiar to me.

GW: I like and admire technical writers, if they're good. When I was an editor, they were the people I was buying the articles from, very largely when I didn't write them myself. It's a greatly underrated skill.

LP: And a reasonably well paying one in modern society.

GW: I'm glad to hear it.

LP: This year you're up for a Hugo for 'No Planets Strike', which might be summarised as 'talking animals in the Holy Manger on another planet'.

GW: Yes.

LP: What gave you the idea to write that?

GW: I have to think for a moment. I was reading a book on clowns, and I came across this quotation from Shakespeare about the sacredness of Christmas Eve, and how fairies have no power to wound, no planets strike, meaning this is a reference to astrology, where Saturn and things like that are the evildoers. Saturn enters your astrological house and you have all sorts of troubles, etc. And I thought [*laughs*] well, isn't that interesting. Shakespeare felt the aliens could not attack on Christmas Eve. And that cooked in my brain for a while, and somehow I mixed it up with the legend that animals could speak on Christmas Eve. And in fact, until I went back and looked at the Shakespeare quote again, I thought that was in there. But there is this legend that at midnight on Christmas Eve, the animals in the barn or wherever discuss in human voices the birth of the Christ child. And that seemed like something I could work with. So I worked out real talking animals, and had them be clowns, because I had been reading about clowns, and a reason for them not to speak most of the time, and then a reason for them to speak on Christmas Eve, and so on. And I came up with a story I really like, and am very happy with. At this point I don't know whether it's going to win the Hugo, but I sure hope it does. That would be great if it did. I've never won a Hugo. I've won three World Fantasy Awards, and two Nebulas, and a lot of other awards: the British Science Fiction Award, the British Fantasy Award, the Prix Apollo, which is the French award, and so forth, but I've never won a Hugo and I'd like to. [*Original Editor's Note: This was not to be, as Mike Resnick's 'The 43 Antarean Dynasties' won the Hugo for Best Short Story.*]

LP: Just as long as they don't announce you and go 'Sorry, no award!' That would be a bummer.

GW: Yeah! Well, I wish Isaac Asimov were back to do it. But I don't think they do 'No Award' in the Hugos, which I think is a good idea.

LP: Well they do, but you have to beat out all the other nominees, which is almost an impossibility under the Australian Rules Ballot. You've often talked about Homer as both an influence and a fountainhead for the storytelling tradition. Do you think there's insufficient appreciation of Homer and other classical authors in the modern world?

GW: Oh yes, absolutely. Classical studies are something we have, by and large, dropped. That means we have put behind us an awful lot of good stuff. We are becoming less able to understand our own culture. We have this assumption in science fiction, I think, and in ordinary life, that people somehow understand their culture. You know, the man from the spaceship lands, and runs into a farmer with tentacles, and the farmer could explain everything about how his society works. That ain't necessarily the truth. Our society has been evolving at least since ancient Greece. You could make a pretty good case for the idea that western civilisation began with the ancient Greeks. And the people who would object to that would not say that it began later, they would say that it began sooner. And it has gone so far and gathered so much momentum that we are losing sight of its roots. There's an oriental gentleman over there whose roots are probable Japanese or Chinese, but he is wearing western clothing, and I'm virtually certain he's speaking English. We need to know where all these things came from. The business suit; we talk about suits for management and so forth, the business suit was originally the hunting costume for a squire. And we know a little but more about how that started.

LP: Final question! Homer, of course, is one of those writers whose work is remembered, at least in his case, thousands of years after his death. How well do you think your own work will be remembered?

GW: Oh Lord! [*Long pause.*] Goodness sake. [*Pause.*] This is really, *really* a mean question that you're asking.

LP: [*Laughs.*] That's why we put it last.

GW: Well I'm glad you did. Uh, I don't know. Two or three hundred years possibly. It's very hard to answer that without being either falsely modest or braggadocios. I would guess, a couple, three hundred years. That's only a guess.

LP: And how do you think you'll be remembered? As a science fiction writer? As a writer? As a late 20th century American writer?

GW: As a late 20th century American writer probably more than anything else. I doubt science fiction as a concept will be still around in 300 years from now. But they will have a number of other concepts, a number of other genres that grew out of what we now call science fiction. They will have forgotten very largely that there was this thing called science fiction, and what they are really dealing with is sprouts put out by this thing. Ancient writers had no such thing as fantasy. They wrote what we now call fantasy, but they didn't know it was fantasy, and they didn't consider it a genre. The genre Homer worked in was the epic poem, something we've pretty well dropped.

13

A Magus of Many Suns:
An Interview with Gene Wolfe

Nick Gevers

In 2001, Wolfe completed *The Book of the Short Sun*. Three new anthologies, *Strange Travelers* (1999), *Innocents Aboard: New Fantasy Stories* (2004) and *Starwater Strains* (2005) collected the best – and the majority – of Wolfe's recent fiction. In 2004, he published *The Knight*, the first volume of a two-novel fantasy, *The Wizard Knight*. In the following interview, a somewhat inscrutable Wolfe discusses – to borrow Nick Gevers' phase – the 'Briah Cycle'.

When I interviewed Gene Wolfe by e-mail in January 2002, I came to the conversation aware that Wolfe the person is not unlike his books: genial (of course), accommodating, plain-spoken at times to a surprising degree; and yet a magician, a poser of paradoxes that, however simple on the surface, are in fact like the Labyrinth at Knossos, the mazes so many of his characters tread, as enormously involved and logically convoluted as reality itself. One cannot expect direct answers, at least about his books: they will speak for themselves, or not at all, and any candour is deceiving. But on certain practical topics (publishing, possibly engineering problems), all is clarity. For allowing me to be the latest interviewer errant to tilt at the windmills of his mind, a tourney of much fascination, I am very grateful to Mr Wolfe.

NG: With *The Book of the Short Sun* complete, and new, unrelated projects such as the fantasy epic *The Wizard Knight* underway, have you finished with the Urth/Whorl fictional universe? Or do you contemplate further novels – or short stories – set there?

GW: In brief, no. At this point I have nothing planned beyond completing *The Wizard Knight*. Frankly, there is no point in planning that far in advance. I'll start planning when the end is a month or two away.

NG: You've previously commented at length on the creative genesis of *The Book of the New Sun* – its growth from novella into novel into trilogy into tetralogy. Did *The Book of the Long Sun* also burgeon, from a single-volume novel into a multi-decker one? And how, in its turn, did *The Book of the Short Sun* evolve?

GW: No, *The Book of the Long Sun* was planned as a multivolume work –

three or four. It turned out four. *The Book of the Short Sun* was always intended as three books, one for each planet.

NG: You've remarked before that, in contrast with the baroque first-person narrative of *New Sun*, you shifted to a more transparent, or in your own term journalistic, style for *Long Sun*. Yet *Long Sun* has its fair share of wonderfully eloquent prose – in many of its descriptive passages, in the speech of quite a few of the clergy, and so forth. How, precisely, does it seem to you that your style has changed since, say, the late seventies?

GW: My style hasn't changed at all. I write in a voice appropriate to the story I have to tell, that's all. I may be doing it a bit better now, or a bit worse; but that's always been the idea.

NG: Speaking currently, then: you're noted for the versatility of your prose style: you can write with deceptively simple minimalism, or in a folksy, expansive way, or in a rich, mythic register. Which mode do you like to use best, and which do you find most demanding?

GW: There really aren't any answers. I use the style suited to the story. If it's the right style for the story, I like it. If it isn't, I change it. A style becomes difficult when it is not suited to what is being said.

NG: Your command of dialogue is outstanding, and never so much as in *Long Sun* – in your dialogue-intensive text, so many of your characters are *defined* by how they speak. As examples of your technique here, how did you fashion the priests Pateras Remora and Incus, and their idiosyncratic modes of speech?

GW: I can't tell you a lot. I listen to people, what they actually say as well as what they mean, and how they say it. Both Patera Remora and Patera Incus speak as slight exaggerations of people I've met. Very few people really talk alike. Both my daughters were raised by my wife, so it would be reasonable to suppose that all three would speak pretty much alike. They don't. Their characteristic modes of expression are quite different.

Of course all of us speak differently to different audiences. Auk [a criminal turned messiah] talks like I do when I'm talking to the dogs. Almost no one seems to notice how Oreb [the night chough, a talking bird] talks, but Oreb can manage only two syllables: 'Good bird! Watch out! Bad boy. Iron girl. Good Silk!'

NG: Running right through the Long Sun/Short Sun sequence – seven volumes! – a fascinating relationship between your major characters, Silk and Horn, develops: that of teacher and pupil, original and mimic, subject and narrator, and ultimately, an overlapping of identities. When you began to trace these bonds (in the first scene of *Nightside the Long Sun*), were you yet anticipating quite how important and sustained they would become?

GW: No, I had no idea. For about half the first draft, I didn't know who was writing *The Book of the Long Sun*, and considered various characters –

Maytera Marble, for example. I finally settled on Horn, and did the re-writes with that in mind. I did not plan to write *Short Sun* until *Exodus From the Long Sun* was accepted. I anticipated a big fight with [editor at Tor Books] David Hartwell over the ending; if that had happened there would have been no *Short Sun*. To my pleased surprise, he loved the ending.

NG: If David Hartwell *had* disliked the ending of *Exodus From the Long Sun*, would you have tried to wrap up the entire Whorl sequence in *Exodus*? Would that have been possible, without leaving too many loose ends?

GW: To begin with, if David Hartwell had disliked the ending I would have argued a lot. After that – I don't know. It would depend in part on just what he disliked and why he didn't like it.

NG: The scriptures employed by the augurs of the *Whorl* – the Chrasmologic Writings – of what are these meant to consist? Are they a melange of Biblical and classical quotations (for example, from Marcus Aurelius), plus later accretions, or are they more definitely structured than that?

GW: A melange, as you say. Typhon [the tyrannical builder and chief 'god' of the *Whorl*] has told some secretary to put together a sacred book that will leave him plenty of elbow room. The book is sacred to Silk, not to me.

NG: Is *Long Sun* a political novel? Does the revolution in Viron follow a course you would practically sanction, the coercion of corrupt, unprin-cipled leaders into obedience to an original Constitution, and thus to the will of God and the People?

GW: Yes, and yes. When the people rebel against a bad government (try to think of a revolution that unseated a good one) they need a unifying principle. For America in the Eighteenth Century, it was no taxation with-out representation. For the French, Liberty, Equality, and Fraternity. For Viron [the city state where *Long Sun* is set] it was the Charter.

NG: What does the female-dominated state of Trivigaunte represent, the-matically speaking? The ability of people (here women), notwithstanding apparent disadvantages, to achieve anything they wish? The dystopian character of any lop-sidedly dogmatic (in this instance feminist) system? Or both?

GW: I don't see Trivigaunte as a dystopia. I wanted to show that in a female state women will act pretty much like men. See Margaret Thatcher, for example. Or Catherine the Great. France once had a general who was a girl in her teens. She was a good general, too, but it was still war.

NG: When I began reading *Short Sun*, I, like many others, was struck by the new work's resonance of location with earlier novels [*The Fifth Head of Cerberus; New Sun*]. Twin worlds, with respective blue and green associa-tions: St Croix/St Anne; Urth/Lune; Blue/Green. Not that these are liter-ally the same planets; but why this repeated pattern? (I should add that

Joan Gordon, and I myself, have speculated on an allusion in *Short Sun* to Kim Stanley Robinson's colour-sequenced Mars novels ...)

GW: At the time I first brought in Blue and Green, I didn't know about Stan's books. Nothing of that kind was intended.

NG: [*Trying again.*] Can your readers usefully view *The Fifth Head of Cerberus* as being set in the same science-fictional universe as *New Sun*, *Long Sun*, and *Short Sun*? Why does *Fifth Head*'s pattern of blue/green sister worlds recur so tantalisingly in Urth/Lune, Blue/Green?

GW: I don't know.

NG: Are the Neighbors, the indigenous, now largely departed, inhabitants of Blue, identifiable as Hierodules [the manipulative 'Holy Slaves' in *New Sun*]? Or at least as conscious co-participants with the Hierodules and Hierogrammates in the (Divinely ordained) reshaping of humankind?

GW: No, the Neighbors are certainly not Hierodules. Nor are they cooperating with them.

NG: [*This is where an interviewer grows a little desperate. I go for broke, with direct, literal questions regarding major textual enigmas in* The Book of the Short Sun.] Is Pig a godling?

GW: Certainly. There are telltale signs all through the book.

NG: [*Hooray! But* ...] Are the Cumaean and/or Merryn inhumi? Possibly, or definitely?

GW: No. The Cumaean is an alien but not an inhuma. Merryn is a human being.

NG: [*All right. But many uncertainties remain* ...] After the action of *Short Sun* closes, does Silk/Horn take an active part, via astral projection, in the events in *New Sun*? Specifically, as the 'ghost' of Master Malrubius?

GW: Yes, but not a leading part.

NG: [*Hmmm* ...] The narrative structure of *Short Sun* is extraordinarily complex, a very involved interweaving of past and present events, with some uncertainty as to the narrators' precise identities. Why did you choose this approach, and how difficult was it to execute?

GW: This is one of those questions that are almost too simple to answer. I chose to do it because that was what I had to do to tell the story. Okay, I could have done everything in third person, but it would have been dead there on the page. The chief difficulty was balancing the stories – not letting one storyline run away with the book.

NG: A more specific question about narrative technique and agency: a large part of *Return to the Whorl* is an account of Horn's (or Silk's) experiences back on the *Whorl*, written in the third person, not by Horn/Silk, but by Horn's two younger sons and his daughters-in-law. How reliable is their reconstruction of events? On page 366 of *On Blue's Waters*, Horn states clearly that Quadrifons was a god he encountered and spoke to; the four make Quadrifons simply a figure referred to or invoked, almost as if they're deferring to Q's dislike of publicity. The godling in the four's chapters seems physically impossible, far too large for the *Whorl*'s gravity field. Have Hoof, Hide, Daisy, and Vadsig got major details wrong, deliberately, or out of ignorance?

GW: Daisy is the principal writer of the storyline back on the *Whorl*. She is basing what she writes on the others' accounts of their conversations with Horn/Silk. She has done her best to string the incidents together and make everything plausible. She has deliberately falsified nothing. As for the size of the godling, he is far too large if he is structured along familiar lines, but who said he was? As an aside, I am always suspicious of arbitrary limits put on living organisms. When I was young, we were repeatedly told that a condor was about as big as a bird could be and still fly. Then scientists dug up an extinct pterosaur as big as a light plane.

NG: Speaking as an engineer, how might the godling be constructed so as to walk as a giant on land, where the undines [submarine giantesses] cannot?

GW: There are a number of ways you could go. First, get rid of the notion that the godling is going to be proportioned like a human being. Changes in size always mean changes in build. (Dr Crane touches on that.) A man fifty feet tall, proportioned like you or me, would sink into the ground a lot – had you thought of that? Take a look at the really big dinosaurs. Bone density could be increased, and the legs and pelvis made more massive, and so on. The problem is a lot like the problem of making a really huge building of concrete or cut stone. If you don't watch out, the weight of the walls crushes the stones at the bottom. You fix that by making the lower walls very thick, and by using stone with a lot of compressive strength.

The undines are proportioned like normal women – as long as they stay in the water, there's no problem with that.

NG: [*Going back to a larger issue.*] Does Horn/Silk actually encounter the god Quadrifons, in some fashion that Daisy cannot report for want of information?

GW: I'm not certain.

NG: The Secret of the Inhumi is a complex matter, relating to how they breed, how they acquire intelligence, how humans interact with them. Apart from obvious precautions the humans of Blue and Green can take against inhumi attack – safeguarding the elderly and very young, maintaining a vigilant outlook, becoming less sinful – how is the Secret to be applied? Could bilocation [astral travel in dreams] be employed, to facilitate direct attacks on inhumi breeding areas?

GW: If human beings did not prey on one another, the inhumi could not prey on us. That's all. It isn't complicated, and I thought that everyone would get it. Maybe the thought of human beings not preying on their own kind is just too foreign.

NG: Why did you choose in *Short Sun* to have your characters cross over into the milieu of *New Sun*? In particular, do the meetings of Horn/Silk and Severian have a decisive impact on the destinies of both?

GW: Because the books would have been lame if they had not. Once you see that Pas is or was Typhon, and know the Rajan can travel by astral projection, he's *got* to do that. There's a wonderful bit in the Roger Rabbit movie nobody seems to get. Roger goes around with handcuffs on his wrists for half an hour. Then he pulls one hand out of the cuffs and does something with it, and sticks it back in. Bob says, 'You mean to tell me you could get out of those whenever you wanted to?' And Roger says, 'No, only when it's funny.' That is a profound expression of the law that governs all writers and performers. The audience doesn't have to think about that, but writers are bound by it. If there's a gun on the wall in Act I, it must be fired before the end of the play. Etc.

NG: Your output of short stories has become quite prolific again in recent years. How, typically, do you construct these precisely-honed tales, with their wealth of subtle clues – how, for example, did you put 'In Glory Like Their Star' together? And: is another collection in prospect?

GW: Thanks. Thank you! I really can't tell you a lot. I have one or more ideas, and an ending – a space ship takes off, and the blast fries someone who's been waiting outside. Who was that? What was he waiting for, and why did the ship take off? Did the pilot know he was out there? When I had answered those questions, I could write the story, and I did.

No new collection is on the way, I'm afraid. I've got an awful lot of uncollected material to put into one, sometime.

NG: You're very good at parody, as witness recent stories like 'The Walking Sticks' and 'A Traveler in Desert Lands'. How deep does this parodic streak of yours run? Many of the stories in *Strange Travelers* appear to be homages on some level, some obvious (Borges in 'Useful Phrases') but others more fugitively so (John Crowley in 'The Haunted Boardinghouse', M. R. James in 'One-Two-Three For Me') ...

GW: I'm amazed that you saw M. R. James in 'One-Two-Three For Me.' You're very perceptive. [Actually, this was pointed out by somebody else, whose name presently escapes me – *NG*] I'd say that the depth of my parodic streak is about five and half feet.

NG: Your current work, *The Wizard Knight*, is rumored to be a big High Fantasy novel. Can you say something about the conception and writing of this book, and the likely time and format (several volumes?) of its publication?

GW: It is a big fantasy novel. I'm not sure I would call it high fantasy. Let's get real – I don't know that it will sell. Nobody's seen it, and that includes me because it doesn't exist in final form. I'm hoping for two big, thick books. I'll settle for what I can get.

NG: More generally, now: who are your favourite contemporary sf and fantasy writers? Are there any authors you see as your conscious disciples?

GW: No disciples that I'm aware of. For the rest – I hate the question. I always leave somebody out. Neil Gaiman. Harlan Ellison. Kathe Koja. Patrick O'Leary. Kelly Link.

NG: And the wider, the 'real world'? You had corrective laser surgery on your eyes recently, and the state of America apparently worries you …

GW: My doctor says I'm not going to go blind. I pray to God he's right. America is in trouble (as it always is). The chief problem is that it is ruled by an elite that is out of touch with the mass of the governed. It's a fairly recent problem, and will be fixed in one way or another. America is still the greatest nation on Earth.

14

Some Moments with the Magus:
An Interview with Gene Wolfe

Nick Gevers, Michael Andre-Driussi and James B. Jordan

In this final interview, which predates *The Wizard* (2004), Wolfe is, perhaps, at his most enigmatic. His occasionally terse responses should remind any critic or commentator that he or she is in the presence of a writer every bit as unreliable as his narrators.

The following interview was conducted with Gene Wolfe by e-mail between August and October of 2003. Henceforward, Wolfe is GW, Michael Andre-Driussi is MD, James B. Jordan is JJ, and Nick Gevers is NG.

MD: Read any good books lately?
GW: Yes. *Adventures Among Books*, by Andrew Lang; *Being Gardner Dozois*, by Michael Swanwick; and *The New Wave Fabulists*, edited by Peter Straub.
MD: What would you do with NASA?
GW: What would I do with NASA? Obviously that would depend on how much money I had to work with. But basically I'd put more effort into spaceboat development and less into flying missions of dubious worth. NASA has suffered two disastrous crashes, the *Challenger* and the sainted *Columbia*. Both were vehicle failures. It needs a better boat.
MD: What conventions are you planning to attend? Would you go to one overseas?
GW: The only convention on my schedule now is Windycon. That's quite near here, in November. I wouldn't attend an overseas con, or any distant con. Rosemary isn't up to travelling, and I'm not about to go away and leave her here alone.
MD: Tell us about your dogs.
GW: We only have one dog now. Calamity Jane had to be put down. She was very old, and her medicine no longer controlled her seizures. Dilly is five now, I think. He's a neutered American Pit Bull Terrier, very gentle, about the colour of buckskin.
MD: What are your thoughts on the US military actions going on around the world (Afghanistan, Iraq, Liberia)?
GW: The US military is already spread too thin. Sending American troops into Liberia was not only foolish but foolhardy.
MD: In the last few years world events have brought a new urgency to a

few stories that you wrote in the 1970s: 'The Blue Mouse' [1971, collected in *Gene Wolfe's Book of Days*]; 'Hour of Trust' [1973, collected in *The Island of Doctor Death and Other Stories and Other Stories*]; and 'Seven American Nights' [1978, also collected in *IODDAOSAOS*]. 'The Blue Mouse' is, in part, about the willingness to fight in murky, international conflicts; 'Hour of Trust' involves the same, but adds suicide bombers; 'Seven American Nights' is set in a fallen America that could well be a result of the conflict in 'Hour of Trust.' 'Hour of Trust' is the most haunting: it shows not only suicide bombers, but also their recruitment from an incoherent mass of variously disaffected people, and how they are used as tools for a coherent policy of terror; it shows a schism between Europe and the US; it shows the power of amateur video being broadcast. These stories were all written before the hostages were taken in Iran (1980), another moment which seems a part of the same picture. What inspired 'Hour of Trust' in particular, and do you think that this 30-year-old nightmare is unfolding today in the post-September 11 world?

GW: 'Hour of Trust' was inspired by a Damon Runyon story, 'A Light in France'. It's basically an early WWII story, written when most people expected that world war to be much like the first one. (We tend to forget that the first and second world wars were only about twenty-five years apart. We are losing the last WWII veterans; when Hitler's army marched into France, there were still a whole lot of WWI vets around, including Hitler.) Anyway, I read 'A Light in France' and started playing with the idea in an SF setting.

I think you're the only person who has ever asked me about that story, Michael.

MD: You've had several stories published online – how do you like it? Is the technology up to speed, really 'consumer-ready'? Is there a stigma or barrier about online publications with regards to reviews and award considerations, or does it seem like it is equal with print sources?

GW: Online publication is fine with me, in part because I hope to collect those stories later. Whether the medium is ready for consumers is better judged by those consumers. I sometimes read online – but not often. The stigma is attached to pay scales. Much online publication is no pay or small pay.

NG: Is ambiguity a necessary property of your work? Does the richness of a Gene Wolfe novel or story depend, to some extent, on its simultaneous stimulation of multiple interpretations in the reader's head, so that thematic closure is never attainable?

GW: Ambiguity is necessary in some of my stories, not in all. In those, it certainly contributes to the richness of the story. I doubt that thematic closure is never attainable.

NG: A number of your readers have speculated on how your Korean War experience has fed into your writing. Certainly the events of 1950–1953 seem to find resonance in the war of Severian's Commonwealth against the Ascians, and in the war of Blanko against Soldo in *In Green's Jungles*. Your comments?

GW: My whole life experience feeds into my writing. I think that must be true for every writer. Clearly the Army and combat were major influences; just the same, you need to understand that many of the writers we have now couldn't load a revolver. I've crossed the Atlantic and the Pacific on ships. I've crewed on a sailboat. I've ridden a lot of horses and one camel – his name was Tank – and we loped across the Australian desert. I've flown in a light plane and a helicopter. (As a passenger. I'm not a pilot.) I've boxed, though not professionally. And so on and so forth.

NG: An interesting distinction between the *New Sun* and *Long Sun* novels relates to the directness of divine presence or intervention. Severian learns the will of the Increate via intermediary beings – Hierodules, Hierogrammates – while Silk appears to communicate directly with the Outsider, as his people term God or the Increate. Is Silk more intrinsically holy than Severian?

GW: I don't think anyone is more intrinsically holy. People experience God in many ways; and it seems to me that God does what the rest of us do: he chooses the means that best gets his message across. He's not rewarding us by talking to us. He's talking to us because He has something to say to us directly, as opposed to the things He says to all humanity.

NG: At the recent Readercon, many observers were impressed by your impromptu rendering of the inner nature of a 'bad man'. In your view, does evil genuinely, consciously, exist? Can you perhaps expand on the points you were making at Readercon?

GW: You seem to think that the only genuine existence evil can have is conscious existence – that no one is evil unless he admits it to himself. I disagree.

NG: Although the *Latro* novels have no declared connection with the *New Sun/Long Sun/Short Sun* sequence, the gods of Latro's Hellenic world do recur to some extent in the *Long Sun* and *Short Sun* books, the same pagan archetypes acquiring far future flesh as prevailed before Christianity. Pas is Zeus, or aspires to be, etc. Is this recurrence simply a reflection of inevitable similarities between pagan pantheons, or is a more literal, material, continuity of 'divine' pagan personae involved? Is Pas Zeus indeed?

GW: Pas is certainly not Zeus. (No doubt he would like to be.) The classical gods are, in general, not as people today imagine them. Ares is the soldier god, not the war god, for example. Aphrodite is the sex goddess, not the love goddess; the love god is Eros, her son.

NG: There's a lot of uncertainty as to how the twelve *New Sun/Long Sun/*

Short Sun volumes should collectively be titled. Would *The Briah Cycle* be an acceptable overall moniker?

GW: *The Briah Cycle* seems to me to be as good a label as anyone is apt to find.

JJ: Angel-like creatures interact with Severian; the Outsider grants direct illumination to Silk; the Narrator of the *Short Sun* books is applying Silk's life in multiple ways. This looks like an extended 'spin' on the Old Testament, the New Testament, and the Church afterwards. There are numerous parallels between Jesus and Silk, and after Silk's burial and 'resurrection' we find in *Exodus From the Long Sun* long sections of 'evangelism' for the 'message of Silk,' finishing with a fiery apocalypse – all of which looks like the Gospels, the *Book of Acts*, and the Apocalypse. Did you have this kind of overall scheme in mind, either at the very beginning or when you came to write *Long Sun* and *Short Sun*? And if not, do you think it is a useful way to think about these works?

GW: No, the Biblical parallel had never occurred to me. I think it may well be a useful way to look at those books, however.

JJ: J. K. Rowling is writing fairly sophisticated stories for young people in her 'Harry Potter' series, reflecting her attachment to C. S. Lewis. Have you read these? Do you have any comments on their literary quality and general worth?

GW: I have read only the first 'Harry Potter' book. I thought it excellent, perhaps the best thing written for older children since *The Hobbit*. I wish the books had been around when my kids were the right age for them.

JJ: Could you tell us about your and Rosemary's general health these days?

GW: Rosemary is diabetic and has difficulty walking any great distance. Stairs are very hard for her. I have glaucoma. We're well otherwise.

JJ: What things inspired you to move into writing the 'Wizard Knight' books? Was this a long-time desire, or were you jogged into doing it by one thing or another, as thinking about costumes jogged you into creating Severian?

GW: I met a nice little boy named Nick. (He's not quite so little now.) He was very, very bright, and crazy about knights and the whole medieval scene. I tried to figure out what attracted him to it so much, and began to write a book.

JJ: Many of your books, particularly the *Latro* and Briah books, portray a dimly-seen conflict or at least interaction of 'higher powers' that is in part 'behind' the human events. One sees the same kind of thing in the *Book of Daniel*, Chapter 11, and also in the *Iliad*. I'm wondering about the origin of this interesting theme in your writing, how you came to think of writing this way.

GW: No comment.

JJ: Could you comment on some of the things that motivated your creation of the story of Patera Silk – such as (possibly) (a) disappointment over people's misunderstanding of the Severian narrative; or (b) a desire to write your own version of *The Diary of a Country Priest*; or (c) some specific event in your life; or (d) something else altogether?

GW: None of those you suggest. I began with the idea of writing about a good man in a bad religion. That's all.

JJ: Aww, why not? I might as well at least *ask* one of the $64,000 questions, so I'll just go for broke. [*Hmm. I've gotta be very precise here. Okay, here goes.*] Which of the following, if any, are physically (not in some merely literary or symbolic sense) the same planets as Blue and Green, in the same order?:

  Ushas and Lune
  Urth and Lune
  Lune and Ushas
  Lune and Urth
  Two Urths
  Two Ushases
  Two Lunes

GW: None.

NG: On *The Wizard Knight*: apart from your aforementioned meeting with young Nick, what first got you interested in writing a novel incorporating knightly chivalry and Teutonic myth?

GW: The short answer is that I don't know. I started thinking about knighthood, and wondering why that period has an eternal fascination for us. Greek myth is laid in the Golden Age. The Dark Ages are our Golden Age; most fairy tales, and all the best ones, are laid there. I start thinking about a lot of things, including dinner, but I needed a new book just then and wanted to get away from the universe of the *New Sun* books.

NG: Why did you choose to make the narrator of *The Knight* a contemporary American? More broadly, why in your opinion are so many authors of Arthurian fantasy (from Mark Twain in *A Connecticut Yankee* to Poul Anderson in *Three Hearts and Three Lions*) inclined to insert modern viewpoint characters into novels set in the Dark Ages?

GW: I've no good answer. I felt I needed to bring in someone from outside, who would not have heard about the Aelf and Angrborn from childhood.

NG: You have narrated a number of stories and novels from the perspectives of children, but *The Wizard Knight* is by far your most ambitious exercise in a youthful vein. What, for you, are the particular challenges of assuming a young, or teenage, narrative voice?

GW: A youthful American voice isn't particularly challenging – I've been a young American, and they're all around me. I can walk from my house to Barrington High School.

NG: *The Knight* describes a hierarchy of worlds, the two highest very possibly the realms of God and the angels, the lowest hellish terrains like Muspel. Does this scheme emanate from Teutonic and Celtic myth, from the Kabbalah, or primarily from Christian theology?

GW: I began with Teutonic Myth: Valhalla above, the elves below. When I needed another layer, I added one. The lowest is not Muspel.

NG: Although *The Knight* is very much a Gene Wolfe novel, packed with cunning clues, oblique touches, unusual viewpoints, searching dialogues, and brilliant prose, it seems more transparent, less veiled, than your previous epics. Could *The Wizard Knight* be employed as a sort of explicatory Rosetta Stone for the wider Wolfe oeuvre, your open statement of themes explored with greater disguise in the Briah and *Latro* books?

GW: Perhaps it could be. I'll be interested to see whether anyone does it.

Part II

The Wild Joy of Strumming
A Collection of Gene Wolfe's Essays

15

Books in *The Book of the New Sun*

We have books here bound in the hides of echidnes, krakens, and beasts so long extinct that those whose studies they are, are for the most part of the opinion that no trace of them survives unfossilised. We have books bound wholly in metals of unknown alloy, and books whose bindings are covered with thickset gems. We have books cased in perfumed woods shipped across the inconceivable gulfs between creations – books doubly precious because no one on Urth can read them.

We have books whose papers are matted of plants from which spring curious alkaloids, so that the reader, in turning their pages, is taken unaware by bizarre fantasies and chimeric dreams. Books whose pages are not paper at all, but delicate wafers of thin jade, ivory, and shell; books to whose leaves are the desiccated leaves of unknown plants. Books we have also that are not books at all to the eye: scrolls and tablets and recordings on a hundred different substances. There is a cube of crystal here – though I can no longer tell you where – no larger than the ball of your thumb that contains more books than the library itself does.

Which is a paradox, to be sure, since Master Ultan's library contains the crystal and is itself the Library, or perhaps the Bibliotheque, of All Books. What does it mean?

Primarily, it seems to me, that the library is folded in upon itself like a Klein bottle, though in a more profound sense. This folding in of the library, this sense that the library is larger than the world that contains it, is modern as far as I know. And yet there is some flavour of the ancient about it, of books that have not been read since before they were written, of the worm and the dust. Jorge Luis Borges's 'The Library of Babel' has rightly been called Kafkan in its sense of enormity and oppression: 'In the entrance way hangs a mirror, which faithfully duplicates appearances. People are in the habit of inferring from this mirror that the Library is not infinite (if it really were, why this illusory duplication?); I prefer to dream that the polished surfaces feign and promise infinity ...' But both Kafka and Borges are twentieth century writers. Since the wrong direction is so often found to be the right direction in the end, let us begin by looking in the wrong direction for the meaning of this modern notion: backward to the words themselves.

Bibliotheque comes to us from the Latin *bibliotheca*, a library, or perhaps (more directly) from *bibliothecula*, a small collection of books. (You can see that French *qu* in the *cu*.) But there are meanings behind the meaning: *biblius* is papyrus, an Egyptian reed, and *theca* is a case, a cover, an envelope, that which envelops and contains. Surrounded by our little collection of books, then, we sit in the middle of a swamp on the Upper Nile. The green and slender tongues of the papyrus, higher than our heads, whisper about us in their millions of millions as they whispered before time was invented in the town we now call El Kab (anciently Nekheb) near Thebes. And though we cannot see them, we know they whisper of crocodiles.

Library takes us to Europe and that vast European forest of which only the traces of the traces remain, but that marked so many of us so much more than we realise, giving to those who dwelt there blue eyes and white, paper-like skin, eyes and complexions suited to skulking through its green shades.

For that word *liber* is only 'bark', the inner bark of those ghostly trees upon which the first books known to the inhabitants of Latium were written. Our little library, then, is a forest too, a place of bark. The very paper of our books is made from the wood of countless trees; the word *book* itself means *beech*, and the innumerable leaves of those beeches whisper forever in our minds. I said a moment ago that only the traces of the traces of that ancient forest remain. But that forest, which we call by custom vast, was really not so vast after all. It covered what are now France, Germany, England and Poland, with a few other countries and parts of a few more, such as Italy – only a small fraction of the land area of this inconsiderable planet of ours. (The largest forest of our world is still existent, though most of us have never heard of it. It is the Taiga of Siberia, and with an area of about three million square miles it is nearly as large as the whole of Europe.)

Yet among the traces of the traces we must count the world of books, and that world is already larger by far than the original forest that gave it birth, and it is growing larger every day.

Now having glanced toward the past, let us look to the future. In *The Sword of the Lictor*, Dr Talos says, 'Look about you – don't you recognise this? It is just as he says!'

'What do you mean?' Severian asks.

'The castle? The monster? The man of learning? I only just thought of it. Surely you know that just as the momentous events of the past cast their shadows down the ages, so now, when the sun is drawing toward the dark, our own shadows race into the past to trouble mankind's dreams.'

What shadow is this? At present our history extends back about five thousand two hundred years. (Pharaoh Menes ruled in Nekheb in 3200 BC.) Let us assume that humankind and civilisation as we know it endure ten percent longer than they have already, that is, for another five hundred and twenty years. Roughly thirty thousand *titles* are now being published every year. (*The Literary Market Place* lists one thousand four hundred and fifty trade publishing companies for 1982, and there are another six thousand or so publishers who are not trade publishers; you are now reading a book produced by one of them – a title that is probably not even included in the thirty thousand.) Let us also assume that the number of titles published each year does not increase, though it has tended to increase throughout most of history. By those assumptions, another five hundred and twenty years will produce fifteen million six hundred thousand new titles.

Suppose that by 2054 the span of human life has increased sufficiently to give a scholar a career of a hundred years. Suppose that during his hundred-year career this centenarian scholar reads a book every day. He will read thirty six thousand, five hundred and twenty five books, or less than three percent of new books produced since our time. Imagine then what the situation will be in Severian's time for the scholar-heirs of a sequence of civilisations that may be over a million years old.

But you already have. All of us already have, I think, and that is the shadow that has come to haunt us. Critics and reviewers (perhaps the most fallible of men) speak of a certain book's dying. If you go to the huckster room in which you bought this excellent book and talk to the dealers a bit, you will discover that few books ever do. (Undoubtedly, many titles we would very much like to have for our collections were lost forever when Caliph Omar ordered the three hundred thousand volumes in the Serapeum burned to heat the public baths of Alexandria; but astonishingly little has been lost since. We have several manuscripts of *Gilgamesh*, for example, a sword-and-sorcery novel more than five thousand years old.) The rarer a book becomes, the more zealously existing copies are guarded, and when a book is sufficiently old, it is likely to be reissued, and certain to be microfilmed, simply because of its age.

But if we were to say all this to Master Ultan, he would only laugh. He must deal also with books imported from other worlds, books that are often in strange forms, as we have seen. The experience of the conquistadores in the New World of Earth should serve as a warning to us; in Peru, they found books written by knotting string. These, like so many of the books in Master Ultan's library, are books no one can read now.

Two hundred years ago, Dr. Johnson said that a man would turn over half a library to make one book. Today, no one could possibly turn over half of any one of the many thousands of large libraries on Earth. In the future the task of turning over large libraries will have to be left to computers; and those of us who have had trouble getting to sleep, as I do, can amuse ourselves with the image of those mainframes of the coming decade, equipped with optical character readers and book-feed and page-turning mechanisms, reading, reading, through the night. (Cyriaca speaks of the ultimate fate of these computers and the books they will read in *The Sword of the Lictor*: 'When the last machine was cold and still and each of those who had learned from them the forbidden lore mankind had cast aside was separated from all the rest, there came dread into the heart of each. For each knew himself to be only mortal, and most, no longer young. And each saw that with his own death the knowledge he loved best would die. Then each of them – each supposing himself the only one to do so – began to write down what he had learned in the long years when he had harkened to the teachings of the machines that had spilled forth all the hidden knowledge of wild things. Much perished but much more survived, sometimes falling into the hands of those who copied it enlivened by their own additions or weakened by omissions ... Kiss me, Severian.')

The library, or at least the large, public building, has ceased to be a place for human beings and become a place for machines. We humans are now confined to the little library, to the bibliotheque or small collection of books; so let us examine what I believe is the only truly small collection to be found in *The Book of the New Sun*, the four volumes that Severian brings to Thecla in *The Shadow of the Torturer*. In the chapter titled 'The Master of Curators', Master Gurloes, you will recall, writes to Master Ultan:

> 'By the will of a court we have in our keeping the exulted person of the Chatelaine Thecla; and by its further will we would furnish the Chatelaine Thecla in her confinement such comforts as lie not beyond reason and prudence. That she may while away the moments until her time with us is come – or rather, as she has instructed me to say, until the heart of the Autarch, whose forbearance knows not walls nor seas, is softened toward her, as she prays – she asks that you, consonant with your office, provide her with certain books, which books are –'
>
> 'You may omit the titles, Cyby,' Ultan said. 'How many are there?'
> 'Four, sieur.'
> 'No trouble then. Proceed.'
> '"For this, Archivist, we are much obliged to you." Signed, "Gurloes, Master of the Honourable Order commonly called the Guild of Torturers."'
> 'Are you familiar with any of the titles on Master Gurloes's list, Cyby?'
> 'With three, sieur.'
> 'Very good. Fetch them, please. What is the fourth?'
> '*The Book of the Wonders of Urth and Sky*, sieur.'

A few pages later in the same chapter, Severian describes two of the four, neither of which is *The Book of the Wonders of Urth and Sky*:

> One of the three volumes Cyby had brought was as large as the top of a small table, a cubit in width and a scant ell in height; from the arms impressed upon its saffian cover, I supposed it to be the history of some old noble family. The others were much smaller. A green book hardly larger than my hand and no thicker than my index finger appeared to be a collection of devotions, full of enamelled pictures of ascetic pantocrators and hypostases with black halos and gemlike robes. I stopped for a time to look at them, sharing a little, forgotten garden full of winter sunshine with a dry fountain.

That paragraph is full of the 'funny words' I have often been taxed with using; so for the benefit of those of you who have not seen *The Castle of the Otter*, I would like to quote some of the definitions given there:

Saffian: a leather made from goatskin or sheepskin (goatskin is better) and tanned with sumac. It is often dyed in bright colours.

Ascetic: uninclined to Urthly pleasures.

Pantocrators: those who have mastered the physical. Also, incarnations of the Pancreator. Those fit for spiritual and philosophical 'wrestling'. Originally, the word designated what we would call all-around athletes; but its figurative meanings have overwhelmed its literal ones.

Hypostases: the persons whose union constitutes the Increate.

It seems to me that we can reasonably make two assumptions about these four books. The first is that they are books Thecla might reasonably ask to borrow, and the second is that they all must have something to do with Severian. Note, for example, that the pictures in the book of devotions are enamelled and that Severian will soon encounter Dorcas; Dorcas comes from a family once engaged in the manufacture of cloisonné, and she once lived in a shop where it was sold. Cloisonné is a coloured decoration of enamels. In the rest of this essay, however, I will concentrate on the first assumption, not wishing to deprive you of the legitimate pleasure of deducing the connections.

The large book, which is so big that Severian, in Chapter VII, cannot slip it through the slot intended for food trays, is almost certainly a history of Thecla's own family, its wide pages occupied by genealogical charts. (If she had been at the point of marrying at the time of her arrest, it might conceivably have been that of her husband-to-be's; but since she never mentions a future marriage, we must assume that none has been arranged.)

This book, then, leads us to ask who the exulted families are and what it means to be an exultant.

In the time of Severian, the Commonwealth is a poor country growing poorer. Its economy is based on agriculture, on small farms like the one from which Melito has plainly sprung and ranches like the one from which Foila must have come. It is in the farmland to the north and west of Nessus where the lowlands receive the greatest amount of rain and the rain can be supplemented from the River Gyoll and its tributaries. It is grain from these farms and water from Gyoll that keep Nessus alive, of course. Although so much of the city is deserted, like the ruins Severian sees as he journeys up the river on the *Samru*, and much of it is only thinly inhabited, like the district to which Dorcas goes when she leaves Severian, there are still many districts (largely to the north) that are home to millions of people.

And yet these millions are only a remnant of those who once lived in Nessus. The pampas are encroaching year by year upon the farmland, and in time the pampas will turn to deserts. As Urth's sun cools, more and more of Urth's water is being tied up in its glaciers, and less and less is entering the atmosphere from its cooling and increasingly ice-covered seas. Eventually, as Severian sees in the house of Master Ash, the glaciers may come down from the mountains. By that time there will be few to mourn their coming in the once-fertile lands about Nessus.

In such a society as this, poor and relatively stable over hundreds of years, power becomes concentrated in particular families. Because we have the word *economics* and the word *politics*, and no word to mean the two together, we think of them as completely different things. The fact is that their interaction is more than strong enough to justify our calling them one thing, just as we call education (in which the student interacts so strongly with the institution, although we have no word for his action upon it or its action upon him) one thing.

Change, Wealth, and War are the great democrats. Change means that yesterday's solutions will no longer work on today's problems. Wealth, that education can be made available even to the poor. War means death for a generation of the aristocratic officer class that is expected to lead the troops, and brings change (and often wealth) with it. The great Russian and German aristocratic systems were destroyed by World War I. In England, the wealth created by industrialisation (England was the first industrialised nation) stripped the aristocracy of all but the trappings of power, so that wealthy nobles today are noble because they are wealthy, and not wealthy because they are noble. The changes introduced by contact with the West toppled the Chinese Empire and ended the power of the Japanese aristocracy.

Conversely, Stagnation, Poverty, and Peace are the creators of aristocracy. Reviewers of *The Book of the New Sun* often say they are surprised to find a 'medieval' or 'European' aristocracy governing the countryside. The truth is that there is nothing particularly medieval or European about such aristocracies – they evolve everywhere when conditions are right for them for a period long enough for them to develop.

I grew up in Texas, which was a wilderness a hundred and fifty years ago but now has a fairly well developed ranching aristocracy. Ranches are passed from father to son, and cattle brands are used as coats of arms were in the middle ages and as each (great) family's *mon* was in feudal Japan. Landless imitators of the aristocracy are said to be 'all hat and no cattle'; it is surprising how seldom Easterners recognise, in the wheelin', dealin', bellerin' Texas millionaire they joke and complain about, the brawling nobleman in embryo.

In the U.S.S.R., it is already noticeable that the managerships of collective farms remain in families and are frequently passed from father to son. This is, of course, not a matter of Soviet policy but of expediency. Managers sent out from Moscow return to Moscow at the first opportunity, while the established local manager can use his political connections to get his son a superior education and use his own position to train him in administrative duties that are basically unchanging.

When the manager dies, his son is on the spot and clearly the person best qualified to administer the farm. It is pointless to protest that he does not 'in fact' own the farm, which belongs to the Soviet Government, which (in theory) administers it as the deputy of the Proletariat. The noble of the high middle ages did not (in theory) own his estate either. He held it from the king in return for feudal service that was seldom given, and the king in turn held the whole country as the vassal (this word originally meant 'servant boy') of God. This is not to condemn (or praise) Soviet society; I am merely saying – no, insisting – that certain social patterns will emerge when conditions are favourable to them, just as the availability of certain types of musical instruments will result in the composition of certain types of music.

In aristocratic societies inheritance is the best way of getting money, and the reliance on it strengthens the bonds of blood. If you do not help your relations, they may leave their money to someone else or influence other relations to disinherit you. Thecla's concern for her family and its history is thus entirely logical and practical. Her best chance of release is through the influence of her relatives.

The second book Severian describes is a euchologion or formulary of prayers, and our opinion of its practicality depends on our opinion of the efficacy of prayer and the reality of the deity addressed. In America today, the first question is (properly, I think) left to private belief. We may pray or not, as we choose. And if we choose, we can believe in the existence of a deity, but choose not to pray, like the character in one of L. Sprague de Camp's Krishnan novels who feels that the gods are most apt to favour those who refrain from pestering them. Or we may pray without belief in any deity on the grounds that it does no harm and it is possible we are mistaken. This last has always struck me as the only logical choice for an agnostic, and I would more than suspect that Thecla prayed in this fashion, were it not for the nature of one of the remaining books.

If she addressed her prayers directly to the deity and not to some intercessor, the deity involved was probably the Increate. The designation is derived from the most common argument for the existence of God. Briefly, it is this: To all tangible objects we can assign some cause; individuals are the children of some parents, for example, though we may never have known those parents. Similarly, animals are derived from earlier animals, and plants from the seeds of earlier plants. Stones are spontaneously engendered from the earth, rivers rise from springs, springs are born of rain, rain descends from clouds, clouds condense from air, air is brought by the wind, and so on indefinitely.

However, the chain of causation cannot be infinite, because an infinite universe would be required to contain it, and for the infinite universe there is no cause. Therefore, at the end of the chain of causation there must be some being that created all the rest by creating beings that created others; and this being we will call the Increate – that which is not itself the creation of another.

That is the name most commonly used in *The Book of the New Sun*. In *The Shadow of the Torturer*, Chapter VII, Master Gurloes says, "But with the passage of time I have come to understand that the Increate, in choosing for me a career in our guild, was acting for my benefit. Doubtless I had acquired some merit in a previous life, as I hope I have in this one." Although Master Gurloes is an old hypocrite, this speech of his tells us a good deal. The Increate is thought to govern the course of human lives; yet human beings are believed to possess free will, since they could not acquire merit without one. Perhaps most important, the people of the Commonwealth believe in reincarnation.

Perhaps we should also note here that there seems to be a belief in luck, chance, or fate as well, though not wholly apart from the Increate. In Chapter XIV, when Master Palaemon gives Severian the sword *Terminus Est*, he says, 'May the Moira favour you, Severian.' *Moira* in this sense means a sacred lottery – luck as an instrument of deity.

We should note, too, that *Increate* is only one of several 'names' used to refer to the Ultimate Power. The sweepsmen Severian hears as he trudges up the Water Way in Chapter XIV use ours, singing:

Row, brothers, row!
The current is against us.

Row, brothers, row!
Yet God is with us.
Row, brothers, row!
The wind is against us.
Row, brothers, row!
Yet God is for us.

Their song shows that *God* may also be in common use, if only among slaves and the very poor. However, it is possible that the word is preserved only in this immemorial rowing chant. In the entire length of *The Book of the New Sun* I believe it occurs only there, although Severian hears the song again in *The Citadel of the Autarch*, in Chapter XXXIII, when the crew of the *Samru* rows him up Gyoll.

One more point seems worth observing. It is that the sweepsmen appear to believe that adversity itself can be a sign of the favour of the deity. And how can you argue with them? If the wind and current were always with their vessel, no sweepsmen would be needed.

I am occasionally asked to translate the Latin (that is to say, they are given as Latin in my translation) inscriptions on the sundials in the Atrium of Time, which Valeria mistranslates. They are *Lux dei vitae viam monstrat*; *Felicibus brevis, miseris hora longa*; and *Aspice ur aspiciar*; and they mean 'The light of God shows the road of life'; 'Happiness is brief, misery's hours long'; and significantly, 'Look at me so that I may be looked upon', which Valeria does not translate. Before we leave these old dial mottoes, it may be well to quote Valeria's mistranslation of the first. It is 'The beam of the New Sun lights the way of life.'

Which brings us back to the enamelled pictures. Who are those pantocrators? If human beings are reincarnated, are they thus greater than the Increate?

Briefly, in the time before Ymar was Autarch, when the sun had begun to cool, there appeared on Urth a man now called the Conciliator, an intercessor and mediator who healed the sick and attempted to teach the people; his stories form what is now called *The Book of the New Sun*. It is thus titled because the Conciliator promised that in time he would return bringing Urth a new sun. (Dr. Talos has seen this 'lost' book and based his play 'Eschatology and Genesis' upon it.) In his second appearance, the Conciliator is thus called the New Sun.

Of the remaining books I need say little. The book Ultan finds for Severian is of course *The Book of the Wonders of Urth and Sky*, which Severian carried with him on his wanderings as a memento of Thecla. One reviewer has called it a sort of future science-fiction anthology. The truth is that it would be more accurate (though not entirely accurate) to call it a future *Bullfinch's Age of Fable or Beauties of Mythology*. It was, as Master Ultan tells Severian 'a standard work, three or four hundred years ago.' He goes on to say, 'It

relates most of the familiar legends of ancient times. To me the most interesting is that of the Historians, which tells of a time in which every legend
could be traced to half-forgotten fact.' In writing the legends, I have supposed facts and old stories to have become confused with others, a rascally
technique which has earned me at least one vehement accusation of pla-
giarism. Thus, for example, the custom of an academic thesis is confounded
with the legend of Theseus in 'The Tale of the Student and His Son.'

The fourth book, as the astute reader will have guessed long ago, is *The
Book of the New Sun* itself. And now we are come again to the notion of
recurrence, of the library folded in upon itself like the Klein bottle. This
notion of recurrence seems to me to circle our Earth (you may spell it as
you like) like the Midgard serpent which clasps its tail in its mouth and is
brother to the wolf Fenris. For the library of Master Ultan is in *The Book of
the New Sun*, and *The Book of the New Sun* is in his library. And you are the
readers of that book.

16
Wolfe's Rules:
What You Must Do To Be a Writer

Write your story. No quantity of graphs, outlines, and timetables will help if you do not write the piece itself.

Complete your story. You must not only start it, you must finish it; 'finish' means bringing your story – on paper, not merely in your mind – to a satisfying conclusion.

Revise your story as needed. Read it over, and when you find something wrong, fix it. When your story is rejected, read it over again. If nothing is wrong, leave it alone.

Submit the story in proper form to a suitable market. When it is rejected by the first such market, submit it to another. When it is rejected there as well, submit it to a third. Continue to revise and submit it as long as you have faith in it – plus two.

Begin a new story as soon as the first one is on the way to its first market. Waiting for your story to sell before beginning your next is the royal road to failure.

Sell your story when someone wants to buy it. If it is a book, you can try for better terms; but NEVER issue ultimatums. Be mindful of my father's sage advice: 'Take the money and run for the train.'

17

Balding, Avuncular Gene's Quick and Dirty
Guide to Creating Memorable Characters

Rid your mind of the notion that characterisation is hard. There are two reasons why you find few good characters in the stories you read, and the first is this superstition that you have to be able to fly on a broomstick to do it. The hard things about writing are telling a good story, and writing skilful prose. The rest – plotting and characterisation, particularly – are easy.

The second reason is that far too many writers are interested only in themselves. It's good to be interested in yourself, but it's fatal to be interested ONLY in yourself.

Characterisation aims at three things. If you do any two of them pretty well, you've got it whipped.

First, characterisation distinguishes one character from another, particularly in dialogue. Mousy Janice does not talk (or act) like Brassy Jane or Heroic Joan. 'Do it! Once you start, you'll find yourself wondering what you were so afraid of.' 'But what will people say? My mother … ' 'Screw your mother. And screw Ralph, too. Get out there and get yourself a life, kid.' Can you tell who said what? Sure you can.

Second, characterisation takes the reader into the character's psyche; it makes us feel we've known the character for years: 'Another mouth to feed. Well, hell.' Jake pushed his sweat-stained old hat onto the back of his head, picked the ginger kitten up and scratched its ears. 'You don't look like no big eater to me,' he muttered.

Third, characterisation makes the reader care what happens to the character – his or her successes and failures become the reader's:

> Even if he succeeded, he too might be hoisted to the top of the tower. Who would come for him them? Only stinking vultures.
>
> He fingered the worn rope. It wouldn't fetch a copper in the market, but it was still strong enough. It would do.
>
> But no. He was a fool. There were a thousand smarter, richer friends in the city, friends just waiting to be found; and when Lian could no longer fight off the vultures, he himself would feel nothing. No, he would not go. Nobody but a green fool would try it.
>
> By the time he had completed the thought, however, he was already loping along Saddlemakers Street; and it was too late.

In brief – you characterise by SHOWING the character acting, speaking, or thinking in a characteristic way. You do not TELL the reader about the character, you SHOW. This is vital. No other point so clearly distinguishes the seasoned writer from the beginner.

Because it does, I'm going to beat it to death for you. You do not say that Jock is a brave and obedient dog. You show Jock being brave and obedient.

Nor do you show him being brave and obedient then say that he is. *You do not say it at all.* You simply show it.

This is NOT a small thing. It is NOT a minor point. It is enormously important. I said that good characterisation is easy, and it is. I also said that it was rare, and that's true too. If you'll do it, your stories will rise head and shoulders above the average slush-pile story. If you'll do it consistently, and market your stories assiduously, it won't be long before you have to look at your records to find out whether this is your sixth sale or your seventh.

Successful writers are asked from time to time what the secret is – how is it that they can write stories and sell them when other people cannot. This is it. It's right up there on this paper you are holding. Read it again.

Remember the Simon story? Don't say nobody ever told you.

18
Wolfe's Irreproducible Truths about Novels

Anyone who can write a good novel can write a good short story; but manyone who can write a good short story cannot write a novel at all. A novel takes sustained effort over a period of months or years. Harlan Ellison and Gardner Dozois are fine short-story writers, but cannot – apparently – write novels.

All writing is an act of courage. A novelist is like a cop or a soldier. To be brave is not enough. He or she must be brave today and brave tomorrow, and brave the next day, and the next.

If at all possible, you should work everyday, even if it is only for ten minutes. You can't do much in ten minutes, but ten minutes of real work will keep your mind focused on your novel. And that's vital.

Forget yourself. It doesn't matter what the agent, the editor, or the reader thinks of you.

Don't worry about your mother. If your book isn't published, she won't see it. If it is, she'll think you're wonderful, and so will I.

People who wait for inspiration write one book in the course of a lifetime, if that. Work hard and fast, and inspiration will hurry to catch up.

A 'normal' novel is about 80,000 words, or approximately 320 pages of typescript. Longer is better. The minimum is 40,000. There is no maximum. However …

Really long novels make more money if they are cut up into trilogies, series, or whatever.

Novels are where the money is. Thus, writers who have made a name for themselves write novels, mostly, leaving the short story field open for you.

It is very difficult to sell a short story collection without having at least one successful novel.

Novels can be published electronically, but there is no money in it so far.

All successful novels are about character, except for those that are about plot. Or place. Or dogs or something.

Plot is better than no plot, but no plot is better than too much plot.

Great novels are concerned with love and death, lesser novels with sex and violence.

Love and death are sex and violence, handled by a great novelist.

Love without sex is better than sex without love.

It is very hard to sell a novel on a chapter and an outline unless you have already written and sold a complete novel. Many people (see above) can write a good chapter and a good outline who cannot write a good novel. Editors know this.

If you submit a chapter and an outline, the chapter must be Chapter One. This is senseless but true. It's a waste of time to send another chapter, no matter how good it is.

If the chapter you send isn't good, it makes no difference how good your outline says the rest of your novel's going to be, since the outline will not be read.

If your novel is boring to write it will be boring to read. Crying, giggling, and jumping up and down at the keyboard are good signs, all of them.

When you have finished the first draft and are ready to revise, print it out and mark it up with a pencil while sitting in an easy chair. If you don't find yourself surprised, sometimes, by what happens next, you have a problem.

It is only when you have finished that you can begin.

The magic is in the second draft.

Amateurs are afraid of shocking, pros are afraid of boring.

Only intentionally should you ever be ambiguous.

You can't be at your best all the time. But you can go over your book again and again, until every page has been exposed to you at your best.

Editors look for flip strength. To win the game, look for it yourself before you send your novel it. If it isn't there, rewrite and improve.

Start something new the day after you put your novel in the mail. Think about it as little as possible; think about your new story instead.

Success does not consist of selling or getting good reviews any more than failure consists of not selling or being attacked by reviewers. Success is continuing to write. Success is speaking in silence.

19

Nor the Summers as Golden:
Writing Multivolume Works

How do you write stories too big for one book?

That is the question I am supposed to answer here, and I ought to confess at once that I may know no more about it than you do. Indeed, I may well know less. My only credential is that I have completed two such works – *The Book of the New Sun* (four volumes and a coda), and *The Book of the Long Sun* (four volumes). I, myself, would not read an article on novel-writing by someone who had written two.

Fundamentally, you create these large works by writing something that is more like life itself than the other forms are. Or so it seems to me. In short stories we typically separate a few hours – a single day at most – from the years of the characters. (In 1972, Gardner Dozois edited an anthology called *A Day in the Life*; that is it, exactly.) A carriage will flee, through ever-deepening snow, a French town occupied by the Prussians; in it ride a great nobleman and his lady, some rich merchants and their wives, a red-bearded beer-swilling radical – and the plump and patriotic little whore the townspeople call Boule de Suif. The driver cracks his whip; a full half dozen horses lunge against their harness; our carriage flounders and skids, and we're off!

The story, as the reader realises at once, begins with the cracking of the whip and will end when the passengers reach Le Havre.

No doubt one out of the half dozen members who read this will want to be told what a novel is as well, with *Huckleberry Finn* or *For Whom the Bell Tolls* as examples. I apologise and beg to be excused. The vast majority of our members, including the other five, read nothing else, and most write nothing else. They do not need to be told what a novel is; they need to be told what the other things are; and that, after all, is what I'm supposed to do here.

One of the other things, to pedants if to nobody else, is the series; but a series is nothing more than a succession of novels that are all too often progressively weaker. You write a novel, and because it sold, another about the same person or persons, until at last your editor warns you Not To Do That Any More. (I cannot present myself as a model of virtue in this regard, much as I'd like to; I've done it, and I'll probably do it again if I get the chance.)

A trilogy, tetralogy, hexology or whatever is very like a series, superficially – so much so that it is often mistaken for one by reviewers; but there are deep-seated differences. And a series, which is much easier to write, is actually much harder to write well.

A multivolume work sets out to tell a multitude of stories under the umbrella of a single overshadowing story. You will be tempted to quibble here, if only with yourself. Telling 'the story of Main Character's life' doesn't count. Everyone is born at the beginning and dies at the end, although it would be both possible and legitimate to write the story of how Main Character came to die; *The Lord of the Rings*, which is a genuine trilogy, comes very close as it tells how Frodo rid himself of the one Ring.

By now you have come to see – I hope – why a series is at once easier, and more difficult to write well. It is easier because the author need not worry throughout several books about the overshadowing story that should be lurking in the background of all the subsidiary stories. Contrariwise (as Tweedledee says somewhere in the two-book Alice series), a series is harder to write well because its individual books lack the unity and sense of purpose that an overshadowing story would confer.

From what I have said, it should be obvious that one of the first things the author of a multivolume work ought to do is decide upon the overshadowing story *and tell the reader what it is to be.* Thus Homer sets out to tell – and does tell – the tale of the rage of Achilles, with a multitude of subsidiary stories about funeral games, the fighting before the walls of Troy, and so on and so forth. Have you forgotten the opening?

Here it is:

> Achilles's wrath, to Greece the direful spring
> of woes unnumber'd heavenly goddess sing!
> That wrath which hurl'd to Pluto's gloomy reign
> The souls of mighty chiefs untimely slain;
> Whose limbs unburied on the naked shore,
> Devouring dogs and hungry vultures tore;
> Since great Achilles and Atrides strove,
> Such was the sovereign doom, and such the will of Jove!

Notice how much Homer has packed into those few opening lines. What is the overshadowing story? Achilles' wrath, mentioned in the first line. Who is Main Character? Achilles, of course, who is mentioned twice in this brief beginning. Can we expect divine meddling in the story? Yes, indeed! 'Heavenly goddess sing', and 'the will of Jove'. Those unburied bodies promise war, and 'the naked shore' hints of the sea. If, after reading all that, you do not understand that Homer was of our trade, you do not understand our trade. Here are a few lines from someone who understood it perfectly:

When 'Omer smote 'is bloomin' lyre,
He'd 'eard men sing by land and sea;
An' what he thought 'e might require,
'E went an' took – the same as me!

Yours is a higher and holier calling, perhaps; all honour to you. But I am of Homer's trade, and Kipling's, admittedly on a rather more modest plan; and the moment Homer opens his *Iliad*, I recognise a member of our lodge. If you have not read him, you ought to, remembering always that he knew exactly what he was doing. (Yes, almost three thousand years ago.) He knew it, because he had recited those verses scores of times to live audiences. If he bored or otherwise displeased his hearers, there would be no soup and no bread for the blind minstrel who wandered from great house to great house. The *Iliad* is, of course, a multivolume work; if you don't believe me, examine its structure. If you still don't, compare its length to those of other poems, including Greek poems.

Now we have reached the hard part, for all the familiar chores of the novelist are the same. You must chose a time and a setting, create engaging characters, provide dialogue that will be succinct and interesting, and the rest of it. You know the drill. You must conclude each of your books in a way that will provide a sense of finality, obviously without prematurely ending the overshadowing story, which will furnish an ending for the last.

Thus in *The Book of the Long Sun*, the first volume ends with Silk's recognising his need to confront his own nature, the second with the death of Doctor Crane and Silk recognised by officers of the Civil Guard as the legitimate head of the city government, the third with Silk installed and functioning as head of the government, and the fourth with his salvaging the people originally committed to his care from the ruin of their city and their world – this last being the overshadowing story told in the four books.

But all that is easy enough. Your own psychology presents the chief difficulty, and frequently requires a good deal of doublethink. You must keep in mind that the overshadowing story is to be told in half a million words or so – while forgetting that years of steady effort will be required to write them. There is a temptation, often severe, to wind the various plots up too quickly. There is another, often insidious, to pad. Half a million is a very large number indeed.

But not as large as you might think. It is necessary to cultivate the notion that half a million words will scarcely suffice, because that is the truth. What you are trying to do is depict not a few hours or a day (that is the short story), not a single significant series of events (that is the novel), but the most significant portion of Main Character's life. In this sense, the novel is like a screenplay, the multivolume work like a documentary. You are free to do or show whatever you wish – there is plenty of room for all of it. But like the man with the monkey's paw, you had damned well better wish wisely, and not once or thrice but literally scores of times.

Because if you lose sight of the overshadowing story, or any of the other plots, you are doomed to sweeping revisions or failure.

Let us say you are thinking of letting Main Character go fishing. His fishing trip must, at the very least, exhibit some aspect of his (or her) character not seen previously. It should also begin a new plot line or end one, and it should in some fashion move the plot of the overshadowing story – because he meets another angler who later proves to be an important character; because he loses track of the time and returns late, or whatever. Ideally, your reader should feel, 'Ah, that little fishing incident was much more significant than I thought at the time. And that bit about the horse show gave him the clue to the real nature of the aliens. Wow! I was tempted to skip them both, but I'm sure glad I didn't.' Obviously, the more the fishing incident and the horse show incident have to contribute, the longer they should be.

That is really it, but there is all that white space down there so let us double back and fool around with some of the stuff you novelists already know.

Main Character must be large enough for the role. He (or She) must be able to hold your interest through three or four, or even five, books; if he does not, he cannot hold the interest of your readers. Be very, very careful here; it is a point at which many fail. He must have come from somewhere, and brought with him a certain education or lack of education, and certain feelings, values, customs, and prejudices, which are not likely to be precisely the same as ours. That is true in the short story as well, and in the novel too. But as the length of the work increases, it becomes increasingly important because there is so much more room in which to make mistakes.

Popeye the Sailor boasts, 'I'm Popeye the Sailorman!' Do you know what a sailorman is, and how a sailorman differs from an ordinary seaman? If you were going to write the sort of stories Joseph Conrad wrote, it would be knowledge of value, and if you intend to write a trilogy about sailors and their ships, about islands and ports and seas, and

> 'Before you come on board, sir,
> Your name I'd like to know.'
> With a smile upon her countenance,
> She answered, 'Jack Monroe,'

it will be exceedingly dangerous for you not to know it . In science fiction and fantasy, we frequently make up these things for ourselves; but it makes no difference – you must know it. There are no empty cultures and no empty subcultures.

Speaking of sailors and such, how does Main Character earn his bread?

And how do his friends and foes earn theirs? The man who turns into a cockroach in Kafka's story is a salesman, but we need not see him selling because the story is so short. In a longer work we must, if the work is not to fall prey to a creeping sense of unreality. In a multivolume work, we will have to see more of the second string earning theirs, as well. Thus in *The Book of the Long Sun* you not only see Silk at the pulpit, but see Maytera Marble in the classroom and Spider the spycatcher snaring a spy.

Neglecting this aspect of our characters means throwing away one of the strongest supports our stories can have. Some people are interesting in bed, although most are not; but virtually everyone is interesting at work, even when the work itself is not. We meet people at work, too, and they meet us.

Think about it. How many of the people you know socially are or were co-workers, suppliers, or customers?

We bring skills and habits of thought and speech home from work as well, and sometimes use them to solve the problems we face in our private life. Sherlock Holmes could tell a weaver by his tooth; we should be able to exhibit one – or an uanhk driver – showing how he talks and acts.

Note here that making Main Character independently wealthy may give him more control over his time, but really changes things very little. Independently wealthy people have their own work, and if they leave it to managers and investment councillors who operate without oversight, they will not be independently wealthy very long. Imagine yourself arranging a wedding and reception for six hundred guests – many from each of the three known intelligent races – without gravity. Catering? Security for three or four hundred gifts? Most will be valuable and some will be very valuable indeed. Flower girls? Rest rooms? What about parking? (You may kick the next person who talks about 'the idle rich' hard and frequently.)

Up there I mentioned setting. One will often suffice for a short story, but rarely for a novel. Three novels with a single setting? Well, that may be possible, but it had better be a real world-beater. You will most likely require several big, complex, and well-thought-out settings, with a good deal of contrast between them. I once told a beginner to put up a little sign facing his desk: I AM GOING TO TELL YOU SOMETHING COOL. A work spread over several books deserves a bigger sign. If your settings do not interest you, they will not interest your reader, and in a long work that is fatal.

How much of this must you know when you begin? None of it, actually; you can work it out as you go along, revising as needed. But it is important – vital, even – that you *think* you know it. You do not have to make notes or outlines in a neat hand in a little spiral notebook before you begin Chapter One; but they may be of value. What is absolutely essential is that you continue to research and make notes and outlines (even if they are only mental) as the story proceeds. You cannot possibly know all that you need to know at the beginning; and if you try to complete the entire work knowing no more than that, you cannot succeed.

I said the end of the overshadowing story would provide an end for the final volume. Perhaps I should add, 'if you are lucky'. It must wrap up its own volume, obviously. It must also wrap up the entire work in a satisfactory way. In general, it should not undercut the endings of any of the earlier books, rendering them, in retrospect, trivial. Rather it must validate them, assuring the reader that they were indeed important points in the overshadowing story – that you did not cheat. Thus in *The Book of the New Sun*, Severian leaves his native city at the end of the first book, reaches the distant city in which he is to be employed at the end of the second, and reaches the war toward which he has been inexorably drawn at the end of the third. At the end of the fourth book (when he returns to his city) I attempted to show that all that had been significant, moulding his character and contributing to his rise to the Phoenix Throne.

There is one final point, the point that separates a true multivolume work from a short story, a novel, or a series. The ending of the final volume should leave the reader with the feeling that he has gone through the defining circumstances of Main Character's life. The leading character in a series can wander off into another book and a new adventure better even than this one. Main Character cannot, at the end of your multivolume work. (Or at least, it should seem so.) His life may continue, and in most cases it will. He may or may not live happily ever after. But the problems he will face in the future will not be as important to him or to us, nor the summers as golden.

20
What Do They Mean, SF?

To a geographer, I suppose it might be San Francisco, and to a dean, senior fellow. To a writer, SF means *science fiction*; but to a science fiction writer, SF (or s.f., or sf) can mean any of three overlapping genres – science fiction, speculative fiction, and science fantasy.

Needless to say, the name is not the thing named. You might write and sell all three without having any clear idea of the nomenclature involved and without having heard the terms; when Mary Wollstonecraft Shelley wrote *Frankenstein* back in the early years of the 19th century, she could not possibly have had any idea she was originating 'science fiction', which is a 20th century coinage. But if you understand how the three differ and know the basis of each, you will possess a considerable advantage.

Science fiction has the oldest name (although it is not really the oldest form), so we'll deal with it first. It may well be the hardest of the three to write; it is certainly the easiest to sell, when it is written competently.

Science fiction is fiction that turns upon the assumption of at least one breakthrough in one of the 'hard' sciences. (A hard science is one in which theories are subject to *rigorous* test, usually by experiment. Physics, chemistry, biology, and mathematics are the principal hard sciences.) Mary Shelley, for example, extrapolated from experiments in galvanism and assumed, for the purposes of her book, that the time would soon come when life could be restored to dead flesh. In other words, she assumed a certain breakthrough in biology or biochemistry. When H. G. Wells assumed that a machine capable of travelling through time could be built, he was assuming a breakthrough in physics.

In both of those books, 'we' – members of western civilisation – were supposed to have made the breakthrough; but it doesn't actually matter who makes it. Wells's *The War of the Worlds* assumes that Martians develop interplanetary flight and come to Earth; it is just as much science fiction as Stanley Weinbaum's 'A Martian Odyssey', in which Americans go to Mars.

Too often, would-be science fiction writers suppose that any story that has a rocket ship, a ray gun, or a robot in it is science fiction, and that any story that lacks all three is not. It just isn't so. L. Frank Baum's *Tik-Tok of Oz* is fantasy (very good fantasy, I might add), although the title character is a robot. It is fantasy because Tik-Tok is fundamentally a large, magical, mechanical toy, and not a triumph of physics and engineering. If you want to examine some contemporary science fiction that does not make use of rockets, ray guns, or robots, you could hardly do better than to read *Who?* and *Michaelmas*, both by the redoubtable Algis Budrys.

Speculative fiction is undoubtedly the oldest genre of the three SFs, although as a term, it is the newest. To the best of my knowledge, the phrase originated with Damon Knight, a fine writer who usually produces science fiction. Knight seems to have meant it as a general broadening of science fiction; but it has rapidly come to designate stories in which one or more changes are assumed in the 'soft' sciences. (Soft sciences are, obviously, sciences that are not 'hard'; psychology, history, economics, and sociology are soft sciences.) The granddad of all speculative fiction is probably *Utopia*, by Thomas More, written almost five hundred years ago. Sir Thomas (who has since become Saint Thomas, the undoubtable patron of all SF writers) imagined a way of life radically different from life in the England of his day and wrote a book to answer the question, 'What if people lived like this?' A superb modern example of the same type of story is Ursula K. Le Guin's *The Dispossessed*, which compares future capitalism and future communism.

Stories that speculate about the effects of a nuclear war next week or a stock market crash next month are speculative fiction; so are those that wonder what would have happened if the South had won the Civil War, or if England had crushed the revolution in her colonies. In the language of the counterculture, speculative fiction is well described by the title of Thomas M. Disch's story collection *Fun With Your New Head*. Another good collection is *Interfaces: An Anthology of Speculative Fiction*, edited by Le Guin and Virginia Kidd.

If this article were to stick strictly to plan, the next genre to be discussed would be science fantasy; but nothing is more typical of the old, unmodified fantasy than that it turns up in unexpected places and in unexpected guises, and some feeling for fantasy – I won't say an understanding, because nobody can really understand it – is necessary to explain science fantasy.

Fantasy is mankind's oldest literature. And yours. *Gilgamesh*, written on clay tablets 1500 years before the birth of Moses, is fantasy. The first book you ever read was probably some dreary text about Dick, Jane, and Spot; but the first book ever read to you, your real first book, was very possibly fantasy – *Puss in Boots* or *Alice in Wonderland*. It might be said that any story laid in Wonderland is fantasy, but it is by no means true that all fantasy must be laid there; James Thurber's 'The Unicorn in the Garden' is fantasy, although the only fantasy element is a unicorn.

For twenty years now, modern fantasy has been almost overwhelmed by J. R. R. Tolkein's *The Lord of the Rings*, the book that proved that fantasy in the 20th century A.D. was no more limited to children's stories than it had been in the 20th century B.C. When our twentieth century is done and the 21st rolls around, *The Lord of the Rings* will probably remain what it is today – the one book every modern fantasy writer must read, and the one book that no modern fantasy writer should try to imitate.

Science fantasy is both the newest term and the newest thing. Fathered by virile science fiction, it is the youngest child of ever-lovely, ever-young fantasy, and it has its father's hands on its mother's eyes. In other and less fantastic words, a science fantasy story is one in which the means of science are used to achieve the spirit of fantasy. Like fantasy, science fantasy turns upon, and often abounds with, 'impossible' creatures and things – girls fall asleep for centuries, one-eyed giants, weapons that can speak and may rebel. But it uses the methodology of science fiction to show that these things are not only possible but probable.

Let's take one of those girls for example. As I write these words, hundreds of medical researchers are seeking a way to achieve suspended animation in human beings. We know it can be done, and indeed among the lower animals it isn't even particularly uncommon. Those goldfish you saw the last time you went to the dime store probably arrived in a cake of ice. That's the usual method of shipping goldfish, and though some fish in each shipment are dead when the ice is thawed, the fish suffer fewer losses that way than they would if they spent the trip sloshing around in a portable tank. If a goldfish, why not a golden-haired princess?

Alas, there is a reason – we don't know how to do it. But if we could we could vastly reduce the difficulty of – say – an expedition to Mars by princesses. Furthermore, if a golden-haired princess (or anybody else) fell ill of a disease science has not yet learned to cure, she could sleep until a cure was ready.

But now suppose that, for whatever reason, no one came to wake her. Perhaps a war was fought – not a war of hydrogen bombs, but a war of deadly viruses. With her biological functions suspended, the princess would not die, though the hospital staff would. When they were gone, she would slumber on, unknowing, while the forests cut by the first settlers grew back around the crumbling walls of the International Medical Centre. Until one day ...

You get the idea now; or if you don't, you never will. That's science fantasy.

Or at least, it could be. It would be if the treatment spoke of the mystery of things, even while the words talked among themselves of disease vectors and cryogenics.

Here's a slightly more advanced example from my own science fantasy novel *The Shadow of the Torturer*. Perhaps you already know that mankind may someday traverse space in vessels driven by the pressure of starlight on immense, tissue-thin, metallised sails. A mad old voyager speaks:

> 'Lords,' he said. 'O lords and mistresses of creation, silken-capped, silken-haired women, and man commanding empires and the armies of the F-f-foemen of our Ph-ph-photosphere! Tower strong as stone is strong, strong as the o-o-oak that puts forth leaves new after the fire! And my master, dark master, death's victory, viceroy over the n-night! Long I signed on the silver-sailed ships, the hundred-masted whose masts reached out to touch the st-st-stars, I, floating among their shining jibs with the Pleiades burning beyond the top-royal spar, but never have I seen ought like you! He-He-Hethor am I, come to serve you, to scrape the mud from your cloak, whet the great sword, c-c-carry the basket with the eyes of your victims looking up at me, Master, eyes like the dead moons of Verthandi when the sun has g-g-gone out …'

That's purple, of course; but then Hethor is a purple character. For contrast, here is Severian (the character Hethor called Master in the passage just quoted) describing the tower of the torturer's guild, to which he belongs:

> It is situated toward the back of the Citadel, upon the western side. At ground level are the studies of our masters, where consultations with the officers of justice and the heads of other guilds are conducted. Our common room is above them, with its back to the kitchen. Above that is the refectory, which serves us as an assembly hall as well as an eating place. Above it are the journeymen's cabins, and above them the apprentices' dormitory and classroom, and a series of attics and abandoned cubicles. Near the very top is the gun room, whose remaining pieces we of the guild are charged with serving should the Citadel suffer attack.
>
> The real work of our guild is carried out below all this. Just underground lies the examination room; beneath it, and thus outside the tower proper (for the examination room was the propulsion chamber of the original structure) stretches the labyrinth of the oubliette …

Cabins? Propulsion chamber? What kind of tower is that, anyway? (The answer, naturally, is that it is a science fantasy tower.)

I don't know for certain who invented what we now call science fantasy, but you can actually watch it taking shape in Jack Vance's *The Dying Earth*. The same author's award-winning *The Dragon Masters* shows it fully developed.

Science fantasy is still sufficiently new that it's hard to lay down rules. Writers are still experimenting, still trying to find out just what works. If you're considering the genre, my advice is to reflect on the science fiction you've already read, and the fantasy too. If you absolutely loved the science fiction, as science fiction, and thought nothing at all was wrong with it or lacking in it, you should write science fiction. If you loved the fantasy, as fantasy, and were never irritated or disturbed by its habit of making up the rules as it went along, then you should write fantasy. But if you liked both, but were dissatisfied with both, for different reasons, then perhaps science fantasy is for you. Marry the two. If you're doing it right, you should often find yourself using science elements and fantasy elements in the same sentence.

Don't cheat on the science. Learn what's going on in the various scientific fields, and eliminate the flatly impossible from your stories. When you pull rabbits out of your hat, you have to be able to tell your reader – entertainingly, not in a dry lecture – just how they got there.

Don't cheat on the fantasy either. Your horrors should shock, your beauties should thrill, your clowns should be funny, and a trifle sad. Everything should be *solid*, and everything should be *fresh*. That's what SF really means.

21

The Special Problems of Science Fiction

Like all fiction, science fiction rests on the four sturdy legs of theme, character, style, and plot. For practical purposes, it includes all stories and novels in which 'the strange' is the dominant characteristic. Sf's particular problems result from the author's need to make this element – the strange – acceptable to the reader.

Theme

In the broadest sense, theme is the story's central concern. In a science fiction story, for example, the theme might be the effects of a system of embalming so improved that the dead could be distinguished from the living only with difficulty. (This was the theme of my story, 'The Packerhaus Method', in which the chief character's father was proven dead only by the fact that he could not get his cigar to draw.) Notice that the theme has nothing to do with what happens to the character. Theme is what the story is *about*.

In science fiction, it is imperative that the theme of each story be fresh or treated from a new angle. If the theme is not original or given a fresh treatment, it cannot be 'strange'. The most common – and the most disastrous – error beginning sf writers make is to assume that editors want more stories on the same themes as the one they have already published. The writer reads the collected works of Isaac Asimov and Jack Williamson, for example, and tries to write a robot story like theirs. His story cannot be 'like theirs' because their stories were fresh and original when they appeared; an imitation cannot be either.

On the other hand, it is still possible to write original robot stories. In 'It's Very Clean', I wrote about a girl who posed as a robot because she could not find work as a human being. I like to think that was original. In 'Eyebem', I wrote about a robot forest ranger, and in 'Going to the Beach', I described an encounter with a robot streetwalker down on her luck.

The trick (and I think it one of the most difficult in writing) is to see things from a new angle. I have found three questions useful in stimulating story ideas.

The first is: *What if something new came along?* Think of something some people (not necessarily everyone) would like to have, and imagine that it has been invented. During the Vietnam War, for example, it occurred to me that the Pentagon would probably like to be able to grow soldiers in laboratory flasks. I added an almost inevitable near-future development, the unmanned, computer-controlled battletank, and came up with a story called, 'The HORARS of War'. (This story originally appeared in the Delacorte collection *Nova 1*, edited by Harry Harrison, and as a Dell paperback; it has since been reprinted by Doubleday in *A Pocketful of Stars*, edited by Damon Knight, and was selected for reprinting again in Doubleday's *Combat-SF*, edited by Gordon Dickson. Many sf stories are reprinted – and paid for – repeatedly.)

The second idea generator is: *What if it gets better?* Take some existing art, skill, or what-you-like, and imagine that some brilliant technician is to spend his life improving it. What will it be like when he is finished? What will the social consequence of his improvements be? *What if it gets better?* – the source of my 'The Packerhaus Method'. A less macabre example is 'The Toy Theatre', in which I had life-sized marionettes equipped with remote controls.

The third question: *What if those two got together?* Combine two existing customs, practices, sciences, or institutions. In 'Beech Hill', I merged the writers' conference (where people who write fiction assemble) with the class of the poseur, the person whose life is his fiction. What I got was an annual gathering of those who pretend to be what they are not – a 'secret agent', an 'international adventuress', a 'wild animal trainer', 'the richest man in the world', and so on. My 'secret agent' was really a short-order cook, and he wrote the rest of the story.

Character

Science fiction's fictional people are hard to make believable because they are likely to be remote from the writer's experience. Who has known a Martian? A starship captain? A woman who has published scientific articles intended to prove that she is not a human being? If the writer cannot empathise with people who do not yet exist – and may never exist – he must stay out of science fiction.

In addition to empathy, there must be plausibility. A man sent to explore a new world, for example, is not likely to be a complete fool or a hopeless neurotic, though someone who finds himself in that position by accident may be either. As with other kinds of writing, character is manifested in speech and action, or by admitting the reader to the character's mind. In both these techniques, the broad scope of sf comes to the writer's aid. In 'Alien Stones', for example, I provided my laconic starship captain,

Commander Daw, with a young assistant named Wad. Wad was actually a computer simulation of Daw's own personality twenty years before. This juxtaposition generated insights that could not have come from the use of a conventional younger officer acting as a foil.

But science fiction holds a number of traps for the writer trying to invent a fictional cast. People in the twenty-second century must not use current slang, for example. Yet if they belong to different social levels, or have been nurtured in different worlds, or possess radically differing personalities, their speech must reveal these differences. Sometimes the writer can coin his own new words. (A smattering of these have entered the language; Karel Capek's *robot* is an example – it did not seem exotic when I used it a few paragraphs earlier, did it? Some others are entering it now, like Robert A. Heinlein's *grok*.) In most cases, however, this is a dangerous expedient, with limited usefulness. Style of speech and habitual cast of thought are surer tools. I tried to use them in '"A Story" by John V. Marsch':

> 'We had no names before men came out of the sky,' the Old Wise One said dreamily. 'We were mostly long and lived in holes between the roots of trees.'
>
> Sandwalker said, 'I thought we were the ones.'
>
> 'I am confused,' the Old Wise One admitted. 'There are so many of you now and so few of us.'
>
> 'You hear our songs?'
>
> 'I am made of your songs. Once there was a people using their hands – when they had hands – only to take food; there came among them another who crossed from star to star. Then it was found that the first heard the songs of the second and sent them out again – greater, greater, greater than before. Then the second felt their songs more strongly in all their bones – but touched, perhaps, by the first. Once I was sure I knew who the first were, and the second, now I am no longer sure.'
>
> 'And I am no longer sure of what it is you're saying,' Sandwalker told him.
>
> 'Like a spark from the echoless vault of emptiness,' the Old Wise One continued, 'the shining ships slipped steaming into the sea ...' But Sandwalker was no longer listening. He had gone to lie between Sweetmouth and Seven Girls Waiting, reaching out a hand to each.

Style

Science fiction has its own stylistic rules, to be broken only in exceptional cases. For example, characters must not lecture each other about things both would know. Your own small talk does not consist of explaining to your neighbour that cars must drive on the right, and that red means *stop* and green *go*. In the same way, a citizen of the year 3000 cannot expound the commonplace mechanics of his culture unless he is talking to someone who could reasonably be expected to be ignorant of them.

Frequently, writers who are aware of this prohibition try to circumvent it by having the hero discover a book (tape, vision cube) that just happens to provide the necessary data. This ploy is out of bounds, too. Of course, if the character has made a search for this 'Pnakotic Manuscript' and finding it is a vital part of the plot, that's different.

Many science fiction stories require coining new names. They should not be unpronounceable. (After all, one of the characters may have to pronounce them: 'Come on Xev'tbq, it's time we met Bwbblnmx.') Furthermore, new means *new*, not taken from the work of some other writer (as in 'Pnakotic Manuscript'). Writers unfamiliar with sf often discover a novel or story they believe to be completely unknown and forgotten, and only much later find that it is a 'classic' work, still revered by a fanatic few and known to almost everyone in the field.

Gadgets should have logical names (in most cases) and they should be used logically. If your character has invented a 'hyperspace phasor interrupter', he will probably call it a 'phasor' in casual conversation; and he – and whoever controls him – will utilise it to achieve whatever goals are logically theirs.

Plot

There are only two plot rules, as far as I know. The first is that it is better to have a plot (though the story can probably do without it in a pinch, if theme, characterisation, and style are good enough), and the second is to avoid the old hack plot, unless you give it a brilliant new twist. *Plot* concerns the adventures of the characters – what happens to them. Do not let the editor discover at the end of our story that the man and woman are Adam and Eve – he makes that discovery twice a week. Do not have your characters die and go to some strange new place, not unless your name is Roger Zelazny. Do not have a neighbourhood tinker invent a time machine in his basement – H. G. Wells could get away with it, but no one can today.

Above all, do not convert some other type of story to science fiction by making changes in background and detail. A cowpoke buckled into a pair of ray guns (now more likely to be laser pistols) is a cowpoke still. This admonition does not mean that the theme of the lone individual fighting for life in a half-tamed wilderness is excluded from sf. But the hero's opponents should not be crooked gamblers, or livestock thieves, or claim jumpers. The theme should be fitted with an sf plot.

Similarly, Joseph Conrad's great stories of the sea will not be improved by being shifted into space. The officers and crew of spaceships will have their own problems – solar storms might pour out deadly radiation, but they will not toss the passengers about; mutinies may break out, but they will not be fought with belaying pins or be sparked by floggings.

Going to the stars

Up until now I have been pointing out the difficulties of writing science fiction. It would not be fair to close without making some mention of the wonderful ease of it. The science fiction writer has escaped from the mundane world and entered the infinite universe. At various times I have wanted a girl who was a real cat, a living man without a head, a lady's maid who looked like a chest of drawers, and a world that was in fact a vast human body; and I have had them. Every writer, in sf, can have whatever he wants, if he can imagine it and make it his own.

22

How to be a Writer's Family

We writers are cowards. Give us any choice, and nine times out of ten we'll take the easy way out. That is why we're always telling you how to be writers – we're afraid to face the fact that you don't want to be writers. Many of you, however, dream secret dreams even more honourable. You would like to be the family of some writer, and I don't blame you a bit – I myself have often wanted to be Harlan Ellison's father.

Don't give up. If you keep plugging away, someday your big break will come. An important editor from New York will call you and say, 'Let me speak to Ursula, please.' That's it! You've made it, and from here on it's downhill all the way.

Or is it?

No, the rough stuff is only beginning. Being a member of a writer's family takes know how. Let me give you a little test. Suppose that you are a writer's wife and mistress of a kitchen equipped with electric stove, electric refrigerator, mixer, blender, trash compactor, kitchen sink, and three thousand dollars worth of groceries. When you stroll into the writer's study and walk around the furnace, do you say: a) I have a headache; b) I can hardly wait for the movie; c) I'd like to help you with that correspondence; or d) Give me some of your coffee …?

That's right, the correct answer is d. That really wasn't so hard, was it?

Here's a little tougher question, a two-parter. Suppose that you are a writer's small son. It is one week until Christmas. What do you tell the writer: a) If there's really a Santa Claus, why can't you get a grant? b) Eddie's dad lets him play Rudolph the Red-Nosed Reindeer real loud all the time; c) Can I type my list for Santa? d) All of the above.

Now for part two. After your father has agreed to type out your list, which of these items DON'T you ask for: a) TV rollerball game; b) The crash-and-burn race set they have on Saturday Night Live; c) A real car; d) A book.

You see, it's not really as easy as you thought. Perhaps before you go into this thing any deeper you should ask yourself whether you are truly qualified. To find out, complete the following statement: Many of my best friends are: a) Black; b) Jewish; c) Catholic; d) Noisy.

Those of you still with us – you know who you are – now need to determine what part of a writer's family you are best suited for. Answer this, and try to be brutally honest with yourself. Are you good at: a) Giggling; b) Sneaking up behind; c) Putting hands over Daddy's eyes while he types; d) Saying with a perfectly straight face, 'My teacher says science fiction is trash ...?' If you answered a, b, c, *and* d, you have found your vocation. You were put into the world to be a writer's younger daughter. You should practice the following phrases: 'The washing machine won't work.' 'The washing machine won't work unless you slam the lid down real hard.' 'I need all that white paper for school.' 'I'll bet you don't know who stepped on your typewriter.'

On that last question, there were probably some of you who got only three out of four. Let us face facts – you may not be perfect for the younger daughter part. There's a chance, however, that it's because you are perfect for Older Daughter. Would you feel comfortable: a) Organising a Lorne Greene fan club; b) Asking Mom why Dad gets mail from a girl named Anna Log; c) Asking Dad how many people came to his signing in the Wee Owl Book Shoppe in Korn King Mall; d) Saying with a perfectly straight face, 'My teacher says written communication will be obsolete in another five years.'

If you scored four out of four, try saying these: 'I went by the post office and I think there was some mail in your box, but probably they're closed by now.' 'They're starting a science fiction course at school; Old Lady Higgins is going to teach it – they're calling her out of retirement,' and 'I left your typewriter on the floor and guess what Therese did?'

Now for the heavy stuff – being a writer's older son. I'm not going to kid you, this is tough. It takes more stamina and guts than a beer commercial, and there is no room for 'nice guys'. You must be tough. You must also be broke, or at least, willing to appear broke. To discover whether you qualify, complete the following sentences: When I have all day free, I enjoy: a) baseball; b) rock; c) reading; d) nothing. When I grow up, I want to be: a) a doctor; b) a lawyer; c) a scientist; d) a crazy, like you. And finally, (look out, this is a tough one): When I need hot water for tea, I: a) get it from the tap; b) heat it on the stove; c) build a solar collector; d) ask dad.

Got your answers marked? ... Okay, those of you who got straight Ds qualify for older son.

Now, what about the rest of you? You've flunked as younger sons, younger daughters, older daughters and older sons. You feel like hell. Well relax, it's Cinderella time! You qualify as husbands or wives, or as a college professor would put it, spice.

Your job breaks down into three major areas – meeting the writer of your dreams, marrying him (or her), and keeping the fathead you married alert. Let's take meeting first.

You need not read the writer's work – in fact, it's better if you don't: any writer would rather talk to somebody who wants to read him than to somebody who has. Practice the following lines: 'Oh, Mr. Tucker, I hear you've started to write! I can't wait until your first book comes out!' That one was for you older ladies. Now for the younger ones, 'Oh, Mr. Haldeman, my father is Secretary of Defence, and he says *The Forever War* practically taught him his job!' Now this next one is only for younger ladies who know how to wiggle. If you're a really good wiggler, it can't miss. 'Oh, Mr. Spinrad, my girlfriend says everything you write makes her feel,' (wiggle), 'oh, you know!'

But memorising lines like these is not enough. You must also learn which lines NOT to use. Here are three: 'Mr. Farmer, your book made me feel like getting plowed.' 'Mr. Budrys, when are you going to start writing again?' and of course the unfailing, 'Dr. Asimov, can I call you Ike?'

But what if the target writer is a woman? Women would never fall for the kind of flattery that sweeps innocent men off their feet. If one were to say, 'Oh, Mr. Tiptree, my father is Secretary of Defence, and he says "Love is the Plan, the Plan is Death" taught him all he knows,' one could hardly expect more than a gale of mocking laughter. No, if you want to meet and impress women writers, you must drill yourself on these lines: 'Perhaps sometime I can take your children to the ballpark for a doubleheader.' 'I am a licensed typewriter mechanic.' And of course the unfailing, 'You won't believe this, but I'm one guy who absolutely loves to cook and do dishes.' If she's Jewish, by all means use: 'My name is Alex.'

Congratulations! You've met your writer and you're well on the way to becoming his or her spouse. Now is the time, as we writers say, to 'finalise' the deal. Fortunately, the same lines can be used for both writing sexes. You might try: 'My father owns an office supply store.' If your chosen writer specialises in fantasy, you could say: 'At my christening a faerie said that whoever married me would achieve improved typing skills.' On the other hand, if your chosen writer goes for the hard stuff: 'I have a $15,000 mini-computer with advanced editing capabilities, but I never use it myself.'

By the time you're back from your honeymoon – whether it be three fun-filled days at Cape Kennedy or ten glorious weeks in the writer-in-residence dorm of the University of Iowa – you should be ready to *teach* Writer's Family instead of taking it. You will be an expert at clogging drains just as the robot turns upon the survivors of the crash; and with a little practice you may even be able to arrange for the dog to have her puppies when the generation ship is falling into the black hole.

The danger, quite frankly, is that you may get *too* expert. You may forget the basics. So you can check on yourself, I give you this last, brief question; you can look it up in your notes when the time comes. When the writer has at last finished the final page of his novel and carried the manuscript to the post office, do you say: a) It must be a wonderful feeling – how about helping me paint the kitchen? b) The robot is stuck in the drain; c) My father doesn't really own an office supply store – he's being thrown off welfare; or d) Gene, don't forget you've got to write a speech for I Con …?

23
Libraries on the Superhighway –
Rest Stop or Roadkill?

You see before you a man suckered by his publisher. I thought my wife and I were going to get an expense-account trip to Miami in return for eating dinner and signing a few books. If I had known I was going to have to give this talk, I would never have agreed. I know nothing about the information superhighway said to be lurking around the next bend – and neither does anybody else, don't let them kid you – and what little I know about libraries I have learned from you. If I were a carny, I'd call this a 'cold reading'. It's what we science-fiction persons do.

Putting my fingers to my temples (without dropping the speech, I hope) and rolling up my eyes in a frightening manner I peer into the future.

Library, Dewey Decimal, Stacks and stacks and stacks and stacks, cataloguing, pettifogging ... Preservation !!!

Looks bad. Most of the trends are against you, so let's do roadkill first.

To begin with, free public libraries are a 19th century phenomenon. Andrew Carnegie died in 1919 – if you don't know who Andrew Carnegie was, ask old Mrs. Hwiggins at the Research Desk. The 19th century notion was that it was your duty to educate yourself, and it was nice for the public to help you. Since the poor could not afford to pay tuition, free schools were provided. Since they could not afford to buy books, free public libraries were provided, too.

To underline my point, I'd like to quote here from Cobbett's *Grammar of the English Language*, published in 1819, exactly one hundred years before Carnegie died. This is how it begins – the first paragraph of the dedication to Queen Caroline: 'May it please your Majesty, a work having for its objects, to lay the solid foundation of literary knowledge amongst the Labouring Classes of the community, to give practical effect to the natural genius found in the Soldier, the Sailor, the Apprentice, and the Plough-boy, and to make that genius a perennial source of wealth, strength, and safety to the kingdom; such a work naturally seeks the approbation of your Majesty, who, amongst all the Royal Personages of the present age, is the only one that appears to have justly estimated the value of The People.'

There you have it. Remember, please, that Carnegie was born in Scotland and began his career as a bobbin-boy in a textile mill. Free public libraries are, or were, the weary bobbin-boy's dream.

All this is, of course, utterly alien to the mental habits of the 20th century, and seems sure to be antithetical to those of the 21st. The new idea,
the current idea, and the future idea – exemplified by drafting me to speak
to this group – is that it is society's duty to adapt itself to the ignorance of
its members, and it's a good idea for them to force society to do it. Faucets
that used to read HOT and COLD are now red or blue – and I do not mean
that those words are written on them.

We are in the process of reinventing hieroglyphics. The hood release of
my car has a picture of an automobile with its hood up, and the cigarette
lighter has a picture of a smoking cigarette. A week or so ago I was con-
fronted by a large and intimidating sign that showed a hand dropping a
handkerchief overlaid with the circle-and-slash thing that looks like the
top of a slot-head screw. Its meaning seemed plain: I had wandered into
the realm of Gilbert and Sullivan's *Mikado*, and the sign meant 'Do Not
Flirt!'

Other signs I have encountered recently include a tiger, meaning 'Bring
more babies to the zoo'; a knife, a fork, and a plate, meaning 'Get gas
here'; and a person peering into an open book above an arrow pointing
back toward Chicago, meaning 'Readers go home'.

All of these are bad signs for libraries.

But, I hear you object, I'm supposed to be talking about the future and
the information superhighway, not highway signs. Bear with me.

The proponents of hieroglyphics tell us we must have them because so
many people – immigrants, visitors, even native-born Americans – have
been educated in a language other than English, particularly Spanish. Think
about that for a moment. Suppose that you were to visit Spain, Mexico, or
some other Spanish-speaking country. How long would it take you to learn
that *caliente* means hot and *frio* cold? Honestly now. Isn't that something
you'd pick up on the first day? And be proud of yourself for having learned
so easily and quickly? How much difficulty would that esoteric Spanish
word *restaurante* give you?

I bought the rationale myself for years, right up until I read a little book
called *Fish Whistle*. In it Daniel Pinkwater tells us that he had grown up
listening to his father's broken English and being told – and believing –
that Polish was his father's native language. At last the Cold War broke
up, and he (a successful author of books for young people) was able to
take his father back to the Old Country, where he watched as native speak-
ers of Polish struggled to understand his father's Polish exactly as people
here had struggled to understand his father's English. Horrified, Daniel
Pinkwater realised that his father was fluent in no language whatever.

That gave me the clue to what is going on with the knife, the fork, and
the empty plate. And with the dead man in bed, the handkerchief drop-
per, and the rest. They aren't there, really, for people who read and

understand Spanish, or Chinese, or any other language. They are there for Daniel Pinkwater's dad.

There are more and more of him, and there will be still more in the coming century, because (as I have said) we have chosen to adapt to ignorance. Education was a privilege once. Today it's a chore, and tomorrow it will be a pointless chore. Most students' attitude is 'Prove to my satisfaction that I will need to know this subject – otherwise I won't learn it.' And as our society adapts further and further to the needs of its illiterates, the proofs demanded will become harder and harder to provide. What the hieroglyphics are *really* saying is 'there is no need for you to read'.

That brings me to the first thing I want to say about the information superhighway. It is that superhighways are great only if you own a car, a motorcycle, or a truck. No tractors, no skateboards, no horse-drawn vehicles, no bicycles, and no pedestrians. You've all seen the signs.

The information superhighway is going to leave a lot of people behind, in other words. I think that they'll resent it. They'll take out their resentment on any institution concerned with literacy – including what is called computer literacy – that is open to political control. If you haven't realised who that is yet, ask old Mrs. Hwiggins at the Research Desk. She knows.

Now it's time to ask what's really meant by an information superhighway. It is, pretty obviously a 'buzzword' – a term that I prefer to 'slogan' because I can't rid my mind of the knowledge that a slogan was originally a Scottish battlecry.

In so far as 'information superhighway' means anything, it means that everyone with a computer can be linked to everyone else similarly equipped, and thus that all of the digitised information that is generally available will be available to them. The image, in other words, is that of a coast to coast tollway – you didn't really think this was going to come free, did you? – connecting hundreds of stretches of local roads, streets, and by-paths.

It goes without saying that not ALL digitised information will be available. Governments and corporations will continue to hide nearly everything, and many individuals will at least try to conceal various matters.

What doesn't go without saying, I'm afraid, is that a lot of the data available on the superhighway will be false. It's currently estimated that one quarter to one half the research reported in scientific journals has been faked. This is a relatively new phenomenon and a dangerous one, and the amount of faking is increasing.

Furthermore, this faked data has been filtered for us, like cigarette smoke. It has had to pass the staff and the editorial board of the journal that published it, and these staffs and boards are very much alert to the problem, turning away masses of ill-conceived, poorly-executed, or suspicious-looking research. The information superhighway will bypass the filters.

Anyone looking into a hypothetical connection between hamburgers and child molesting will get research sponsored by what used to be called the beef trust and research promulgated by Hindus and vegetarians.

Wait, it gets worse.

Most faked research today comes from Ph.D. hopefuls and bush-league scientists angling for grants. Think what it will be like when the hackers and the pranksters get to work. Wait till the bush-league scientists start writing papers under new names confirming their fictitious 'discoveries'. Public libraries have little to worry about in this regard, perhaps; but I'm afraid that those of you who work in university libraries are going to find yourselves hip deep in it. Did a Dr. Smith at your school in fact confirm that it was not the onions, the beef, or the bun, but the special sauce that best correlates with an uncontrollable urge to fling infants to tigers?

Do you in fact have a Dr. Smith? Yes, you do. Do you have a record of this paper? Yes to that, too – although not ON paper, it's a computer listing. Did Dr. Smith in fact write it? No, he did not, and good luck in finding him to ask.

Most of you have labelled me as a hopeless technophobe by now, scratching out bewildered accounts of dystopias in which monstrous self-propelled juggernauts with wide chrome smiles kill more babies than tigers and scarlet fever combined.

Naaah.

It's just that – well, let me tell you about my freshman math teacher. His name, well as I can recall it now, was Prof. Schleswigholsteinuntgottdamnerrung; and he was young and plump, and spoke English with an almost impenetrable accent. He rode a bicycle and was in those benighted times the only faculty member to do so, and he wore a knit cap in which the knitter had made some major mistakes and a knit scarf that was plainly a product of the same hand.

We were young too, and easily frightened in those days, a mixture of country boys who were thoroughly cowed at finding themselves amongst environs so very learned and sophisticated as a cow college, and city boys like me who were terrified to find themselves marooned for four years in a huddle of run-down buildings on a barren and trackless prairie.

We were afraid of upperclassmen, campus cops, cafeteria food, each other, and even (though I blush now to admit it) the English Department. Of the Chemistry Department, the Physics Department, the Dean's Office, and – above all the rest – the Department of Mathematics we stood in abject and mind-numbed terror.

Nevertheless, after the first class or two, we voted to keep Prof. Schleswigholsteinuntgottdamnerrung as a pet. The rowdy crowd might steal his knit cap and throw it on the roof or let the air out of his bicycle tires. We would have none of it, though we perpetrated various minor hoaxes, wheezes, and swindles involving thefts from the old, scuffed briefcase in which he transported his lecture notes, and conspiracies to misinform him about American holidays.

He had numerous peculiarities and eccentricities, but of the things I recall most vividly now is that he wore both an old brass pocket watch that appeared to have been inherited from the same unsuccessful German attorney who had supplied his briefcase, and a new and very cheap wristwatch. When he wanted to know the time, he consulted both, added their readings, and divided the result by two – usually getting the answer wrong.

His most enduring quirk, however, was his habit of using his slide rule for every possible computation, reading it to five mostly inaccurate figures. If he had to double seventeen, for example, he used his slide rule and arrived at thirty three point nine, nine, seven. It is good enough for engineering purposes.

Fifteen years later, the company that employed me, having established that I was worthless at everything else, made me a computer programmer. This, you understand, was way back in the pioneer days, when the memory of walk-in vacuum-tube computers was yet bright and home computers were still undreamed-of. I spent the last years of my engineering career as a programmer, and left the job in 1972. I was supposed to be telling the computer to tell a numerically-controlled milling machine how to make things, and mostly telling it how to make blow-moulds for plastic bottles.

Our computer, as I soon discovered, had no interest in bottles. It was out to fake its way through the whole project, something I had done occasionally myself. I would tell it, very clearly and distinctly, to outline a bottle rather like a dress-maker's dummy, and it would proceed to rough out a Klein bottle.

Or something.

Before long, I recognised that computer for what it was. Cybernetic science, for which science fiction had given me such immense respect, had laboured mightily for whole decades with silicon and germanium, rubber, copper wire, tin siding, plastic and God knows what else, and has at last triumphantly produced a Frankenstein Prof. Schleswigholsteinuntgottdamnerrung.

That computer knew far more mathematics than I would ever know, and that computer knew nothing else at all. It could be misled by a child. It could be misled by me even when I was doing my utmost not to mislead it.

Furthermore, we had a keypunch operator – in our gross ignorance and primitivity we then used people called keypunch operators, and when I've got more time I'll tell you about IBM cards – named Bobbi Beavers. I'm not making this up; that was her name. She was small and cute, and could do an imitation of Shirley Temple, skipping rope while singing *On the Good Ship Lollipop*, that I have never seen equalled. And when Ms. Beavers and I combined our formidable creativities, we could tie that computer in knots well before the middle of the program.

I left programming in 1972, as I said, and took an honest job. It was a strain at first, and there have been times – though mercifully few – when I have felt a pang of nostalgia for Prof. Schleswigholsteinuntgottdamnerung. I mean that darn computer. But I find that if I shut my eyes really tight and think hard about plastic bottles, the feeling goes away.

When the rage for writing on computers began, Algis Budrys and a dozen other friends told me I simply had to get one. I asked them to name one useful capability a computer would give me, and they named scores of neat ones. Unfortunately, they were *only* neat. Useful is something else.

That computers are wonderful machines, I do not in the least deny. If you want to hunt submarines using statistical methods – which is what electronic computers were in fact built to do, originally – they are truly marvellous. They are unequalled at calculating orbits for NASA. But give them a simple job –

Well, the library I frequent has done away with the old card catalogue and installed computers, and they are wonderful. Say that you are interesting in snipe hunting. These computers – and I use the plural advisedly, for there are frequently as many as two in service at one time – will produce a list of every single book on snipe hunting held by every single library in the north-west Chicago burbs. They will even tell you which of these books are in the library in which you happen to be sitting.

But there is one thing that they will not do under any circumstances. You can cuss and sweat, and pound the table until the library closes; but they will never, ever, tell you where that book is. For that you need a librarian.

And eventually it dawns upon you that you can bypass the computers completely, just going up casual-like to a librarian and saying, 'Where are the snipe-hunting books?'

In a way, this is rest stop – librarians are not about to go the way of the key-punch operator. In another, it is just more roadkill because librarians have to deal all day long with people maddened by their failure to access (as computer folks say) the simple information they need.

I've done some reading in order to write this little talk – reading is often needed, I find, when you know nothing about your subject – and as a way of sliding from roadkill into rest stop, I'd like to read you some sentences and paragraphs I've come across, and of course argue with them and find fault, and carry on as I always do when I read just about anything.

Here's a fine science-fiction writer, David Brin. 'On the other hand, no author before 1979 came even close to predicting something as fundamental to our modern world as the home computer.'

The reason – and Brin should have had no difficulty at all in deducing it – is that authors are not in the business of predicting irrelevancies. The people I know who own home computers are reading and send e-mail, the greatest majority of it cocktail-party chatter. They enjoy it, and that's good. But it isn't anything a writer can make a story from. They are playing neat-o games; that's fun, but ... They are keeping financial records and playing the stock market; neither, alas, is new. My writer friends who write on computers all tell me that they are writing more and better. I read them, and they are indeed writing more.

But not better.

In fact, not as good – possibly a story could be made out of that fact, but it would interest few people who were not writers themselves.

I have racked my brains to find something really relevant that some owners are using their home computers for, and the only thing I've come up with is that home computers are letting some people who used to drive to an office work at home. I'm all for that, but it's basically a revival of cottage industry.

Here's another quote. This is by Stephen P. Brown, the editor of *Science Fiction Eye*, and is one of those interesting statements in which the idea itself is correct, although almost all the details are wrong.

'Right now everyone is infatuated with technology itself with little thought as to the results. It's as if early auto theorists spent all their time on engine and road design without a clue regarding the massive changes made in society by putting total mobility into the hands of everyone.'

That of course is exactly what the early auto theorists did. And they did NOT put 'total mobility' into the hands of 'everyone' – try to drive from here to France. Try to drive if you're blind, or too poor to afford a car and gasoline.

And of course not 'everyone' is infatuated with this sort of technology. I for one am not. Rather, I am fascinated by the hold it has upon its devotees, and how little real, usable capability it has given them to date.

For my final quote, here's one of the best cyberpunks, Bruce Sterling. '[Computer] bulletin boards excel at minor aspects of social housekeeping, such as swapping addresses, spreading headlines, breeding rumours, and, especially, exchanging insults.'

I think that makes very plain what the worst of the 'roadkill' aspects of the superhighway will be for libraries. In place of that bewildered-looking man who wanders up to you and asks where you keep the snipe-hunting books, you're going to have hundreds (I'm lying here, because I'm afraid that you wouldn't believe me if I said thousands) of inquiries, inputs, and complaints, nearly all of which will have to be dealt with in some way by somebody. In the 25th century, my old pal Buck Rogers assures me, that somebody will be a computer. In the 21st, I fear, old Mrs. Hwiggins will have retired; but you will still be there.

Did I say that bit from Bruce Sterling was my last quote? I lied about that, too. Let's return David Brin for a minute. Brin asks, 'What will be the consequences when, as some predict, the personal computer will be so cheap that the average citizen of the Third World owns one and has a greater access to *data* than to clean water?'

My late friend Jim Friend taught English at a college in Chicago. And a few years before he died, Jim visited China. He dropped in on a university in Beijing to compare notes with his Chinese counterparts, and they grabbed him and demanded that he speak to their students. The students, they said, would never forgive them if they let a western professor leave without giving a lecture. They would provide a translator, a hall, a mike, and in short whatever Jim wanted but he *had* to speak. What about tomorrow night?

That gave poor Jim something like ten minutes in which to rack his brain and come up with a topic of interest to Chinese college students – one that he knew enough about to speak on without references. The topic he came up with was the capabilities of Chicago-area colleges and universities: which ones were strong in English, which ones offered what foreign language, which had well-regarded journalism departments, and so on. There are roughly sixty institutions of higher learning in the Greater Chicago Area, and Jim was familiar with most of them. He told his Chinese colleagues, and they put up little notices around the campus. 'Prof. James Friend of Chicago State University will speak tomorrow night on the capabilities of Chicago-area colleges.'

Jim said he figured nobody would come because the notices were in Chinese.

Seriously, he expected forty or fifty students at best, those who had some reasonable expectation of becoming exchange students and thought that they might like to come to Chicago.

He got fifteen – hundred. That is not an exaggeration. The room in which he spoke was intended to hold four or five hundred.

And the students knew it. They had begun arriving about four for his six forty-five talk. Every seat was filled, and they were seven deep in the aisles. They filled the windows, sitting and standing on the windowsills.

Brin speculated that the *average* citizen of the Third World will eventually have his own home computer in which to cruise the superhighway. I don't believe it, but I do believe this: suppose that every *college student* in the Third World gets access to a computer and the superhighway. Forget about the millions upon millions of toiling peasants. Let's just suppose every college student.

Well, it's not as bad as you might expect. There are only 600,000 of them in all China. That's only ten times as many as attend the university of Illinois, or twenty times as many as attend the university of Florida. It could be a lot worse. Teachers are another kind of people in China who may well get onto the net before long, though I doubt that they'll be quite as active there as the college students. Anyway, there are only about 700,000 of them.

Now that we've begun looking at the bright side, let's switch to the good stuff, the rest stops. Sure, there are going to be problems. And we can be certain that the rosiest predictions of the technophiles are pipe dreams, as they always are – I remember when they said that electricity generated by nuclear power would be so cheap you wouldn't need a meter.

But there are going to be some real benefits for all of us, including libraries. Say that someone needs very badly to have a look at *The War in Florida*, by a Late Staff Officer. It was published in Baltimore in 1836, and it's not likely that your library has a copy. Your computer will be able to tell you within a few seconds that there's a copy at Bethune-Cookman in Daytona.

Furthermore, you'll be able to print up a facsimile of it on the spot, including all the drawings and maps. Pretty cool, huh?

It won't be cheap, though. I suspect that you'll either charge your patron a fairly stiff fee and let him keep the book, or (if he prefers) a lesser fee and loan him the book. When he returns it, you can catalogue and shelve it for the next researcher.

Nor is that all. About thirty years ago, I had the very enlightening experience of watching two librarians trying to help a patron who wanted to read ghost stories. Their library had no category – it distinguished only between juvenile and adult fiction, as I remember – and they did a great deal of fumbling around.

That's already a thing of the past, as you know. Today you can perform a key-word search that should yield all the titles that include the word *ghost*. Tomorrow you will be able to compile your own anthology, if you choose. Or your patron can. 'Let's see. "The Ghost", by Richard Hughes. I have to have that. And here's "The Woman's Ghost Story", by Algernon Blackwood. I've heard of him, so I'll put it in, too. What about "The Ghost Ship" by Richard Middleton? Why, that could be about a German raider in the First World War or something. Let's just pull it up onto the screen and have a look. Dear, dear! I wish the library didn't make everything so difficult.'

All the participating libraries in the world will become, in effect, parts of one vast library. If you work for, let us say, the Savannah Public Library, you will be able to think of the Library of Congress as a branch of yours.

Far more important, you are ideally positioned to make the benefits of the information superhighway available to those to whom they would otherwise be denied. I said a while ago that a highway is of benefit only to those who can own and drive a car, a truck, or a motorcycle. You can be the Greyhound and the Trailways of the information superhighway.

No, you *are*, because if you aren't nobody else is going to do it. You can make 'home' computers available to the people who cannot have them in their own homes. Using them, people whom the educational system and the economic system have failed will be able to explore the bewildering array of programs that are available to them on the city, county, state, and Federal levels, and can be coached by software though the completion of the necessary applications, which they can then submit over the net.

That will not just give them a reason to learn to read, it will actually teach them computer skills that may permit them to land a job.

And in the process they will have *learned* to read. Think of it; at the same time they see the need, they will be acquiring the skill.

Furthermore, they will have acquired it *in the library*. *Your* library. It will no longer be an alien place, a place frequented by the educated elites whom they believe are their oppressors, but a known and friendly place.

The world has turned away from Carnegie's dream, and it's quite possible that it believes it's done away with Carnegie's dream once and for all.

I don't agree. Dreams are weak things, as every writer quickly learns. They are nebulous – we who hawk them on the streets know that only too well. But dreams, I notice, always play the second half.

And the second half has just begun.

24
The Handbook of Permissive English

Introduction

The Handbook of Permissive English is the first grammatical and syntactical guide ever published with a non-snob purpose. This book – I mean this one here – is to help you write like everybody. If you use it good, the boss will never read one of your reports and say the deadly, 'Why he/she writers better than me!'

Just like our having sex has been freed up from the no fun ideas of old fashioned ancient times, writing and talking needs to be freed up from it to. *The Handbook of Permissive English* does it. Permissive English is just exactly like permissive sex, except not so much fun and/or worrying.

a, an One of those Ant Annie distinctions that is rapidly starting to be dead. (See *who, whom,* its worse.) If your going to be a Ant Annie about it, at least be consistent all the time. Use *an* before all the words that start with a *H*. Like this: 'An hotel, an herpes case, usage as an hole.'

amateurs People that do what they do do out of love. The other way is *hookers*. (See *prose*.)

among/between Puzzling because one way means among two people and the other one means between three or even more than that. But no one can remember which one is the other one. The solution is to write them both like here, with a slash. (See slash.) In the middle. Like this: 'Just among/between you and myself ...'

and/or People that have not got their shots for enough Progressive English say *and/or* is silly because if you say and or for the slash. (See slash.) It's and and or or. It's not because the slash in *and/or* is upside down (pretend like). So what it really is is and or and or. It means one and/or the other one to. For instance, if a menu has got on it ham and/or eggs, it means that if you just only want ham or eggs you can get it. (See *slash*.)

ante-bellum Against the civil war, especially Southern bellums like Scarlet O'Hara.

apostrophe A comma upside-down at the top. It's most common usage is for making plurals. Like this 'The 9's stick in this typewriter.' 'I am Mr. Hopkins's's secretary, Senior and Junior both.'

assassin A not too smart word for people its not a real good idea to talk a whole lot about them. *Double hippy* is a nicer way, but they don't appreciate it much either. In Chicago its better to not talk about 'The Boys'. In Los Angeles don't call anybody 'Vader's Raiders' if it fits. They aren't 'the Company' in Washington either.

at A troublesometimes word that is easily tamed by knowing that the Old Middle English (dialect of the middle of England like Leicester) had it with a *H*. It being not incredibly polite (see *assassin*) to inquire the where of some person's whereabouts position. Like this: 'Where is Giles (h) at?' The headcover clothes type itself serving *in rerum natura* – means behind the natural person.

awful Means the same as *very*, but a lot more. A girl that is very cute probably isn't very cute, but a girl that is awful cute is really terribly cute. Used with words about time, awful means it will be a awful long time 'till you forget about it. Like this: 'How was your date?' 'Awful!'

because The word to use after 'the reason is'.

disinterested Could care less.

ellipsis Three little dots ... for something you left out. They get their name because they are supposed to remind you of those 1,2,3 pictures when the sun gets in the way of the moon.

fan Somebody that likes whatever it is they are a big fan of. For instance a politician might say, 'I am as big a fan of clean air as someone, but ...' etc. A fanatic is a super-fan, but super-fan is more polite.

gay This word must always be used, because it is the only one accepted by all gays except for Gore Vidal and other who don't. Like this: 'He danced with Gay Abandon.' (Gore Vidal is just an old troublemaker, and everybody knows it.) (See *queer*.)

hopefully A good word to put in front to show you care. Using it a lot will get you promoted in most companies. Like this: 'Hopefully people will start writing memos a person can understand now.'

I and **me** You can waste a lot of time trying to decide which one is right, but it really doesn't matter. The reason is because your boss doesn't know either. Here's a time-saver tip: *I in front, me in back.* These words almost never turn up in the middle of you're sentence, so if the problem is in front, say *I*. If its in the back, say *me*. Important exception – if its in a list of people's's names, say *myself*, front or back. Like this: 'George and I will do it. It will be done by George and me. It will be done by myself, Betty, George, an Howard.'

national names When the names of countries are written down in Permissive English, they should be the one on your map, even if the other one is no longer or even shorter. Like this: 'Our Poland account.' 'There

Philippines plant.' Not *Our Polish account* and *There Philippine plant*. As this rule shows, its really Permissive England.

Permissive English What you are speaking (and writing) if you have read this right straight and not peeked ahead to here to start. Permissive English is England (see *national names*) as a live language used like by police, sanitary engineers, hookers and the other street-type people. Its always getting simpler, so its okay if you say PermEng, but pretty soon according to the rule by Orwell (the great England writer) everybody will say MisSpeak. Its the way you talk (and right after three drinks).

prose Professional persons that have got jobs.

queer Because it means *gay*, this word should never be used. *Odd* is the best other word. Like this: 'She saw Chesterton's *The Club of Odd Trades*, but didn't pick it up.'

quotation marks Named for the Marks Brother who became a stock broker, and they are the ones that look like tiny little vampire teeth. Like this: 'Really Mr. Hopkins, what you did was "all right".'

slash A mark like this: /. Also called a virtual because its virtually (means without giving in) impossible to choose between each side. When reading out loud, pronounce as 'and/or'.

sob A useful word because it means somebody's mother was a dogperson, but between little stars it looks like your crying. Like this: 'Mr. Hopkins you *sob* don't want me to retype that whole letter *again*?' You'll feel a whole lot better.

unique Saying *unique, uniquer,* and *uniquist* is just fine in Permissive England (after all, everything are), its better to do it right. Like this: *unique, most unique,* and *incredibly unique*.

who, whom Another just about dead distinctions, but one the careful writer of Permissive English may still find he and/or she likes. The rule is to write *who* in ordinary talking, only *whom* when an air of more formal is wanted to be imparted. Like this: 'Hopkins, I wish you to discover in whom's rooms these sheets originated at.' The phrase *to whom it may concern* is considered sexist now.

25

More than Half of You Can't Read This

But the Writers of the Future Contest has asked me to read your palm nevertheless. Twenty-five years is no great length on the scale of history, and thus I am conservative, limiting myself to the following five predictions – one for each finger. And indeed, they are less prediction than certainty.

- The Thumb – Power: America and the U.S.S.R. preserve an uneasy accord, each testing the other's will within well-defined limits. No *major* nuclear war has taken place. Soviets are more like Americans (and Americans more like Soviets) than anyone else.
- The Index Finger – Learning: Vestiges of reading, writing, and spelling remain in the curricula of the public schools. Those who can read a few common words are counted literate. The schools train their students for employment – how to report to computers and follow instructions. (Called *interaction*.) Fifty million adult Americans are less than fluent in English.
- The Fool Finger – Entertainment: Sports and televised dramas are the only commonly available recreations. The dramas are performed by computer-generated images indistinguishable (on screen) from living people. Scenery is provided by the same method. Although science fiction and fantasy characterise the majority of these dramas, they are not so identified.
- The Ring Finger – Love: There is little sex outside marriage, which normally includes a legal contract. A single instance of infidelity is amply sufficient to terminate a marriage, with damages to the aggrieved party; this is a consequence of the two great plagues of the past twenty-five years. (I do not include the one we call AIDS, because it began well before this was written.) The population of the planet is below six billion. People live in space and on the moon, but their numbers are not significant.
- The Little Finger – Minority: A literate stratum supplies leadership in government and most (though not all) other fields. Its members are experimenting with sociological simulations that take into account the individual characters and preferences of most of the population.

Its aim is to increase the power of the literate class and further limit literacy, without provoking war with the U.S.S.R. or alienating the rising powers – China and the Latin American Block. A literate counterculture also exists.

Its products, too, are largely science fiction and fantasy; it tries to broaden the literate base, in part in order that its output can be read. It is of course to you of this counterculture that I write to say, take heart! Twenty-five years is no great length upon the scale of history. In my time too, the age was dark. But we are summoning the sun.

Gene Wolfe
Palm Sunday 1987

26

Wolfe's Inalienable* Truths About Reviewing

Reviews provide a supplemental success path that can, to a limited extent, do the same things that short stories do for your writing career.

It is very difficult to get good reviewing slots unless you are a good reviewer – interesting, literate, knowledgeable.

You submit reviews to newspapers and magazines just as you would short stories. HOWEVER, the review you submit is rarely accepted and published. What generally happens is that the review editor gives you assignments if he likes your work.

Top markets like *The Washington Post* pay quite well – three hundred and seventy five dollars for under two thousand words. Most others pay little (two or three cents a word) or nothing.

HOWEVER, you aren't in it for the money. You are in it to make a name for yourself, to become a well-known writer. Remember, novels are where the money is.

You should never describe the plot – tell what the book is about instead. 'This is near-future science-fiction in which an army with intelligent machines fights a seemingly hopeless war in the Martian desert.'

Unless your review is very brief, you should never offer an opinion without explaining why you hold that opinion.

When space permits, quote the book to make your points. For example: if you say the book is clumsily written, give a telling instance of the clumsy writing in your review.

NEVER bias your review to use as a weapon in a feud.

NEVER make up things to make your review more entertaining.

NEVER say anything in your review that you would not tell the author face-to-face.

ALWAYS remember that reviewing is dangerous. You can easily hurt yourself far worse by reviewing than you can help yourself. If you are seen as a dishonest reviewer, you will make scores of influential enemies very, very quickly.

---

* Because they have nothing to do with aliens.

27
A Fantasist Reads The Bible and Its Critics

Let me begin with a string of disclaimers. I am a Christian, but I shall not write here to promote Christianity. I am a Catholic, but nothing I say here should be taken as Catholic doctrine or as the opinion of my church, for which I have no license to speak. I am neither a theologican nor a biblical scholar. I will boast, however, that I possess a couple of advantages most critics lack: I have actually read and reread the book in question. And I am a writer, the author of some twenty-odd books of my own.

There are insights that result from being of the trade, though separated by the ages. The humblest seaman, given an account of Drake or John Paul Jones, will understand things that have escaped scores of earnest historians. They may not be pivotal or even significant things (at least, not in the opinion of the historians), but they are actual things none the less; and the process of writing has changed far less in the past five thousand years than that of sailing in the past two hundred.

If you carry nothing else away from this humble essay, take this: it is not all that different in the doing. Divine inspiration makes an immense difference, to be sure. Nothing that any modern writer writes can claim the dignity of, say, Samuel. But the authors of the books that make up the Bible were not (as I believe and a multitude of details show) stenographers taking God's dictation, but human beings inspired by Him. And it was as human beings that they wrote, conveying the message of inspiration to their fellows.

This is much nearer the practice of the Greeks than is usually acknowledged, by the way. The Greeks believed that their gods spoke to them through the 'makings' of inspired poets, of whom Homer was the first and greatest. The ancient Jews believed that God had spoken through Moses, whom they credited with the authorship of the Pentateuch. The fashion today seems to be to discount both, to say that Moses wrote nothing, and to add that Homer never lived – to contend that the books anciently credited to each were actually written by no one. Indeed, millions of words have been spent to convince us that these books simply grew up of themselves.

A writer dismisses that at once, of course. Try telling a cabinet maker that tables come together by themselves, one generation setting up a leg in the middle of the dining room, and another, a century later, balancing a single leaf on top of it.

Which brings us to the centre of the vexed question of authorship. What do we mean, or rather what should we mean, when we say that Moses did not write Exodus or Numbers? That his own fingers never grasped the pen? Pens were not in use. That he himself did not laboriously scrape off wax or imprint clay? Erle Stanley Gardner dictated his mysteries, yet we do not scruple to call them his. Eisenhower's *Crusade in Europe* was ghost written, as are thousands of other books. How do we benefit by holding Moses to a stricter standard? The end of Deuteronomy describes the death and burial of Moses. Are we supposed to believe the Ancient Jews were somehow blind to that?

There is a test that can be easily applied to the Mosaic books as soon as one realises that the great lawgiver was an Egyptian. (Everyone, I suppose, has heard the joke about the two little Baptist churches standing side-by-side in a remote Kentucky village. A traveller asks why the town requires two Baptist churches, and the town loafer explains, 'Well, that 'un's fer them that says she found Moses in the bullrushes. T'other 'un's fer them that says that's what *she* said.'

(But whether or not Moses was genetically or racially a Jew – whatever that is supposed to mean after centuries of captivity in Egypt – he was surely Egyptian by culture and education.) If then, he was the author of the Pentateuch, we should expect to find a residue of Egyptian customs and dietary laws (yes, the Egyptians had dietary laws) there. As indeed we do. Were you aware that the Ancient Egyptians were circumcised? And that they considered pigs unclean?

You may reasonably ask what all this stuff about Moses and authorship has to do with fantasy. A lot, or so I think. Fantasy provides the best modern paradigm for the writing of the books that constitute the Bible, not because Moses was a fictional character – he was not – but because the writers of fantasy must deal in the same way with the same types of material. Moses was real, and Frodo is fictional. But the scribe who described (what a suggestive word!) the death of Moses was writing about his idea of Moses, just as Tolkien dealt with his of Frodo. This should not make us think less of Moses, although it may lead us to think rather more of Frodo.

Thus the fantasist who comes to the Bible for the first time finds himself among friends. That, I believe, is the chief thing I have been trying to say in this part of this essay. The sailor told of Drake senses that if he were set down on the main deck of Drake's ship he could touch his cap and say, 'Mornin', Cap'n!' and take his place in the crew within an hour. In precisely the same way, the fantasist senses that he could picnic on bread and dried fish beside the Sea of Galilee. These are his kind of people.

He senses too (if he had read them) that most critics of the Bible would quickly gravitate to the Pharisees, and that they would feel equally at home there.

Speaking of critics, they must be rubbing their hands already over that joke about the Kentucky village. On the principle that a foe divided is half defeated, I'm going to tell another one. A priest, a literary agent, and a rabbi were sitting in the same row on a flight over the Rockies. Their plane was getting banged around pretty badly by a storm when one of the engines caught fire. The rabbi, in the aisle seat, lifted his hands and his eyes to the sky and implored God to rescue them; and the priest, in the window seat, bowed his head and began to say the rosary. The agent – as is the custom of agents – did nothing. After five minutes or so, the priest and the rabbi elbowed him to suggest that he, too, ought to try to save the passengers and crew. The agent (who had never prayed before in his life) nodded, gulped, looked up at the ceiling of the plane, and croaked, 'So, God, when's your next book coming out?'

There is, I think, a deep truth concealed in that joke, as in most jokes. In this one, the truth is that the Bible is God's book in almost the same sense that Deuteronomy is Moses's. Just as the fantasist is aware of the human authors who wrote the books of the Bible, he will be – if he is wise – aware of an underlying author whose stature exceeds that of mere humanity. Here he may see – again, if he is wise – the Bible as an analogue of all existence; and this, it seems to me, is the reason that so many modern critics are so fond of the assertion that every writer quickly realises is false.

For if there was never a human author of (let us say) the Gospel According to John, if it was not written by John or by someone who could be accepted by his contemporaries as writing for him, then surely there need be no superintending divine author either. A book that does not require a man to write it surely does not require God to write it. And if human life is a sort of book, too, as it certainly seems to be – a great, sprawling multigenerational saga of the family of Adam and Eve – that book requires no divine author either.

Now it is the hallmark of good fantasy that we cannot always be sure of the demarcation between fiction and fact. When I was a small boy, my mother read *Alice in Wonderland* to me. And though I had no difficulty crediting Alice, or the various talking animals, or the Queen of Hearts and her court (my parents had pictures of all those people, printed on stiff cardboard, in the drawer of the library table), I could not believe in treacle. As far as I could see, it was a substance that existed only in that book; and eventually I came to think of *treacle* as a nonsense word, like *jabberwocky*.

Let me give another example, because I think this is an important point. When my daughter Teri was in high school, we went to a movie about an attempt to assassinate the Pope. In this movie, the Pope was visiting San Francisco, and was to attend the theatre there; a sniper would shoot him as he sat in his box. On the way home Teri announced, 'The show *I* want to see is the one the Pope was watching!' I said something to the effect that I would try to get tickets the next time it was staged around Chicago, and she goggled at me. She had assumed, you see, that there was no such theatrical piece, when the Pope had been watching Gilbert and Sullivan's *Mikado* (Katisha's entrance at the end of Act I). The Pope had been an actor, and the theatre in which he sat a set; but the show on the stage of that theatre had been a real one.

Critics of fantasy who critique the Bible in the light of fantasy risk a hundred like mistakes. They may except David while accepting Goliath. 'David' (they may say) 'was unquestionably a historical figure, and thus somebody with whom we have nothing to do. Goliath, on the other hand, is a giant; giants do not exist, so Goliath is ours.' In point of fact, it is far better established that Goliath lived than that David killed him. But though both lived, the fantasist has more business with David, the hero-king.

Similarly, we may be tempted to separate Mary from the Angel of the Annunciation. But when we have done enough of this, sifted out what we are pleased to call the 'fantasy elements' in the Bible, a different angel (in the guise of a physicist and thus presumably a fallen one) is liable to ask us just what the Hell we think we're doing. 'You say that fantasy will give you new insights into the Bible, and vice versa. But you yourself have no insight into fantasy. When I say that A is a variable and *alpha* is another variable, I will not listen patiently when you tell me that A is a Roman letter and *alpha* is a Greek letter, because neither of your statements is correct. A is acceleration, and *alpha* the angle of the vector.'

So it is with us. Without David, Goliath has no story – that is to say, no meaning. Without Mary, the angel's mission is vain. If we are to understand the story, we must suspend our disbelief in Mary, this Jewish girl with a Greek name, this untutored village maiden who says, 'Behold the handmaid of the Lord.' (The original Greek is actually much better: 'Ιδου ε δουλε Κυριου.' 'See the Lord's slave girl', or 'You're looking at the Lord's slave girl.') We must come as readers in search of wonder, and not as judges eager to weigh plausibilities and approve or condemn.

I can already hear the protests of my fellow Christians, who desire that the irreligious read the Bible in order that they will become convinced of the truth of Christianity. My brothers, I wish it were so! The truth is that no one who lacks faith will come to faith by reading the Bible in the way you suggest – and in fact, the convinced Christian meets with few tests of his faith more severe than the Bible. He comes to it convinced that Jesus Christ is God incarnate, and discovers that Jesus himself called himself the Son of Man, again and again. He comes, that is to say, eager to abase himself in prayer, and finds that his fetish clasps him by the hand and calls him cousin. He comes, too, hoping to be assured that he can bribe God with virtue – that for being good he will be made rich and happy; and there are passages in the Old Testament that tell him precisely that. He brings a case against God, who should not *permit* rape and murder, child abuse, or even cruelty to animals. And he discovers that the greatest and best of men, the Son of God, has been tortured to death.

And as the sky darkens, he condemns God, and would cast him into Hell – if he could.

Nor is that all. He arrives as a convinced monotheist, only to find 'his' Bible filled with gods who are not God: 'For on this same night I will go through Egypt, striking down every first-born in the land, both man and beast, executing judgement on all the gods of Egypt.' 'Now I know that the Lord is a deity great beyond any other.' 'For what great nation is there that has gods so close to it as the Lord, our God, is to us whenever we call upon him?' 'For the Lord, your God, is the God of gods ...' 'God rises in the divine assembly; he judges in the midst of the gods.' King Solomon, or so the Christian has heard, was the wisest of men. What is he to think when he reads, 'The king defiled the high places east of Jerusalem, south of the Mount of Misconduct, which Solomon, King of Israel, had built in honour of Astarte, the Sidonian horror, or Chemosh, the Moabite horror, and of Milcom, the idol of the Ammonites'?

He has explained to his family, to his friends, and to his acquaintances that religion need not embrace superstition – his, certainly, does not. But 'Behold, there is a woman that has a familiar spirit at Endor.' And she conjures the ghost of Samuel.

The truth – this is a matter of plain, historical fact – is that the Church was never made by the Bible; but rather that the Bible was made by the Church.

Let us then read it as we might *The Lord of the Rings* or even *Alice in Wonderland*. Let us ask it the questions we ask of those books. It is more than possible that we shall learn much about it and them.

One of the questions we routinely ask of such books is 'Who is the heroine?' It is easily answered in the case of the second book I just instanced, rather more difficult in the case of the first. Once we have determined *for ourselves* the identity of the heroine of the Bible, a whole host of difficulties vanish.

In every fantasy we can profitably examine the author's use of symbolism, and nowhere will we find it richer or more varied than in the Bible, though often the characters and even the scribe who wrote the account we are reading do not seem to realise what it means.

And of course we may seek to learn the identity of the author – though in the case of the Bible we already have a name, which is generally enough to satisfy us.

Index